ROME

A

PILGRIM GUIDE

MICHAEL

REAR

ROME
A PILGRIM
GUIDE

illustrated by
Hilary Griffiths

G RACEWING

First published in England in 2019
by
Gracewing
2 Southern Avenue
Leominster
Herefordshire HR6 0QF
United Kingdom
www.gracewing.co.uk

ISBN 978 085244 901 1

Typeset by Gracewing

Cover design by Bernardita Peña Hurtado

Cover image drawn by Hilary Griffiths

With love to Caio, Beth, Libby, Will, Daniel, Helen, Tomo, Emi, Lydia and Cara

Amate Roma

CONTENTS

THE PLAN OF THIS GUIDE

Walking around Rome can be bewildering and exhausting, especially in the summer sun. This guide gives the individual pilgrim or tourist the ability and confidence to use the buses and metro for seeing the essential sights of Rome, together with many lesser-known ones: all you need for a few days, a week or more. For those travelling with an organised group it provides background reading.

In an ancient city like Rome there is some sense in following a historical order, and that is the pattern of this guidebook. It begins in the historic classical heart of Rome, among the archaeological remains of the city, whose Empire once governed almost the whole of the known world. Here you will see buildings familiar to the earliest Christians in the city; some erected by Emperor Augustus, whose census for taxation purposes, just before Jesus was born, helped finance his great building projects in Rome. Walking on Roman paving stones around the Colosseum and the Roman Forum, with its temples and triumphal arches, you are in the world of those early Christians; maybe even visiting the house of St Clement, where some of them probably worshipped. There is a prison too, kept as a memorial for Christians who were martyred in waves of persecution under successive emperors.

Another day takes you to the catacombs where those martyrs and others were buried, some in finely decorated mausoleums; and also to the excavations beneath St Peter's where the apostle was laid to rest in a cemetery rich with mosaics and wall-paintings.

The persecutions were ended in the fourth century by Emperor Constantine, and you will see the great churches he built: St John Lateran (still the Cathedral of Rome), St Peter's Basilica and St Paul's. Churches with an English connection may interest you: overlooking the Circus Maximus (Circo Massimo), where chariot races were staged, is S. Gregorio with its monastery from which Pope Gregory dispatched St Augustine to reconvert the English in 597; and there is the Church of S. Maria in Campitelli, where the little Italian congregation prays every Saturday evening for the conversion of England, as they have been doing since 1750.

There are many places to wander in Rome, where ancient remains lay cheek by jowl with Renaissance and Baroque churches, palaces and fountains. The massive Pantheon (now a church), the beautiful Piazza Navona (on the site of a Roman athletics stadium), and the spectacular Trevi Fountain and Spanish Steps should not be missed. You could spend a day in the Vatican Museums, from where the Sistine Chapel is reached, or an evening there with a concert and reception; or enjoy a tour of the Vatican Gardens. As most pilgrims today are also tourists the guide includes some of the most important museums and galleries.

In a city of more than nine hundred churches, only a small number can be included and inevitably they are a personal choice, dictated partly by being in easily accessible parts of the city (so the maximum number can be seen in a relatively short stay), and partly because together they are representative of the long history of the Church.

Outlines of history and culture are provided to put events and personalities into their context. Admission times and websites, telephone numbers where appropriate, details about buses and trains, lists of hotels and religious guest houses, helpful hints and suggestions and more, are all in this guide, together with prayers, to help you make the most of your time in the Eternal City.

Thinking ahead and Booking in advance

The guide offers a daily programme for a week's stay, plus a good deal more besides. On most days the morning and afternoon programmes are separate and interchangeable to suit the visitor's preferences. Someone may like to drop sightseeing one afternoon and go shopping. Having said that, to make a day less tiring, the afternoon programme starts in the place where the morning programme ends.

It is flexible. So, for example, if you wish to go to the International Sunday Mass in St Peter's at 10:30 (getting there very early to ensure a seat) you may wish to spend the afternoon around St Peter's, instead of going there on another day. Alternatively, if you like plainsong, during term time you may decide to go to the Sunday Conventual Mass at 9:00 in the Benedictine Monastery of S. Anselmo on the Aventine Hill. In this case you may prefer to spend the day around the Aventine and Trastevere (p. 108). If you attend the Papal Audience, that takes care of Wednesday morning. If you book to see the *Scavi*, the excavations beneath St Peter's, where the apostle is buried, you will have to fit the rest of your programme around the date and time they assign to you.

Some pilgrims may like to prioritise prayer in the Seven Pilgrimage Churches, even walking to them, a devotion probably started by St Philip Neri. They are listed in the index.

It is a good idea to browse through this Guide Book before you go, because some venues must be booked in advance online or by telephone, and there are others where, by booking, you can avoid long queues. Please note that website addresses sometimes change.

Buses and Metro: Maps, routes and advice are on p. 237.

OMNIA Vatican and Rome Card and Roma Pass: Check out online these 3-day Passes for buses, metro and museums, to see if they are worth it for you:

www.romeandvaticanpass.com

www.romeinformation.it/en/rome-pass/

Note that day one starts on the first day you use it, so don't start using it at 17:00! See also p. 237.

Roma Cristiana Open-Bus Tour: Covers the most interesting historic sites and churches, uses audio-guides, and is probably the best value of the many bus tours. You can have a non-stop overview tour or pay more to hop on and off. You may join the bus at any of the eleven stops, but the

Main Meeting Point, *Opera Romana Pellegrinaggi*, is easy to find on the left of Via della Conciliazione, just before you reach the colonnade at St Peter's. They also organise walking tours. Website: www.operaromanapellegrinaggi.org

St Peter's Tomb: For this fascinating 90-minute tour of the *Scavi* beneath the Basilica, book, if possible, several months in advance. You need to be 15 or over. Full details at: www.scavi.va Click ENG.

Vatican Museums and Sistine Chapel, Vatican Gardens, Necropolis Via Triumphalis, Castel Gandolfo Gardens and Gallery of the Popes: Tickets for individuals and groups can be booked in advance on the Vatican website: w2.vatican.va. Click English at the top and Vatican Museums at the bottom. Click Visit the Museums, then a range of options, which are constanly being augmented, opens. The site also has useful links to the Basilicas of St Peter, St John Lateran, St Paul and St Mary Major, and several virtual tours. Note in particular:

Vatican Museums: The Sistine Chapel can only be accessed through the Vatican Museums. Breakfast and lunch can be booked by those who wish to spend the day there. *For a quiet visit scroll down to Night Openings.* On Fridays from 19.00 between April and October (except August) the Sistine Chapel and parts of the Museum, including the Raphael Rooms, the Pio-Clementine and Egyptian Museums, Upper Galleries, the Modern Religious Art Gallery and Borgia Apartments, are open to a limited number. On many Friday evenings there is also a (free) concert in one of the rooms. For an extra charge there is a buffet-supper in the Pinecone Courtyard. To find this, click Happy Hour. Admission to the Vatican Museums is free on the last Sunday of the month (and therefore frantic).

Vatican Gardens: There is a 40-minute open bus tour and a 2-hour walking tour, which must be booked in advance.

Admission includes the Vatican Museums (without a guide) and Sistine Chapel.

Castel Gandolfo: A train from the Vatican Railway Station at 10:45 runs to Castel Gandolfo. Tickets, which must be obtained in advance, include admission to the Vatican Museums, tours of the Vatican Gardens and Castel Gandolfo Gardens and an audio guide. Tickets for the Gardens and Palace, without the rail journey, can also be purchased.

Tickets (free) for Papal Audiences and Ceremonies: Book on: www.vatican.va/various/prefettura/index_en.html. You will be told where to collect the tickets. Tickets should ensure a seat, though none are reserved. The Audience starts at 10:00 or 10:30, but some people get there as early as 8:00 to secure a place near the front or close to a barrier where the Pope passes by at the end, at about 12:00. On Sundays the Pope speaks, preaches and prays the Angelus from his window overlooking the Square at 12:00. No tickets are needed.

Vatican Information Office, Post Office, Bookshop and Toilets: There is a helpful Information Office on the left side of the Square beyond the colonnade, where you can obtain tickets for the Vatican Museums, Gardens and Castel Gandolfo if you failed to book in advance; there are also toilets, a bookshop and the Vatican Post Office. Cards with Vatican stamps tend to travel quicker than Italian ones, but must be posted in the Vatican post boxes. On the right of the Square there are toilets, and a facility providing showers and clothes for those who are homeless.

Dome of St Peter's: The entrance to the Dome (Cupola) is outside on the right side of St Peter's, near the cloakrooms and bag drop. A most useful website on this and much besides is:
stpetersbasilica.info/touristinfo.htm

Treasury in St Peter's: The entrance is inside the Basilica, through the sacristy, a little way up the left side of the Basilica. Booking is not necessary.

Mass in St Peter's: Catholic Priests may turn up at the sacristy between 7:00 and 7:45 to be given an altar. To book a crypt chapel for a group apply in person a few days in advance or tel: + 39 06 6988 3712 or fax: +39 06 6988 5518. Priests are welcome to concelebrate at Sunday Masses, and weekday Mass at 17:00.

Pilgrimage Masses: Priests with Pilgrimage Groups are welcome to celebrate Mass in most basilicas and churches. It is advisable to book the church.

The American Church, St Patrick's: welcomes and assists all who come to Rome as pilgrims and tourists: www.stpatricksamericanrome.org

Australia: has a Pilgrim Centre offering help, tickets and tours: www.domusaustralia.org Tel. +39 06 488 8781. It has accommodation and welcomes all nationalities and Faiths.

Catacombs: You can just turn up to join an English language group, though it is advisable to book at Priscilla. For a group of people or to celebrate a Mass it is essential to book:

- *Catacomb of S. Callisto.* Open 9:00–12:00; 14:00–17.00. Closed on Wednesday, closed in February. Tel +39 06 513 0151. Fax +39 06 5130 1567. Email: scallisto@catacombe.roma.it Website: www.catacombe.roma.it

- *Catacomb of S. Sebastiano.* Open 10:00–17.00. Closed on Sunday, closed last week of December. Tel: +39 06 785 0350. Fax: +39 06 784 3745. Email: info@catacombe.org
  Website: www.catacombe.org

- *Catacomb of Domitilla.* Open 9:00–12:00; 14:00–17:00. Closed on Tuesday, closed mid-December to

mid-January. Tel: +39 06 511 0342. Fax: +39 06 511 0512. Email: info@domitilla.it
Website: www.catacombedomitilla.it

- *Catacomb of Priscilla.* Open 9:00–12:00; 14.00–17:00. Closed on Monday, closed in January. Tel/fax: +39 06 8620 6272. Email: cat.priscilla@tiscalinet.it Website: www.catacombepriscilla.com

- *Catacomb of S. Agnese.* Open 9:00–12:00; 15:00–17:00. Closed on Sunday morning and Monday afternoon, closed in November. Tel. +39 06 861 0840. Email: catacombe@santagnese.it Website: www.santagnese.org

Chiesa Nuova: the church of St Philip Neri, offers short guided tours of the church at 10:30 and 11:00 on Saturdays. Book at: oratoriopiccolo@gmail.com.
Website: www.vallicella.org/english/

Siesta: One problem you quickly encounter is that many churches close for a siesta at lunchtime, but others don't. Times of closure are included in the guide, but be warned, they are liable to change, and it is a good idea to check opening hours on the internet.

Street Maps, Sights and Hotels are easily accessed:
www.google.co.uk/maps/place/rome
www.aviewoncities.com/rome

Ancient Rome: Tickets for the Colosseum, Forum, Domus Aurea, Pyramid of Caius Cestius, and other archaeological sites and monuments of ancient Rome may be booked at the official site:
www.coopculture.it.
You should avoid non-official sites when ordering tickets because they are often more expensive. Most Monuments and State Museums are free for European Union citizens under 18, and offer concessions to those between 18 and 25. European Union teachers of art or architecture, with proof they are on permanent contracts, often get free admission.

The Italian Tourist Website: www.turismoroma.it is packed with valuable information and 'What's On', including concerts, theatres and sporting events. The online English magazine, *Romeing*, is excellent: www.romeing.it as is www.wheretraveler.com/rome. For concerts and other events, including Baroque evenings in S. Agnese in Piazza Navona with a guided tour, concert and supper: www.romaoperaomnia.com The Art Gallery, Palazzo Doria-Pamphilj, hosts Saturday morning concerts with a guided tour: www.doriapamphilj.it

Palazzo Farnese: visit by appointment only: www.inventerrome.com

Pyramid of Caius Cestius: guided tours, which must be booked, at 11:00 on Saturdays and Sundays (except the first in the month) by telephone: +39 06 399 67700.

Villa d'Este, the Water Gardens at Tivoli and Hadrian's Villa: For full details and advance bookings check on: www.villadestetivoli.info www.villaadriana.beniculturali.it

Villa Borghese Museum and Art Gallery: Booking is obligatory, with timed entry: www.tosc.it/tickets or tel. +39 06 32810.

Hotels and Places to Stay: Avoid too much foot-slogging by staying around St Peter's or the Railway Station (called *Stazione Termini* or simply *Termini*), where you are not far from buses and the metro. Alternatively, stay close to a bus route or near a metro station. For a list of such hotels and religious guest houses see p. 252. There are hundreds to choose from on the internet, and many apartments. Religious guest houses offer good value for tourists as well as pilgrims: www.monasterystays.com

1

IN THE STEPS OF THE FIRST

CHRISTIANS IN ANCIENT ROME

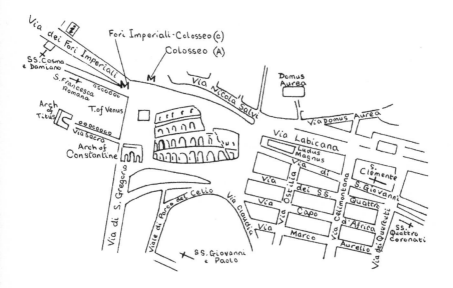

Your tour begins near the Colosseum. Getting there: from Termini take Bus 85 or metro Blue Linea B (direction Laurentina) to Colosseo (Map p. 238) unless you prefer a 20-minute walk down Via Cavour (Map p. 169). Walk on the right side, and towards the end keep your eyes open for Cavour 313: it has the old and narrow frontage of a wine bar going back to 1935, easily missed: 'not just a wine shop, but a meeting point for lovers of good food,' which is not expensive.

If you are staying on the right of St Peter's the metro from Ottaviano to Colosseo (direction Anagnina, but you have to change at Termini) may be quicker, but bus 81 from Piazza del Risorgimento is more interesting (Map p. 240). If you are staying on the left of St

Peter's or in Via della Conciliazione (Map p. 239) take the 64 or 40 to Piazza Venezia and from the stop where you alight catch the 81 or 87 to the Colosseum; alternatively, take the 46 or 916 to Piazza Venezia (their Terminus), and from the stop where you alight catch the 51, 85 or 117 (Map p. 241).

You are in a part of Rome that would have been familiar to the early Christians. In Jerusalem on the Day of Pentecost, in the year AD 30, St Peter, *'filled with the Holy Spirit'*, preached to thousands of people, who included *'visitors from Rome'* (Acts 2:10). Three thousand were baptised, some of whom returned to Rome with the Christian Faith.

In Jerusalem, opposition to Christianity gradually turned into active persecution. The apostle James was beheaded in 43, and Peter was imprisoned but miraculously escaped. The decision was subsequently taken to centre the Church in Rome rather than Jerusalem, probably to avoid persecution, and also because the capital of the Empire was the obvious place from which to fulfil Christ's commission to *'preach the Gospel to all nations'* (Matthew 28:19). St Peter went to Rome, called, perhaps for reasons of secrecy, *'another place'* (Acts 12:17), via Antioch. By the time St Paul arrived in 61 there were so many Christians in Rome that they came to meet him *'as far as the Forum of Appius and the Three Taverns'* (Acts 28:15) on the Appian Way.

Then tragedy engulfed them. All this district where you are, its houses and shops, was destroyed by a fire in the year 64. There had been fires before, but nothing like this, and the fire brigade set up by Emperor Augustus watched helplessly as it blazed for nine days. A rumour swept round that Emperor Nero's henchmen had been seen starting it with burning torches, in a grandiose plan to create a new Rome. Needing a scapegoat urgently, Nero pinned the blame on this new religion, Christianity, which had taken root in the city. St Peter and St Paul, with a huge number, were put to death. Nero's barbarity shocked the pagan historian, Tacitus:

First were seized those who admitted their faith, and then, on their evidence, a vast multitude was convicted, not so much for the crime of burning the city, but for hatred of the human race. Besides being put to death they were made into sports: they were clad in the skins of beasts and torn to death by dogs; others were crucified or set on fire. Nero gave his own gardens for this display and performed in his Circus, dressed as a charioteer, mixing with the plebs or driving about in his chariot. All this gave rise to a feeling of pity … for it was felt they were being destroyed not for the public good but to gratify the cruelty of an individual..

Nero was but the first of many Roman Emperors to persecute Christians over the next 250 years, before Constantine was proclaimed Emperor in 312.

*Walk down Via di S. Giovanni in Laterano near the Royal Art Café. On your left you will notice the remains of the **Ludus Magnus**, a gymnasium where gladiators prepared for their contests in the Colosseum. You soon reach the side door of San Clemente, on the left.*

Basilica of San Clemente

Open: 9:00–12:30; 15:00–18:00.

Who was St Clement? He was the fourth pope after St Peter, the writer of a celebrated *Letter to the Corinthians* in the year AD 95. Origen of Alexandria identifies him as the fellow worker mentioned by St Paul (Philippians 4:3). Like Tacitus, Clement wrote about the persecution under Nero:

> It was for jealousy and envy that the greatest and most righteous pillars [of the Church] were persecuted and fought even to the death. Let us set before us the good apostles: Peter ... who having borne witness, passed to his appointed place of glory; Paul ... bore witness before rulers, and thus passed from the world, and went to the holy place ... To these men of holy conversation we must add a great company of the elect souls who gathered round them ... subjected to countless indignities and tortures. Women were persecuted and were subjected ... to dreadful and unholy violence, until they won the goal for which their faith had struggled, and they received ... a noble prize.

Entering this twelfth-century church, you are standing on a lovely Cosmati mosaic floor. You will soon recognise the beautiful work of the renowned Cosmati family all over Rome, and may have seen it in Westminster Abbey too. There were seven craftsmen in four generations of the family, working from 1140 for about a century. Their colourful mosaics were made of Roman marble that was found lying around or buried.

In front of you in the apse is a stunning mosaic of the Cross, the Tree of Life, surrounded by saints, and also ordinary folk in their everyday occupations, like a girl feeding poultry and a shepherd patting his dog. The cross is planted on the hill of Paradise; the doves represent redeemed souls. Christ, the Lamb, is raised to the Cross in sacrifice and victory. This iconography is fourth century, yet it was made in the twelfth. In the band below are twelve lambs, symbolising the apostles, with the Lamb of God at the centre—you will find this feature in other churches which have apses decorated with early mosaics. Before you is a marble enclosed choir, which you may think also looks older than the church. Walk on the right of it towards the high altar, beneath which are the remains of St Clement and St Ignatius of Antioch, and from the gate look closely at the ancient chair in the apse. You will see part of the word 'martyr' engraved on it, because it was recycled from the memorial stone of a martyr. Above the chair is a fine twelfth-century fresco of *Our Lord, Our Lady and the Apostles.*

> Almighty ever-living God, your servants Clement and Ignatius walked with your Son the way to the cross. Bless and give strength to all your servants today who, like them, are suffering persecution. This we pray through Jesus Christ our Lord. Amen.

The church you have entered was not the first to be built here. An earlier, fourth-century church was wrecked by Normans in their 1084 Sack of Rome. Robert Guiscard had come to the aid of Pope Gregory VIII (Hildebrand), who was besieged in Castel Sant'Angelo in a power struggle with Emperor Henry IV, but his 36,000 troops ran amok and gutted buildings around the Colosseum and Lateran, and on the Capitol and Palatine Hills. Rather than clear the whole site, the rebuilders simply filled the shell of the old church with rubble by knocking down the roof and upper reaches of the walls, thereby creating a raised platform on which they built the present church; putting into it the sixth-century choir, baldacchino and chair, which they salvaged, and a copy of the mosaic. In the seventeenth century the church was entrusted to Irish Dominicans and restored by Carlo Stefano Fontana, a late Baroque architect, the nephew of the greater Carlo Fontana, whom you will meet all over Rome. In 1857, with extraordinary daring, Father Joseph Mullooly personally excavated beneath it, and after carefully supporting the church on concrete pillars, removed all the rubble of the earlier church. What he discovered is astonishing.

Tickets for the excavations are sold in the bookshop beside the sacristy.

Going down the steps you pass plaques and sculpture from the first church, and then enter its atrium, where two eleventh-century wall paintings introduce us to the legend that grew up around the saint. Clement was exiled to the Crimea by Emperor Trajan, where he was bound to an anchor and thrown into the Black Sea—the anchor is still his emblem. Later the waters receded to reveal on an island a little chapel built by angels, containing his tomb. Once a year at low tide the chapel was exposed, and in one particular year, a child, who had apparently drowned the previous year, was discovered alive and well inside it. The first picture shows the miracle with the ecstatic parents gathering up their child. Note the lovely fish, octopus and jellyfish. The next picture shows the relics of St Clement being removed from the tomb by St Cyril and taken in a procession, with censers flying, to this church built to his memory in Rome.

Against the atrium wall in front of this picture there is a hinged marble tombstone. The original, sad, pagan, finely-carved inscription translates, *Marcus Aurelius Sabinus, known to us as 'the little wanderer', was a most sweet son whose life was incomparable among the other children of his time.* Personal memorials like this were common among wealthy families. Christians naturally adopted the custom, gradually extending it to poorer people, who would purchase secondhand slabs and engrave the other side. On the other side of this one, by an unskilled hand, is a Christian inscription, *To Surus resting in peace. Erected by his brother Euticanus.*

Passing through the doorway you are now in the fourth-century church. To the left behind you is a ninth-century picture of either the *Ascension of Our Lord* or the *Assumption of Our Lady.* Close to it are damaged paintings of the *Crucifixion,* the *Women at the Tomb,* the *Marriage at Cana* and the *Descent into Hell.* Further along are some of the pillars of this church and a painting of the *Legend of St Alexis* (S. Alessio), whose church is on the Aventine Hill. His parents arranged his marriage, but he ran away to Odessa and lived a life of prayer. Seventeen years later he returned, incognito, and his parents failed to recognise him. But his father employed him in the house, and lodged him in a room below stairs. Another seventeen years later he died, and a paper in his hand, here being examined by the pope, revealed his identity to his stricken family, who are literally tearing out their hair. The next painting shows *St Clement celebrating Mass*. You may be interested to see that the maniple, which priests used to wear on their left arm at Mass, originated as a sweat cloth in their hand. At the far end of the aisle on the right is a ninth-century fresco of the *Descent into Hell*.

Going into the south aisle (on the left) you come to the tomb St Cyril, whom you saw in the painting. He and his brother St Methodius were great evangelists, who brought the Gospel to the Slavic nations. Pope St John Paul II named them Patrons of Europe in 1980. Cyril is honoured as the apostle of Russia, and gave his name to the alphabet of Cyrillic script he invented.

> O God, who enlightened the Slavic peoples through the brothers Saints Cyril and Methodius, grant that our hearts may grasp the words of your teaching, and perfect us as a people of one accord in true faith and right confession. Through our Lord Jesus Christ, your Son, who lives and reigns with you in the unity of the Holy Spirit, one God, for ever and ever. Amen.

Not content with discovering this earlier church, the intrepid archaeologists decided to go down still deeper in order to test the tradition that, like many other churches in Rome, it stands above a house used by the earliest Christians for worship. For in those early centuries Christians were not permitted to build churches, but had to worship in houses or small halls they called *tituli*. Each *titulus* had one or more priests. The excavators dug down and to their astonishment came across a Mithraic Temple with its associated rooms. You can see the altar with Mithras slaying the bull, and the stone benches along which the worshippers lay on their stomachs. In one room there is a fresh water spring.

In another you will hear water rushing into Rome's ancient sewer, the 40-kilometre long *Cloaca Maxima*, which has been draining the Forum ever since the sixth century BC. Why did they build a church over a pagan temple? It could only be that they wanted to build it above the house next door. You pass along a narrow first-century street and then find yourself standing in that house, decorated with marvellous herring-bone brickwork. Most likely it belonged to a wealthy Christian, Flavius Clemens, a consul. He was Emperor Domitian's cousin and married to Domitian's niece. But this did not stop Domitian putting him to death in AD 95 for being a Christian and banishing his niece to the island of Ventotene. St Clement would have known him and almost certainly worshipped in his house.

Returning to the fourth-century church, in the right aisle you will see fragmentary frescoes, and in a niche a sixth-century *Our Lady and Child* with Mary robed as a Byzantine Empress, flanked on the side walls by two saints, perhaps St Euphemia and St Catherine of Alexandria, both wearing crowns of pearls. There is also a pillar from that church, and the hole through which Fr Mullooly first entered this level. Back in the upper church pause for a moment in the right aisle to pray and admire Sassoferrato's devotional painting of *Our Lady* in characteristic deep blue, one of many this seventeenth-century artist painted, including a very similar one in the National Gallery.

Remember to look into the attractive courtyard, often a venue for summer concerts. Leave the church by the side door, perhaps first visiting the Blessed Sacrament Chapel on the right, and the Chapel of St Catherine on the left, with its fine frescoes painted 1425-31 by Masolino da Panicale, riding high after his collaboration with Masaccio in the Brancacci Chapel in Florence.

If it is lunchtime when you leave S. Clemente, you will find many bars and restaurants close by; or else wait a little and have an inexpensive hot sandwich, beer or coffee at the Info. Centre in Via dei Fori Imperiali. Make your way back to the Colosseum. If you wish to go inside you have to buy a 2-day Combo ticket (available online to save a long queue), which also includes admission to the Roman Forum and Palatine Hill. You will have to decide whether you have the interest and time to explore them—and the feet, for the Forum is rough underfoot.

The Colosseum

This immense theatre, built to hold 50,000, even 75,000 spectators, was begun in AD 72 by Emperor Vespasian and finished eight years later under his son, Titus, by prisoners he brought back from Jerusalem.

Imagine people's amazement when they first set eyes on exotic wild animals brought here from all parts of the Empire, especially North Africa. In the opening ceremonies five thousand animals, including crocodiles, elks, giraffes, hippos, hyenas, leopards, lions, rhinos and tigers were killed: and not only animals. In regular shows gladiators and slaves fought to the death, and Christians died there too, along with criminals. The animal shows were in the morning, a warm-up to the terrible slaughter of human beings in the afternoon: all free entertainment for the masses.

It is not known how many Christians were martyred in the Colosseum, and the tradition they were has been disputed. But

Pope Pius IX erected a cross inside to commemorate them, and each year on Good Friday the Pope leads Stations of the Cross there. One who knew the fate awaiting him was St Ignatius of Antioch, who had learned the Faith from the beloved disciple John, and whose remains are in S. Clemente. He was arrested and taken to Rome during the persecutions of Emperor Trajan in 108. On the journey, chained to Roman soldiers, he wrote seven letters to the bishops of different churches en route, including one to the Church of Rome, which he said *'presides in love'*. His words vividly illustrate the faith and composure of Christians facing death in the persecutions:

> I am truly in earnest about dying for God ... to be a meal for the beasts, for it is they who can provide my way to God. I am his wheat, ground fine by the lions' teeth to be made the purest bread for Christ ... let them not leave the slightest scrap of my flesh, so that I need not be a burden to anyone after I fall asleep ... all I pray is that I may find them swift.

Emperor Constantine, the first Christian emperor, under pressure from the Church, tried to abolish gladiatorial contests, but without success, for as Juvenal had written: *'The degraded people of the world clamoured for only two things, bread and circuses'*. But on 1 January 404, a Christian monk, St Telemachus, entered the arena and protested at the butchery; the infuriated crowd stoned him to death. That proved to be the last contest. So moved was Emperor Honorius by the monk's martyrdom that he issued an historic ban on gladiatorial contests. It took another century to outlaw animal fights.

Originally known as the Flavian Amphitheatre (after the family name of the emperors who built it), the Colosseum is thought to get its present name, not from its size, but from a colossal statue some 35 metres high which Emperor Nero built of himself. The base of the statue, seven metres square, is marked out by a raised grassy square with ilex trees, which you will pass between the Forum and the Colosseum. The floor of the Colosseum is long gone, though part has been reconstructed, and you can see the channels from which the men and animals were raised by lifts into the arena. It could also be flooded to re-enact naval battles. You will have to imagine all the tiers of seats from those that remain. Spectators were sheltered from the blazing sun by an immense retractable awning (*velarium*) pulled over the seating area by sailors.

On leaving the Colosseum, make your way towards the Arch of Constantine.

The Arch of Constantine

In AD 312 Constantine was proclaimed Emperor at the age of 24. At the time he was in York, staying in a fort beneath the present Minster. His arch was built about 318 to celebrate his victory over his rival, Maxentius, at the Milvian Bridge on the Tiber. He attributed this to a cross he saw in the sky with the words *in hoc signo vinces* (in this sign you will conquer), a sign that was put on his standards for the battle. Christians had endured persecution for almost three centuries under successive emperors. Thousands had been martyred throughout the Roman Empire, including Britain. Some Emperors had been tolerant, others utterly savage. Constantine's mother, Helena, was a Christian. Her son did not convert for many years, but he showed his sympathy by passing the Edict of Milan in 313, which guaranteed freedom to all religions, and ended the persecution of the Church. Christians could at last live in peace and safety.

On its south side Constantine's arch depicts the Battle of Milvian Bridge, and both north and south sides carry an identical and intriguing inscription, crediting his success to being inspired *'by a divinity'*. The fact that he did not attribute his victory to the *'immortal gods'* (plural) hints at his move towards Christianity. From the year 315 the Chi-Rho, a Christian motif, appeared on his coins.

> We give you thanks, O God, the King of kings and Lord of lords, for all those in authority who seek justice and grant freedom of Faith, and we ask you to give the leaders of all nations wisdom to discern your will.

Make your way to the footpath beside the railings round the Forum, walking on the large black basalt paving stones of the Roman road to the Via Sacra, at the end of which is an entrance to the Forum. You can see the Arch of Titus through the gates at the end, but you will not see its frieze unless you go inside. Otherwise, continue walking towards Via dei Fori Imperiali.

The Arch of Titus

The Jews in Israel had long resented their conquest by Rome, with its consequent oppression and taxation. A large-scale protest led to the Great Revolt (AD 66–73), during which six thousand Jews were executed. Nero dispatched the future Emperor Vespasian (with his son Titus) to crush it. Jesus had wept over Jerusalem, and predicted its destruction because of its rejection of him: *'The days will come when your enemies will raise fortifications around you and hem you in on every side, and dash you to the ground, you and your children within you, and they will leave not one stone upon another'* (Luke 19:41–44).

In AD 70 this prophecy was terrifyingly fulfilled when Titus burnt the city and slaughtered its inhabitants. The Jewish historian Josephus, who may be exaggerating, claimed that more than a million Jews were killed or enslaved. Titus frantically tried to save the Temple, but his army, like the fire, was out of control. The prisoners he brought back to Rome were enslaved to complete the Colosseum; the sacred objects he looted from Solomon's Temple were placed in the newly-built **Temple of Peace** in the Forum, from where they disappeared for ever after Rome was invaded by the Visigoths in 410 or by the Vandals in 445. Inside the arch there is a frieze showing soldiers in triumphal procession leading slaves and carrying items plundered from the

Temple, including the Menorah (the seven-branch candlestick) and its Altar.

Retrace your steps down Via Sacra, and if you would like to visit **S. Francesca Romana** *(also known as S. Maria Nova) turn left just before you reach Via dei Fori Imperiali, alongside the impressive columns of* **Temple of Venus and Rome***, the largest temple in the city, begun by Emperor Hadrian about AD 130 and completed by his successor, Antoninus Pius.*

Santa Francesca Romana (Santa Maria Nova)

Open: 10:30–19:00 (17:00 in winter).

When Roman religions lost ground to Christianity, and temples fell into disuse or were closed, some of them were turned into churches. This is probably the first example, built into the **Temple of Venus and Rome**, though greatly altered over the centuries. In the apse are early twelfth-century mosaics of the Virgin and Child and Saints Peter, James, John and Andrew. A *Madonna and Child* is above the altar. To the right is the tomb of Gregory XI, the last of the Avignon popes, who returned the papal court to Rome. A precious early sixth-century icon in the sacristy, *Our Lady of Tenderness*, comes from **S. Maria Antiqua**, an older, albeit ruined church in the Forum which is often closed for restoration (see p. 38). Also in the sacristy is a sixteenth-century painting of *Cardinal Reginald Pole*, the last Catholic Archbishop of Canterbury, who died on the same day as Queen Mary Tudor.

S. Maria Nova was rededicated to S. Francesca Romana (St Frances of Rome), a woman from the Trastevere district, who was born in 1348. She was always concerned for the sick and the poor, and after her husband's death she founded a community of Benedictine oblates to look after them which still exists today. Famously she wrote: *'A married woman must leave all her devotions when the household demands it'*. Her body may be seen beneath the altar in the crypt, and the chapel there is pervaded by an extraordinary atmosphere of prayer. In the *confessio*, designed by Bernini, is a nineteenth-century statue of the saint, replacing one of bronze removed by Napoleon's soldiers.

*Turn into Via dei Fori Imperiali and you will pass some huge reliefs illustrating the growth of the Roman Empire. Go a little way up the road and cross it if you would like to relax over a light lunch in the Info. Centre. There are toilets too. If you have decided to visit the Forum and Palatine Hill, buy a small specialist guide book there. Otherwise stay on the left side where you soon come to the fine **Basilica of Saints Cosmas and Damian**.*

Santi Cosma e Damiano

Open: 10:00–13:00; 15:00–18:00.

On this site stood the **Temple of Peace**, constructed by Vespasian in AD 70, adjoining the early fourth-century BC **Temple of Romulus**. In 526 the Church of SS. Cosma e Damiano was built into part of them, another early church to occupy a pagan building. From inside the church you can see some of the Temple of Romulus and from the Forum you can see its fourth-century bronze doors between two beautiful porphyry columns—the original entrance to the church. Cosmas and Damian were twins, both doctors, living in Syria, whose willingness to treat patients without a fee led them to be denounced as Christians and martyred during the persecutions of Diocletian.

Like many churches in Rome, this one was remodeled in the seventeenth century, but in the apse you will see a beautiful sixth-century mosaic, one of the finest in Rome. It shows Cosmas and Damian (in brown robes) being presented to Christ by St Peter and St Paul (in white): to the left, holding a model of the church which he built, is Pope Felix IV, and to the right St Theodore. One of the chapels on the right has an eighth-century *Byzantine Crucifixion* with Jesus wonderfully triumphant and open-eyed.

> Jesus, good physician of our souls, bless doctors, nurses and carers, and all who are sick. Be mindful especially of those who live and work in Syria. Saints Cosmas and Damian pray for them.

Before leaving, you must look at the intricate eighteenth-century Neapolitan crib (*presepio*) in the cloister. And then, outside the entrance, if you did not see it when you came in, admire the graceful modern bronze of *St Francis* sculpted by the Franciscan Padre Andrea Martini.

Continue on your way. Statues of Emperors line the road and on both sides there are ruins of the forums they built. The entrance to the **Roman Forum** *is on the left. You will pass a viewing area, but will find a better one later. Unless you are visiting the Roman Forum, cross to the right side of the road to look at the* **Forum of Nerva**, *the* **Forum of Augustus**, *and best preserved of all, the* **Forum of Trajan**.

Trajan's Forum

Started in AD 107, it was completed in 113. Most impressive is the market, a terrace of about 150 shops, which you can visit as part of the **Museo dei Fori Imperiali**. As well as selling oil and wine and other produce, the market was a distribution centre for supplies in the city. Behind them you will notice the **Militia Tower**, known also as Nero's Tower, because Nero is said to have stood on it playing his fiddle while Rome burned. He didn't because it dates from the thirteenth century and was part of a castle built by Pope Gregory IX to protect the city: it is one of the best preserved medieval buildings in Rome.

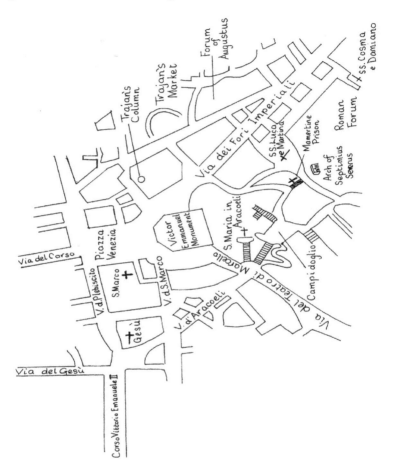

Trajan's Column, standing nearby, is over 30 metres high, and has an intricately carved spiral bas relief depicting his victories in Dacia (modern Romania). It appears to be cylindrical, but halfway up the diameter increases to create that illusion. On top stood a bronze statue of Trajan, which Pope Sixtus V replaced in 1588 by St Peter, making the point that the Church had triumphed over the Roman Empire. In spite of being pagan, the column was never defaced by Christians, perhaps because Trajan was more tolerant of them than his predecessor Domitian (though he did have some Christian leaders, including St Ignatius of Antioch, put to death). There was a legend that Pope Gregory the Great, gazing at the column, and knowing of Trajan's reputation for justice and mercy, and in particular his schemes to help poor and abandoned children, wept and prayed for his salvation.

*Walk over the bridge and cross to the other side of Via dei Fori Imperiali. Towards the left you will see Via S. Pietro in Carcere that leads to the **Mamertine Prison**. Take the left fork off that by the **Museo Centrale del Risorgimento**.*

The Mamertine Prison

Open: 9:00–16:30.

A tour includes a multimedia presentation in the context of Roman and Christian history.

The entrance to this terrible dungeon is beside the Church of S. Giuseppe dei Falegnami (St Joseph of the Carpenters), which was built over it in the late sixteenth century. The upper chamber of the prison was dug out by Ancus Martius, the fourth King of Rome, in 640 BC. The lower chamber, reached by steps (originally only by the hole), was constructed in 578 BC. Notable political prisoners include Jugurtha, King of Numidia, who was starved to death here in 106 BC; Vercingetorix, leader of the Gauls, imprisoned before being strangled in 46 BC; and Simon bar Giora, leader of the Jewish Revolt, brought here by Titus.

A recently discovered eleventh-century fresco of Jesus, with the oldest-known picture of the Campidoglio behind him, and a fourteenth-century fresco of him with his arm around a smiling St Peter, reflect the tradition that St Peter (and perhaps also St Paul) was held here in the reign of Nero. Pope Sylvester I made the prison a place of prayer in 314.

> For all who are in prison for their offences, we pray, Lord, that they may be repentant and converted. And may those unjustly held, like Peter and Paul, be given strength to endure their anguish; and let their innocence be proved.

*Leave the Mamertine through the little bookshop; down the steps you will see the Church of **SS. Luca e Martina** standing on the site of the original Republican Senate House, the **Curia Hostilia**. The brick building close-by in the Forum, the **Curia Julia**, replaced it. You also get near to the **Arch of Septimius Severus**.*

Senate House (Curia Julia)

Julius Caesar began building the Senate House in 44 BC after the Curia Hostilia burnt down, and it was completed by Augustus in 29 BC. It owes its preservation to being used as a church from the seventh century until 1937. Not only did the senators meet here, it was also the place where an augur could reveal the wishes of the gods. Stripped now of most of its marble and other decorations, the building still retains a fine inlaid marble floor (a technique known as *opus sectile*) with stylised rosettes: be sure to see this if you visit the Forum. You will also see the *Lapis Niger*, the Black Stone, a remnant of the *Comitium*, an assembly area in front of it, perhaps marking the grave of Romulus. The original bronze doors may now be seen at St John Lateran, to where they were taken in 1660 (see page 92).

The Arch of Septimius Severus

An able leader, Severus was emperor from AD 193–211. His richly-decorated and well-preserved triple arch celebrates his conquest of Parthia (part of modern Iraq and Iran). In 208 he invaded Caledonia (Scotland) but fell ill and died at Eboracum (York). There were persecutions during his reign, and he issued an edict in 202 forbidding conversion to Christianity, but it not clear how much he enforced it. According to the priest, Tertullian, a contemporary of Severus and like him a native of North Africa, the emperor was well-disposed towards Christians, employed a Christian as his personal physician, and protected several high-born Christians from 'the mob'.

*Go back up the steps to Via S. Pietro in Carcere, and walk straight ahead until you reach a column on the left surmounted by the legendary founders of Rome, Romulus and Remus, who are being suckled by a she-wolf; on the right is a small park. You will also spot one of the innumerable drinking fountains of Rome flowing with crystal-clear water. The trick is to put your finger over the spout allowing a jet of water to spurt through the hole in the pipe into your mouth. Otherwise, fill a bottle. A little further on your right you will come to steps, Scala dell'Arce Capitolina, and off them a short flight to **S. Maria in Aracoeli**.*

Santa Maria in Aracoeli

Open: 7:00–19:00.

On this hill, the Capitoline, stood the huge Temple complex of Jupiter, Juno and Minerva, built *c.*520 BC. Juno's Temple was protected by a flock of screeching sacred geese, which are said to have saved Rome when the Gauls invaded in 387 BC. The watch-word was *Juno Moneta* (Juno warns), from which we derive the word 'money', because next to her temple was the mint. A daughter of Saturn, and wife of Jupiter, the chief god, Juno was revered as Queen of Heaven, and patroness of women, marriage and childbirth. A church was built on the site in the sixth century and served by Byzantine monks. Emperor Augustus, while visiting Juno's Temple, was said to have received a vision of the Blessed Virgin and her Son in heaven, and this gave the name Aracoeli (Altar of Heaven) to the church.

The church has always lacked a finished façade, but inside it is breathtaking, most famous for the little chapel on the left, near the high altar, containing the *Bambino Gesù*, a jeweled statue of the infant Jesus. It is a place to pause and pray. Women come here to ask Our Lady (supplanting Juno) for the gift of a child and a safe delivery. To reach the chapel you pass a domed structure with a porphyry urn containing relics of St Helena, the mother of Constantine. Around her altar are depictions of the vision of Augustus.

When Christianity gained ascendancy over paganism a few temples were turned into churches, but most of them were demolished and their pillars and other masonry re-used. The twenty-two pillars in this church are no exception, and the third on the left from the back, made of Aswan granite, carries the inscription *cubiculo Augustanorum*, (the Emperor's chamber). Franciscans enlarged the earlier church in the thirteenth century, laying down the Cosmati floor, and enhancing it with paintings and tombs of members of the Order, including Brother Juniper (Fra Ginepro), one of the original followers of St Francis. The fine ceiling was gilded and painted to thank Our Lady for the surprising victory over the Turks at the Battle of Lepanto in 1571 which ended the Moslem conquest of Europe, a victory attributed to praying the Rosary.

The nave is full of tombs and memorials of Roman families. On the right of the entrance and easily missed, is the badly-worn tomb slab of Giovanni Crivelli, Archdeacon of Aquileia, carved (and signed) by Donatello of Florence, the most influential sculptor of the early Renaissance, on one his few sojourns in Rome (1432–33). In the first chapel on the right admire the *Life of St Bernardino of Siena*, painted by Pinturicchio from Umbria, another early Renaissance artist. He did much work in Rome, particularly in S. Maria del Popolo, and in the Sistine Chapel and Vatican Library. Pietro Cavallini painted the rather damaged frescoes in the last chapel on this side.

It was here, on 15 October 1764, Edward Gibbon wrote: *'as I sat musing amidst the ruins of the Capitol, while the barefoot friars were singing vespers in the Temple of Jupiter, that the idea of writing the decline and fall of the city first started in my mind'.*

Leave by the side door through which you entered, make your way down the steps, and move to the right until you come into the magnificent square on top of Rome's smallest hill, the Capitoline or **Campidoglio**.

Campidoglio

Campidoglio is old Italian dialect for Capitol, which was so called because the head (*caput*) of a mythical hero *Tolus* was found when the foundations of the Temple of Jupiter were being dug. The discovery was taken as a sign that Rome would become the head of the world (*caput mundi*), and it gave us the word for a principal city or the seat of government. The Campidoglio was laid out by Michelangelo. He designed the façade of the central building, the **Palazzo Senatorio**: dating from the twelfth century it was built over the remains of the **Tabularium**, which may have housed the archives of ancient Rome. The Palazzo is now Rome's city hall. The fountain Michelangelo made, of Roman sculptured figures and ancient Greek basins, represents the gods of the Nile and the Tiber, with the goddess Roma, looking a bit like Britannia. The imposing equestrian statue of the Emperor Marcus Aurelius in the centre of the piazza is a copy, the original having been moved into the **Capitoline Museums** which occupy the buildings on either side (also designed by Michelangelo).

On the right is the **Palazzo dei Conservatori**, and you can see the foundations of Jupiter's Temple inside the hall. Here also is the original of Marcus Aurelius's statue, the only bronze equestrian statue to have survived from Roman times. Aurelius was a cultured philosopher, but in his reign the blood of Christians flowed in torrents; the reason his statue survived is that until the fifteenth century it was thought to depict Constantine. The palace houses splendid Etruscan, Greek, Roman and later sculptures, among them the original Etruscan bronze *She-wolf* and the *Greek Boy withdrawing a Thorn from his Foot* (a Roman copy is in the Uffizi in Florence), and the lovely *Esquiline Venus*. In the art galleries are works by Veronese, Guercino, Tintoretto, Rubens, Caravaggio, Van Dyck, Titian and others. Of particular note is Caravaggio's young *John the Baptist* and Titian's *Baptism of Jesus*. On the left, the **Palazzo Nuova** contains such a wonderful collection of Roman sculpture, and Roman copies of Greek masterpieces, that it is hard to single any out. Among the most famous are a colossal statue of *Mars*, the *Dying Gaul*, the *Wounded Warrior* and the *Drunken Old Woman*.

Now walk round the right side of the Palazzo Senatorio for the best view of the Forum.

The Roman Forum

You are gazing at more than a thousand years of Roman history: five hundred years of the Republic and five hundred of the Empire; ruins of the Forum that was once the civic and religious centre of the western world. At its height the Empire encircled the Mediterranean, stretching from Britain in the north, across much of what we call Western Europe, around the Black Sea, down through Syria and Palestine, and deep into Egypt and Africa north of the Sahara. As you look down you can see the *Via Sacra* which linked the Campidoglio to the Forum below. In the far distance you can just make out the Colosseum and to the right of it the Arch of Titus. On the right is the **Palatine Hill**, which has given us the word palace, because here the Emperors built palaces: their massive ruins still stand. It was below the Palatine Hill that Romulus and Remus, the twin sons of Mars, were washed up after being abandoned beside the Tiber. Saved and suckled by a she-wolf, they were found by a shepherd, Faustulus, who, with his wife, brought them up. Romulus founded the city of Rome, giving it his name, and on 21 April 753 BC he became its first king, or so the ancients, including Livy, believed. The moderns must believe it too, for each year, starting on the anniversary, they gather in their thousands around the Circus Maximus for several days of processions of gladiators, vestal virgins and senators, and other events.

Myth and history are difficult to distinguish. What is known is that, as well as Romans, other tribes including Etruscans and Sabines from the surrounding districts settled on the Palatine and other hills of Rome, fighting one another, making alliances, and even sometimes sharing their kings. In the **Museo Palatino** on the Palatine you can see mock-ups of the ninth-century BC thatched huts they lived in, along with attractive frescoes, mosaics, and sculpture collected from over the years. Rome's position on the Tiber was a huge advantage, and its trading contacts with Greece and Phoenicia brought prosperity. The valley of the Forum had been a marshy swamp, but the Etruscans transformed it by constructing the *Cloaca Maxima* you heard in S. Clemente, and which still keeps it drained. By the sixth century the Etruscans were dominant. The last King of Rome was the Etruscan Tarquinius Superbus who, it is thought, built the great Temple of Jupiter. His son raped Lucretia, a Roman aristocrat, who committed suicide in her distress, and in reprisal a certain Brutus led a Roman counter-attack in the, perhaps legendary, Battle of Regillus, that drove out the Etruscan dynasty in 509 BC, replacing it with two consuls and other officials elected annually. Thus the Republic was born, and it would last five hundred years, expanding by conquests and alliances. The remains of some buildings from this Republican period survive, including the Temples of Vesta, Saturn, and Castor and Pollux, though they were reconstructed and greatly embellished during the years of Empire.

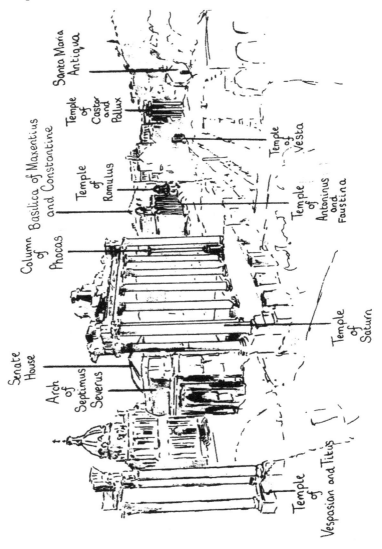

Temple and House of Vesta

The Sabines had a circular hut on the Palatine containing a sacred fire, dedicated to the goddess, Vesta. When the Forum was drained and building began, a Temple of Vesta, keeping its circular hut-shape, was constructed there. Four (later six) priestesses, the Vestal Virgins, were entrusted with making offerings to Vesta, guarding the sacred statue of Athena in the temple, and keeping the fire burning. Unsurprisingly the temple burnt down and was rebuilt many times; to the left of three very tall columns you can just make out the three remaining columns of the last one, built in the third century AD. Next to it was the House of the Vestal Virgins. During the Empire vestals became especially revered. They attended civic functions with the social standing of an empress, the Chief Vestal having the right of audience with the emperor. Appointed by him when they were between 6 and 10 years old, they served 30 years, after which they could leave and marry; but if they broke their vow of chastity while serving they were buried alive, and the lover was flogged to death. If they let the fire go out it was feared disaster would fall on Rome, and the vestal responsible was severely punished.

Temple of Saturn

Dating from 497 BC, Saturn's Temple was rebuilt after a fire in the fourth century AD. The eight Ionic columns of the portico you see in the foreground are all that remains. Saturn was a popular god of agriculture and plenty, and the State Treasury was housed within his temple. Most interestingly, he was unwittingly responsible for the celebration of Christmas, for in late December was held the Feast of Saturnalia, when masters and slaves changed places. Around 336 the Church was seeking a suitable day on which to keep Christ's birth (since no record existed of his birth date): what better day than 25 December to celebrate the incarnation of the one *who took upon himself the form of a slave* (Philippians 2:7), and *who came not to be served but to serve* (Matthew 20:28). On Saturnalia gifts were exchanged as well. Christianity often 'Christianised' pagan festivals, buildings and myths, giving them new meaning, as we shall see in the catacombs.

> Almighty God, grant we pray that by your grace we may be raised to share in the divinity of your Son, who through his incarnation humbled himself to share in our humanity.

Temple of Castor and Pollux

The three tall columns with an architrave on top, to the right of the Temple of Vesta, are all that remains of the temple to the Graeco-Roman deities, Castor and Pollux. It dates back to 484 BC. In the Battle of Regillus at the start of the Republic, two young men on white horses appeared, fighting for Rome. Later that day they were spotted by a pool in the Forum watering their horses, telling of the victory, and were hailed as 'heavenly twins', known also as the *Dioscuri*, the sons of Jupiter, and brothers of Helen of Troy. This temple was raised beside the pool to honour them, and such was their fame they appeared on early Roman coins. The surviving columns of the temple belong to a major rebuilding in the Augustan era.

The Republic prospered under its consuls and senate, and expanded. Early in the fourth century BC the massive **Servian Wall**, 11 kilometres long, was flung round the city to protect it (parts are still visible near *Termini*). By 396 Rome governed the whole of central Italy. The great Mediterranean power was Carthage (near modern Tunis), with an Empire stretching from northern Africa up to Sicily and southern Iberia (Spain); and when Roman armies reached Sicily in 264 Carthage fought back, and a relentless century of Punic Wars almost ended Rome's ambitions. Hannibal brought his great army, which included elephants, up from Iberia over the Pyrenees and across the Alps into Italy in 211. But the Servian Wall defeated him. He had seen nothing like it and was lost. By 146 Carthage was conquered and with it much of the Greek Empire too. Fabulous wealth came with conquest. The Greek Empire surrendered its legacy of art, architecture and culture, which Rome was very quick to adopt. Wealthy Romans purchased Greek sculpture; Roman sculptors imitated it. Temples and public buildings went up all over the expanding city, and the grandeur of Rome was born. But by the end of the second century BC Rome was in trouble. With failure in government, generals acting as warlords, food and water shortages, social unrest and riots, autocracy was being demanded. The ambitious Julius Caesar crossed the Rubicon in 49 BC and marched triumphantly to Rome. In 44 the Senate proclaimed him dictator for life.

Shakespeare's *Julius Caesar* immortalised the Republic's final days; within a month of the proclamation Caesar was assassinated in Pompey's Theatre (see p. 184) on the Ides of March (March 15), in a conspiracy led by Brutus (who claimed descent from the Brutus who founded the Republic) and Cassius. Mark Antony, who tried to warn Caesar, may not have begun his funeral oration with the words, *'Friends, Romans, countrymen'*, but he eloquently praised Caesar in his tribute delivered on the **Rostra**, a wide platform, partly preserved, on the other side of the columns of the Temple of Saturn. Although Caesar had named Octavian as his successor, not until 27 BC, after the death of Mark Antony, did the Roman Senate proclaim him Augustus. He reigned for forty-five years. 'I found Rome a city of bricks and left it a city of marble', he boasted. A 'brilliant tax strategist', Augustus used taxation to finance his building projects, and it was the collection of taxes which led to Jesus being born in Bethlehem. In his reign began the *Pax Romana*, an unprecedented era of peace, albeit won by conquest, voiced in the ancient Catholic Christmas Proclamation:

> In the one hundred and ninety-fourth Olympiad;
> The seven hundred and fifty-second year from the foundation of the city of Rome.
> The forty-second year of the reign of Octavian Augustus;
> the whole world being at peace,
> Jesus Christ, eternal God and Son of the eternal Father,
> desiring to sanctify the world by his most merciful coming,
> being conceived by the Holy Spirit,
> and nine months having passed since his conception,
> was born in Bethlehem of Judea of the Virgin Mary.
> Today is the Nativity of our Lord Jesus Christ according to the flesh.

Five hundred years of the Republic had ended, and five hundred years of Empire had begun. The city prospered. Eleven aqueducts brought plentiful sweet water from the Alban Hills (you may have noticed remains of Emperor Claudius's 40-kilometre-long aqueduct if you travelled by road from Ciampino airport), and by the middle of the third century there were reservoirs and fountains, and nearly a thousand public baths in Rome, which had an estimated population of more than a million and a half. No other city in the world reached that population until London and Beijing in the nineteenth century. New buildings went up all over Rome, and the Forum was filled with magnificent temples and basilicas. From your vantage point these are the main ones you can see:

Temple of Vespasian and Titus

The three elegant Corinthian columns closest to you belong to this temple begun by Emperor Titus in honour of his father, Vespasian. Within two years Titus died and it was completed in AD 80 by his brother, Domitian, who succeeded him. Vespasian is said to have died with these words on his lips: *'Pity, I think I'm turning into a god'*. It was customary for the emperors to be deified after death.

Temple of Antoninus and Faustina

This building appeared in the Forum in AD 140, constructed by Emperor Antoninus in memory of his deified wife, Faustina. When Antoninus died his name was added to the frieze. It is easily identified if you look to the left beyond the Temple of Saturn and spot eight green marble columns, behind which arises the Baroque façade of S. Lorenzo in Miranda (which is rarely open). The sides are rough stone, for the original marble went to embellish the Lateran Palace, when the Forum became a quarrymen's paradise during the Renaissance.

Temple of Romulus

If you can manoeuvre yourself to see beyond the Temple of Antoninus and Faustina you may spot the little round Temple of Romulus, dedicated, not to the founder of Rome, but to the son of Emperor Maxentius, though some now think it was a Temple of Jupiter. You saw its interior in SS. Cosma e Damiano. It may be that Constantine erected it around AD 315 to celebrate his victory over Maxentius.

Basilica (Nova) of Maxentius and Constantine

Beyond the Temple of Romulus is the vast, looming brick Basilica Nova, new because it was the last great building in the Forum. Started by Maxentius in AD 306, it was finished by Constantine after 313.

It may be helpful to explain that pagan temples were shrines rather than places of public worship. Generally they were quite small. The basilica was a large, public, commercial or civic building, with an apse and aisles. When Constantine permitted Christians to build churches to accommodate crowds they not unnaturally adopted the basilica style, as well as the name, as you see in St Peter's Basilica, St Paul's and the rest. You can see the basilica plan in front of you on the right: the long, wide area of grass with the stubs of pillars in it, are the remains of the **Basilica Julia**; originally started by Julius Caesar, it was rebuilt in AD 12 after being burnt down. Here 180 judges sat together to adjudicate serious cases. The remains could easily be taken for the footings of a large early church.

Santa Maria Antiqua

This sixth-century church is the best reason for walking round the Forum, but sadly it is often closed for restoration. You can make it out below the slope of the Palatine, beyond the Basilica Julia: a little brick building with a curious roof, a marble doorway facing you, and a little portico to one side. Wrecked by an earthquake in 847, it was not rebuilt, but some fine eighth-century frescoes survive, especially a Crucifixion in which Christ on the Cross is flanked by Our Lady and St John, and two smaller figures, one of whom is Longinus, the Roman soldier who pierced Christ's side, while the other holds up a sponge of vinegar. Another fresco shows the apostles Peter and Paul flanking the Virgin and Child. A damaged painting of St Anne holding the Blessed Virgin in her arms can be dated to 649 from a Greek inscription. In the same aisle there is a Christian sarcophagus with a relief depicting the resurrection motif of Jonah, which you often find in the catacombs. Next to the church, and originally part of its complex, is the **Oratory of the Forty Martyrs**, named after its apsidal wall-painting of forty Christian soldiers, who were frozen to death in an icy lake in Armenia during Diocletian's persecutions of 303.

Column of Phocas

This was the last construction in the Forum: a fluted Corinthian column standing 13.5 metres high on a white marble plinth, it is one of the few columns to have remained upright since the day it was erected. Try and position yourself to see it on the other side of Saturn's Temple. It was made in AD 608 to honour the Byzantine Emperor Phocas, who had just visited Rome and presented the Pantheon to Pope Boniface IV.

The Forum was now full. Augustus had refurbished the old buildings of the Republican era, and completed great building projects of his own. Successive emperors had made their contributions, and by the third century the city must have looked at its magnificent best, gleaming in white marble with fine carvings. The first two centuries after Augustus were prosperous, but as the Empire expanded by conquest it became too large to govern. Legions could no longer secure its long borders, and there was a shortage of legionaries. Tribes of 'barbarians', particularly from Germany, constantly made incursions, despite the Roman policy of assimilating them and giving their leaders positions of power and responsibility.

Rome was in trouble. In 235 Emperor Severus Alexander was assassinated. There followed him five emperors in five years, then 50 years of civil wars, invasions, plague, massive military expenditure, economic disaster and social distress. Between 271 and 275, to protect Rome from invaders, Emperor Aurelian flung a new, virtually impregnable, wall round the city, which you still see in many places, especially near St John Lateran. Augustus and his successors had distributed free grain to feed the growing population: free olive oil was later given; now to try and pacify the people Aurelian provided five pounds of free pork per month to each citizen. But the unrest continued. There were riots and persecutions against Christians, who were accused of angering the gods by refusing to worship them, thereby being the cause of these calamities.

Diocletian took drastic measures to control the deteriorating situation. He tried to wipe out Christianity with the most systematic and brutal persecution there had ever been. In 285 he gave the Empire two centres of government, with two Emperors, one in the east and the other in the west, assisted by two Caesars, ruling as a tetrarchy. None of them lived in Rome: and even Diocletian, who constructed vast new baths in Rome and kept buildings in repair to please the people, visited Rome only once, spending his time defending the northern border. Constantine reunited the Empire when he became Emperor, but seventeen years later he abandoned Rome and transformed ancient Byzantium into the Empire's glittering new capital, Constantinople, a new Rome; modern Istanbul. Once again there were emperors in the east and in the west, and the division in the Empire inevitably deepened, as Rome declined. Eventually there would even be two Churches, the Catholic West and Orthodox East. In 401 the Western Emperor Honorius transferred his court to Ravenna. The city of Rome was left to its fate.

Alaric the Visigoth attacked in 410, the first time in eight hundred years Rome had been sacked. All over the Empire the shock was profound. The legions were immediately ordered to abandon Britain and other parts to defend Rome. St Augustine, in *City of God*, argued that the sinful nature of Roman society was to blame. The attacks continued. Attila the Hun invaded northern Italy in 452, but Pope Leo the Great, now Rome's de facto leader, persuaded him to withdraw. The next crisis was in 455 when the Vandals attacked the city, and in 476 the last Western Emperor, Romulus, was deposed by the barbarian soldier, Odoacer, bringing the Western Empire to an end. It was now ruled by Gothic Kings, appointed as exarchs of the (Eastern) Byzantine Emperor. The Byzantine Empire flourished, especially under Justinian I (527–65), and gave an immense legacy of learning, law and culture to Italy. You have seen some of the stunning Byzantine-style mosaics in Rome's churches. So life went on quite well in Rome until Justinian dispatched a general, Belisarius, to recapture the city from its Gothic rulers in 536, thereby precipitating the Gothic Wars which culminated in another Sack of Rome in 546 by Totila, the Ostrogoth king. The aqueducts were destroyed, the people had no fresh water and fled to the hills. The population went into freefall. From over a million there were probably fewer than fifty thousand left, maybe only twenty thousand. The city was ruined: the Forum reverted to being a disease-ridden swamp. It fell to the Catholic Church, and in particular to Pope Gregory the Great, whom we shall meet later in the week, to generate Rome's remarkable recovery.

Return to the Campidoglio, and go down the gentle flight steps with wide treads, called a 'Cordonata' in Italian.

At the top you pass the Heavenly Twins, Castor and Pollux, with their pointy hats and their horses, whose Temple you saw in the Forum, and part way down on your right the small statue of Cola di Rienzo who takes us on to the fourteenth century, another period Rome was down on its luck, when the popes lived in Avignon (p. 152). Rienzo popularised himself as a new emperor, called on the Pope to return to Rome, and sought to unify Italy. The nobility turned against his extravagant claims, and this statue, erected only in the nineteenth century, marks the spot where he was struck down in 1354. At the bottom of the Cordonata you see two lions, Roman spoils from Egypt.

Turn right and you will see the remains of a second-century AD five-storey housing block with a shop, known as an insula, home to perhaps 200 people in spacious apartments. The Church of S. Rita was built into it in the Middle Ages, and the insula was re-discovered in 1927 when the church was demolished. You can see frescoes from the church as you pass. Keep along the pavement until you come to the corner of the huge white marble monument, which dominates Piazza Venezia.

Monument to Victor Emmanuel II (Il Vittoriano)

This enormous but undeniably imposing white marble monument to Victor Emmanuel II has always divided opinion: detractors call it 'the wedding cake' or 'the typewriter'. It would have shocked Augustus, dominating and hiding as it does the Forum. Nor would it have pleased Victor Emmanuel himself who was by all accounts a modest man. His great achievement was to do what Cola di Rienzo had no chance of doing. He united the Italian States and made Rome their capital in 1871, becoming the first king of a united Italy, a title he held until his death in 1878. You will find his tomb in the Pantheon (see p. 149). The monument was begun in 1885 but not completed until 1911. The area in the centre, beneath the goddess Roma, has the tomb of an unknown soldier from the First World War and is known as the Altar of the Fatherland (*Altare della Patria*). Within the bowels of the monument is the **Museo Centrale Risorgimento** (Reunification Museum). Like it or not, the monument can be seen from all over Rome, helping you to locate Piazza Venezia if you get lost; from the roof you can enjoy stunning views across the city.

*You now have a choice. There are many bus routes from Piazza Venezia (Map p. 241) to Termini, St Peter's and other places, so you should find your way back. But if you have time for more sightseeing, cross the road, go through the small park, and you will glimpse the façade of S. Marco beyond the trees. If you keep your eyes open in Rome (and that means looking up as well) there is always something worth a diversion to see. To your left in the little **Piazza d'Aracoeli** is a lovely fountain by Giacomo della Porta (1589), the great fountain designer in Rome.*

Basilica di San Marco

Open: 10:00–13:00; 16:00–18:00 (Tuesday to Friday).

Founded in 336 by Pope Mark in honour of St Mark the Evangelist, this is one of Rome's oldest churches. Inevitably it has been rebuilt and refurbished several times after sackings and fires: finally, and very sumptuously, in 1735-50, when the twenty columns lavishly veneered with Sicilian jasper were installed in the nave. The fine coffered ceiling is by Giovanni dei Dolci, who came to Rome from Florence as a carpenter in 1458, and whose name is linked with the Sistine Chapel. But your eye will be drawn to a ninth-century mosaic in the apse: in the centre is Christ, his feet resting on a pedestal or footstool inscribed with the Greek letters alpha (A) and omega (Ω). Christ is flanked by Pope Mark, presenting his church, and Pope Gregory IV, St Mark the Evangelist, and St Agnes, St Agapitus and St Felicissimus; rather unusually, they too are standing on pedestals inscribed with their names. The façade was designed by Leon Battista Alberti, a Genoese priest, architect and philosopher, much involved in the restoration of Rome after the disastrous Avignon papacy. From its double-height triple-arched portico, Pope Paul II, who built and occupied the adjoining palazzo as an official residence, would give his benediction to the crowds in the piazza below. Paul II was a Venetian and since his time S. Marco has been the regional church of the Venetian community in Rome.

In the corner to the left of the church, is a large second- or third-century statue of Isis, known since the sixteenth century as **Madama Lucrezia**. It is one of the Talking Statues of Rome, so-called because satires poking fun at public figures, especially popes, were posted on them in the fourteenth and fifteenth centuries. To everyone's delight, statues would have conversations with one another.

Palazzo Venezia (formerly Palazzo di San Marco)

Designed (according to tradition) by Alberti, this palace was built in the mid-15th century as a residence for the cardinal appointed to S. Marco, Cardinal Pietro Barbo. On being elected Pope Paul II in 1464, Barbo continued to live here and it was a papal residence until 1564 when Pius IV gave the building to the Venetian Republic for an embassy and ambassador's residence (hence Palazzo Venezia and Piazza Venezia). A more recent occupant was Mussolini, who built his secret bunker inside and from the balcony overlooking the piazza harangued the crowds. The apartments now form the **Museo Nazionale di Palazzo di Venezia,** a museum of porcelain, ceramics, tapestries, ivories and sculpture from the early Christian era up to the early Renaissance.

This is really the end of the day with the early Christians, but you may be tempted to visit one more church. The Gesù time-travels you into the seventeenth century, but it is close by; and at 17:30 each day it hosts a kind of 15-minute son et lumière with the restored 'macchina barocca' in the magnificent Chapel of St Ignatius. To get there; go round the Palazzo Venezia to Via del Plebiscito. (Beware of being tempted into Sorelle Adamoli, the marvellous house-and-kitchen shop across the road.) At the end of the block you will come into Piazza del Gesù with a large church on your left.

Church of the Gesù

Open: 7:00–12:30; 16:00–19:30.

St Ignatius of Loyola was one of the great sixteenth-century reformers of the Church and the founder of the Society of Jesus, the Jesuits, which became the most powerful missionary movement of Christianity since the preaching of the apostles. They took the Gospel to the newly-discovered lands of South America, to North America, India, Japan and China, suffering martyrdom in many countries, including England. A soldier, Ignatius was gravely injured in battle in 1521 and endured many surgical operations, but during his convalescence he read a Life of Christ and was converted. On 25 March 1522 he left his uniform before an image of Our Lady, and began his new life.

Gesù is Italian for Jesus, and this church is the mother Church of the Society of Jesus. St Ignatius is buried here, though he never lived to see it built. The architects were Giacomo Barozzi da Vignola, the influential master of the later Renaissance, and his pupil, Giacomo della Porta, who took over both the Gesù and St Peter's, when Vignola died in 1573, and substituted a new design for the façade. The building they produced was hugely influential—in the words of the architectural historian Nikolaus Pevsner, the Gesù 'has perhaps exerted a wider influence than any other church of the last four hundred years'. Its style is so familiar in Rome (and think of Wren's St Paul's Cathedral in London). Combining length with central planning, it allows for the glorious celebration of Mass while providing a huge space for preaching—a single wide nave with the pulpit positioned for the best acoustics.

The extraordinarily rich and dynamic decoration of the interior with its profusion of marble, bronze and gilt, came a century later and caused a sensation: it was scathingly derided as 'baroque', meaning 'misshapen' or 'absurd'. But this period of the High Baroque embraced not only architecture, but painting, sculpture and music too; the Catholic Church became its leading patron, and the style displayed impressive confidence in Jesus and his renewed Church.

> Dear brothers and sisters, may the Lord help us to re-discover the way of beauty as one of the ways, perhaps the most attractive and fascinating, to be able to find and love God ... When faith, celebrated in a particular way in the liturgy, encounters art, a profound synchrony is created, because both can and want to praise God, making the Invisible visible.
>
> Pope Benedict XVI

Raise your eyes to the wonderful *Adoration of the Name of Jesus* by Giovanni Battista Gaulli, the renowned ceiling painter, and his *Assumption of Our Lady* in the dome. St Ignatius's Chapel, in the left transept, is the church's masterpiece: designed, after stiff competition, in 1695, by Andrea Pozzo, a Jesuit brother, architect, painter and theatrical designer. His *macchina barocca* or 'conversion machine' drew on his theatrical experience and the idea of using 'modern media' to communicate and inspire Faith—and it does so again, since its restoration. During the operation of the 'machine' (today accompanied with music and commentary), the painted altarpiece of Ignatius on a cloud being received by Christ, slowly sinks into the altar below, revealing a splendid shining statue of the saint, gilded and bejeweled and brightly illuminated. One advantage of coming to see the 'machine' in operation is that the splendid ceiling paintings in the nave and cupola are illuminated. In the little chapel next to St Ignatius a revered thirteenth-century image of Our Lady, the *Madonna della Strada*, Our Lady of the Way, invites devotion. Opposite St Ignatius' Chapel is Pietro da Cortona's Chapel of St Francis Xavier, the missionary to India and Japan, whose death as he reached the island of Sancian (Shangchuan) on the way to China, is depicted in the painting. Cortona was an exceptional Baroque painter, a contemporary of Bernini and Borromini, who are better known. The marble decoration in the sanctuary and nave were added in the nineteenth century.

Next to the church, at Piazza del Gesù 45, you can visit the rooms of St Ignatius, where he corresponded with the hundreds of Jesuit missionaries around the world. In a corridor Pozzo painted wonderful frescoes of lively events and humorous scenes from his life. You can also see relics, documents and belongings of the saint.

To return you may walk back to the bus stops in Piazza Venezia (Map p. 241), or walk on a little further to Largo di Torre Argentina (Map p. 149), with its ruins of four temples from the time of the Roman Republic. The 40, 46, 62, 64, 81 and 916 buses outside Feltrinelli's bookshop will take you towards St Peter's. To reach Termini catch the 40 or 64 near Deutsche Bank on the Corso Vittorio Emanuele II.

Alternatively, if you are staying near St Peter's, and have the energy, you can continue walking along the Corso Vittorio Emanuele II, which is full of bright and busy shops, and churches open for private prayer and Mass. You will reach Sant'Andrea della Valle and Chiesa Nuova that way (Map p. 138). There are restaurants on and off this road.

2

WITH ST PETER AND ST PAUL

Morning: Basilica of St Peter

Open: 7:00–18:30 (19:00 in summer).

The quietest time to visit St Peter's is around 7:00 or 8:00 am, when priests are celebrating Mass on their own or with groups of people, (even if it means missing your hotel breakfast and having it afterwards in a bar); or in late afternoon. Even in the winter the queues through the airport-type security detectors often stretch all around the Square, and the inside of St Peter's can be like King's Cross Station in the rush hour. (Maps for St Peter's, pp. 239 and 240.)

Viewing St Peter's from the Square you realise the Basilica is built on an incline, the Vatican Hill. Try to imagine a cemetery where the Basilica now stands. The sole reason the Basilica was built is that St Peter was buried in that cemetery. It was a very extensive pagan necropolis, above ground, and was used for burials from the first to the third centuries AD: still in use in Emperor Constantine's time, it contains some very fine tombs and expensively decorated mausoleums. Poorer people, and that included St Peter, were simply buried in the ground, as we do today. Part of it, the **Necropolis Via Triumphalis**, is accessible from the Vatican Museums, but the entrance to the part where St Peter was buried (the *Scavi*) is to the left of St Peter's (see below).

St Peter's was built over the cemetery. Further to the left of the cemetery, now partly beneath St Peter's and St Peter's Square, was the Circus of Nero, formerly known as the Circus of Caligula. The obelisk in St Peter's Square was brought from Alexandria by order of Emperor Caligula and set in this Circus complex in AD 37. If you visit the *Scavi* you may notice a marker where it stood. It was in this Circus in AD 64 that St Peter was martyred, crucified upside down, it was said. This obelisk may have been the last thing he saw.

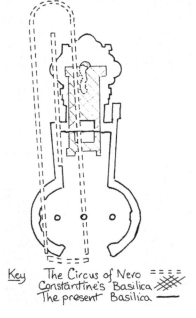

Key — The Circus of Nero ====
Constantine's Basilica ✕✕✕
The present Basilica ——

His body was buried, perhaps hurriedly and at night, during Nero's terrifying purge, in a shallow grave close to the Circus. How it was marked we do not know, but other Christians were soon buried very close to him, like the spokes of a wheel, and one burial (not necessarily the first) has been dated AD 70 by a date-stamped tile. In the year 150, during the long and peaceful reign of Emperor Antoninus Pius, the Christians felt confident enough to raise a small monument above Peter's grave with pillars about a metre high, a Roman *aedicule*, supported by a red-plastered wall. It became known as the 'Trophy of Gaius', simply because a priest of that name happened to mention he had seen it on a visit in 200.

Emperor Constantine decided, in about 314, to honour the apostle by building a basilica over his tomb. To do this he had to be drastic. He cut into the hillside to provide a level surface for his large church, destroying and damaging graves and mausoleums in the process, and burying others. Even pagans resisted disturbing the dead, and to do so was a crime punishable by death. It is impossible to exaggerate the risk he took, even as an emperor. Some of the graves he damaged were of high-ranking citizens of Rome. But he did so because he was determined to place a monument in the Basilica immediately over Peter's tomb. In 1939 Pope Pius XII ordered excavations (*scavi*) beneath the Basilica to try and locate the tomb, and these are open to the public, but you must book in advance (p. 4). Another section of the necropolis has been excavated beneath the Vatican Gardens, accessible not from St Peter's, but from the Vatican Museums (p. 4).

St Peter's Tomb

The entrance to the Scavi is on the left just outside the colonnade, and it has its own quick scanner, security and guards. Do not bring any bags (save a small handbag, maybe) or else you will have to queue with everyone else and deposit them in the free facility to the right of the Basilica. At the end of the tour you will be in the crypt of the Basilica where many popes are buried.

A guide takes you down into the necropolis where you walk along a narrow path that was once at ground level. On both sides you see tombs and mausoleums, some of which Constantine damaged, and others in perfect condition. The decoration and wall paintings are beautiful. It is a pagan necropolis, but some of the mausoleums contain the remains of both Christians and pagans from the same family. A predominantly pagan one has an inscription asking Peter to pray *'for the holy Christians buried beside your body'*. One in particular is most striking. It contains a golden mosaic depicting Jesus as the sun-god, his chariot drawn by horses rising in the sky, which early Christians adopted as a motif of his resurrection (Sunday, the 'Day of the Sun', the day Jesus rose from the dead). In the same mausoleum is a fresco of Jonah, found also in the catacombs as a symbol of Christ's resurrection.

The archaeologists reached the area immediately beneath the Papal Altar and, as expected, found Peter's grave, the Trophy of Gaius, and Constantine's Monument above it. The Trophy is supported by the red plastered wall, and at right angles to it is

another wall they named the 'Graffiti Wall' because innumerable Greek and Latin prayers had been scratched on it by pilgrims visiting the grave between the end of the third and the beginning of the fourth centuries. It was noted that the monument in Constantine's Basilica was not positioned immediately over the grave but, rather curiously, equidistant above the grave and the Graffiti Wall.

The bones in graves around Peter's were catalogued and reverently stored. There were a few bones in Peter's grave beneath the Trophy. These were very carefully examined, and found to be the remains of three people, clearly not the bones of St Peter. The purpose of the excavations had been achieved, St Peter's grave had been found. It was nonetheless disappointing not to find his remains, and surprising, for although it was known that at some date, probably around 258, his bones, along with those of St Paul, had been kept in the Catacomb of S. Sebastiano, it was assumed they had been returned to their original cemeteries (p. 86). The excavations concluded in 1949.

In 1952 the distinguished epigrapher, Margherita Guarducci, was given permission to study the Graffiti Wall, and became intrigued by a Greek inscription which she deciphered as *Peter is here*. She examined a cavity beside it and was surprised to find it lined in marble. She asked one of the archaeological team if any bones had been found in the cavity, and on being given the box she was astonished to see the bones were wrapped in remnants of purple cloth run with gold thread. In ancient Rome colours denoted status and as only the emperors wore purple—indeed ordinary people would have had no access to purple cloth—this suggested that the bones might have been wrapped by an emperor himself. They were subjected to close scientific examination and it was found that the soil encrusted on them matched the marly sand in the grave, while in other parts of the Vatican area the earth is different (blue clay or yellow sand). The bones were of a well-built man, aged between 50 and 60, 1.7 metres tall, but missing feet (as St Peter would have been had he been cut down hastily from a cross after being crucified upside down). Carbon-dating confirmed they were first-century in date.

After all the tests had been concluded Pope St Paul VI was sufficiently assured to announce to the world that the bones of St Peter had been found.

The Basilica

Visitors must go through security, and deposit bags in the free facility to the right of the Basilica, where there are cloakrooms and toilets.

By the fifteenth century the old Basilica of Constantine was too small and in serious disrepair. Pope Julius II made the bold but controversial decision to demolish Constantine's great gift to the Church, which had stood for 1,200 years, and replace it with a modern church, entrusting the design to Donato Bramante of Milan. When the old church was being demolished this earned him the epithet *Bramante Ruinante*. Julius II laid the Foundation Stone on 18 April 1506: it lies under the north-east crossing pier (St Veronica's). Progress was rapid, but in 1514 Bramante died. Work slowed down, successive popes and architects died, the design kept being altered, and Rome was sacked in 1527. In 1546 the 72-year-old Michelangelo was sent for to rescue the project. He adopted and enlarged Bramante's design and began work on his own dome. The Basilica was still unfinished when the great man died in 1564—just a couple of weeks short of his

89th birthday—and Giacomo Barozzi da Vignola constructed the two subordinate domes according to Michelangelo's plans before his death in 1573. Several architects later, in 1605, Carlo Maderno, whose façade at S. Susanna had won wide acclaim, was entrusted with its completion. The design was changed yet again: the nave was made much longer; but finally, on 18 November 1626, it was consecrated by Pope Urban VIII on the 1,300th anniversary of the consecration of the first Basilica. The building can host twenty thousand people and frequently does. Above that number, and Mass is celebrated in the Square outside. The great church was paid for by a worldwide appeal, not least, to the shame of the Church, by the sale of Indulgences, which precipitated Luther's Reformation. And so the building, notwithstanding its magnificence, is a vivid reminder of the division in those tragic days.

While work on the Basilica was underway, the Square was also being constructed. The 327-ton obelisk was moved from Nero's Circus and raised here in 1586 under the direction of the late-Renaissance architect, Domenico Fontana, who became a great favourite of Pope Sixtus V. Raising it took 900 men, 150 horses, and 47 cranes, a complex and dangerous operation supervised by the Pope himself. The story is that he called for total silence. Suddenly a voice rang out, *'water on the ropes'*. A sailor called Bresca had noticed the ropes were heating up. The Pope asked him what reward he would like for saving the day, and he requested that his family might have the privilege of providing the pope with palms from his plantation for Palm Sunday. The obelisk had been topped with a metal globe (now in the Capitoline Museum): Sixtus had this replaced by a cross containing a relic of the True Cross. In the inscription at the bottom he included the words *incredib sumptu*, meaning 'shocking price', referring to the cost of building the Basilica.

The two fountains are fed from Lake Bracciano, the earlier one, on the right, was designed by Carlo Maderno: its pair was added in 1675 by Gian Lorenzo Bernini, the designer of the great colonnade whose welcoming arms draw you into the Basilica. Hailed as the 'Father of Baroque', the Neapolitan-born Bernini was its most famous exponent and the greatest sculptor of his age: his work is to be found all over Rome. The geometry of the colonnade is so accurate that if you stand on one of the porphyry discs set in the paving between each fountain and the obelisk, the four-deep columns close and become as one. Above the colonnade 140 statues of saints remind us of the many witnesses *'in a great cloud on every side of us'* (Hebrews 12:1).

The more recent mosaic of Our Lady (*Mater Ecclesiae*) on the left corner of the Apostolic Palace, was put there on the orders of Pope St John Paul II in thanksgiving for his recovery after the assassination attempt in the Square on 13 May 1981. He attributed this to Our Lady, since it happened on the Feast of Our Lady of Fatima, and told his would-be assassin, *'One hand fired the shot, another deflected it'*. It was copied from an image inside St Peter's which had been in Constantine's Basilica.

From the balcony above St Peter's central door the pope addresses and blesses the people of the world after his election; and on the feasts of Christmas and Easter he gives his blessing *Urbi et Orbi* (to the city and to the world). On Sundays he speaks from a window in the Apostolic Palace.

Inside the Basilica

In the early morning, when the Basilica is quiet, the pilgrim should perhaps first walk up the nave to the *confessio*, the area before the Papal Altar, and pray there close to St Peter's tomb, the goal of a pilgrimage to Rome.

> How many saints have knelt here since the dawn of Christianity! Here St Ignatius of Loyola, St Philip Neri, St Dominic and others prayed in ecstasy and bedewed the ground with their tears. Here kings and emperors have come to lay their homage and even their crowns at St Peter's feet.
>
> Fr P. J. Chandlery SJ

On the way look for the names of other great cathedrals in brass letters let into the marble floor, the position of each name indicating that building's length compared to St Peter's: the next longest is St Paul's in London. The proportions of St Peter's

are so perfect you hardly realise how vast it is. The Latin letters in the dome, of Peter's Commission, *You are Peter and on this rock I will build my Church* are 2 metres high, and give some idea of the scale. Just before you reach the *confessio* you will see on the right the bronze statue of St Peter saved from the old Basilica. Some experts date it to the fifth century, others to the thirteenth. The saint's large right toe has been replaced many times having been kissed and touched so often by devout faithful. The casket on view in the *confessio* contains *pallia*, neck-stoles, woven from the wool of lambs blessed on the Feast of St Agnes; worn by patriarchs and archbishops they signify their calling to shepherd the flock in unity with the pope.

> Lord, you called Saint Peter to be the rock on which you built the Church and made him the Shepherd of your flock. Bless his successor, our Holy Father, with all the graces he needs in his life and ministry.
> St Peter, pray for him; pray for the Church.

The baldacchino over the Papal Altar with its four enormous bronze barley-sugar columns was designed by Bernini when he was only 26. Constantine's Basilica had similar but smaller stone columns and you can see eight of them in the four balconies which overlook the balda- cchino. These are set high up on the four massive piers supporting the dome. Below are niches filled with large statues: St Helena with the Cross; St Longinus, who pierced Christ's side with a lance, designed by Bernini; St Veronica with her veil; and St Andrew, brother of St Peter.

Sections of the Basilica are often closed-off by barriers, and it is not always possible to see all the altars and monuments. If you can, move from the Papal Altar to the Altar of the Chair in the apse, so called because the elaborate bronze throne held aloft above it by four Doctors of the Church, encases an ancient wooden chair formerly believed to have been used by early popes, if not St Peter himself. (It is now thought to be a Carolingian throne: you can see a copy in the Treasury.) The climax of the east end is the luminous *Gloria*, an oval window made of thin alabaster, surrounded by a host of gilded angels among billowing clouds. Gilded shafts represent the light of the Holy Spirit, here symbolised by a dove at the centre of window. All of this was designed by Bernini. Daylight streaming through the orange-yellow alabaster of the window bathes this end of St Peter's in a golden glow.

To the right of the altar is Bernini's monument to Urban VIII who consecrated this new St Peter's. He employed many artists to beautify the Basilica, and the streets and piazzas of Rome are full of wonderful fountains and works of art he commissioned: they all have the 'Barberini Bees' from his family's coat of arms. Bernini was his favourite sculptor. He is said to have remarked to the artist, *'It is your great fortune to see Barberini pope; but We are even luckier that Bernini lives at the time of Our pontificate'*. So close were they that the pope was once seen holding up a mirror for Bernini to make a self-portrait.

To the left of the altar is the monument to Pope Paul III by Giacomo della Porta, a close collaborator with Michelangelo. This pope issued fierce denunciations against slave trading, and convened the reforming Council of Trent in 1545. For him Michelangelo painted the *Last Judgement* in the Sistine Chapel and created other works in Rome, including the architectural setting of the Campidoglio.

Moving towards the left aisle you will see a monument to Pope Alexander VIII, an old man who was pope for less than two years. Facing this is an altarpiece of *St Peter curing the Paralysed Man by the Temple Gate* (Acts 3:1–10), a mosaic reproduction of the original by Francesco Mancini. It is worth noting that the only painting in St Peter's is in the Blessed Sacrament Chapel;

all the other 'pictures' are fine mosaics produced in a workshop, founded in the sixteenth century, and which still exists in the Vatican Gardens.

At the end of the north (left) aisle is the Altar of Pope St Leo the Great, who is shown in Algardi's marble relief persuading Attila the Hun, who invaded Italy in 452, to leave Rome in peace. Preaching soon afterwards he warned the people: *'Lest you incite reproach, return to your Saviour. Remember the marvels he has wrought amongst you. Beware of attributing your deliverance to the stars, as some people impiously do, but refer it only to the boundless mercy of God who softened the hearts of the barbarians. Let us use this respite accorded by our kind master to work at amending our lives'.* To your left is the Altar of Our Lady of the Column, with an image of the Blessed Virgin which had been painted on a marble column in the central nave of Constantine's Basilica. Pope St Paul VI bestowed on it the title *Mater Ecclesiae.* This is the image Pope St John Paul II had copied in mosaic to put on the exterior of the Apostolic Palace.

Moving down the aisle you pass Bernini's flamboyant monument to Pope Alexander VII, with its marble drapery and bronze *memento mori.* Completed in 1676, when Bernini was nearly 80, this was his last work in St Peter's. The figure on the left, with a child on her arms, represents Charity; on the right Truth has one foot on the British Isles. This alludes to the pope's anger at England, which he called that 'snakepit of heresy and regicide', where opposition by Puritans after the Civil War caused the rejection in 1663 of a Plan for Unity supported by Rome, Archbishop Sheldon of Canterbury and almost all the Anglican bishops. Alexander VII is remembered in Rome for some fine architectural projects like Piazza Colonna and Piazza del Popolo. Opposite is the Altar of the Sacred Heart, with Jesus revealing to St Margaret Mary Alacoque the love of his heart for everyone.

The left transept is a chapel for daily Mass and private prayer. Of its three altars, the central one is dedicated to St Joseph. On the right is the Altar of St Thomas, and on the left the Altar of the Crucifixion of St Peter, with a mosaic showing St Peter crucified upside down in Nero's Circus on which this part of the Basilica stands.

A little further on, under the kneeling figure of Pope Pius VIII, is the entrance to the sacristy, part of which you may enter. It was rebuilt in the eighteenth century, replacing a very much older building on the site called the Rotonda of St Andrew, which had been used as the sacristy since the sixteenth century. The polychrome marble statue of St Andrew in the vestibule probably came from this earlier building: on your right is a marble tablet inscribed with the names of the popes who are buried in St Peter's Basilica. A corridor brings you to the **Treasury**, which is well worth a visit if you have time and a few euros to spare (they are used to help the poor). There are ten rooms of treasures, among them artefacts from Constantine's Basilica, including the ninth-century gilded bronze cockerel from the top of the campanile. Here too is the *Crux Vaticana*, a wonderful sixth-century reliquary-cross containing a fragment of the True Cross which was given to Pope John III by the Byzantine Emperor Justin II, and the paleo-Christian sarcophagus of Junius Bassus, a Roman prefect and Christian convert, vividly carved with Biblical scenes from both the Old and New Testaments. Among the many sacred vessels on display is the solid gold Stuart Chalice, made by the goldsmith Valadier, encrusted with 130 diamonds of different shapes and sizes, which belonged to Henry Benedict, Cardinal Duke of York, whose marble bust by a late eighteenth-century sculptor is also here. In the Chapel of the Beneficiaries the inscription on the altar shows that it, too, was the gift of the Cardinal Duke of York.

Opposite the sacristy entrance is the Altar of the Lie, depicting Ananias and Sapphira who lied about their possessions (Acts 5:1–11). Round the corner to your left is the Altar of the Transfiguration, under which lies the body of Pope Innocent XI. Above the altar is a fine mosaic of Raphael's final masterpiece, the *Transfiguration*. This area is part of the Clementine Chapel, named after Pope Clement VIII, who commissioned its decoration with precious marbles, mosaics and stucco, for the Great Jubilee Year 1600. Here you will find the Altar of St Gregory the Great, the pope who sent St Augustine to reconvert England in 597 (after the devastation of the Church by the Anglo-Saxon invasions); and whom he appointed first Archbishop of Canterbury.

To the left is the monument of Pope Pius VII, commissioned by his Secretary of State, Cardinal Consalvi, from Bertel Thorvaldsen (a Dane, and the only Protestant sculptor ever to work in St Peter's). Given the title 'Servant of God' by Benedict XVI, Pius VII was a cultured man and Benedictine monk, who campaigned against slavery, and whose other major concern was the aftermath of the French Revolution, and the suppression of France's monasteries by Napoleon. When he annexed the Papal States, Napoleon imprisoned the sick Pius VII for six years at Savona, close to the French border, until British forces released him in 1814. So forgiving was the pope that he pleaded with the British Government to alleviate the harsh conditions under which Napoleon lived in exile on St Helena, sent a priest to be his chaplain, and offered a refuge in Rome to members of the Bonaparte family.

The monument to Blessed Pope Innocent XI, shows the pontiff with his triple tiara on his knee flanked by statues representing Faith and Fortitude. A curved bas-relief depicts the Liberation of Vienna from the besieging Turks in 1683, a decisive episode in the history of Europe, in which Innocent played a vital role. He strongly disapproved of religious persecution and condemned Louis XIV for his treatment of the Huguenots. He admonished James II for his support of the French King, and also for the forceful way he tried to impose Catholicism on England. Innocent XI is even suspected of helping fund the so-called 'Glorious Revolution' which drove the Catholic Stuarts from the English throne and broke England's alliance with France. Soon you will come to the Stuart Memorial in St Peter's. Then there is Alessandro Algardi's white marble monument to Pope Leo XI, who reigned but 27 days in 1605. When Bernini's patron Pope Urban VIII died in 1644, his successor, Innocent X, preferred Algardi; this was his first major commission.

The next chapel is the Choir Chapel, where many of the daily services are held. Maderno, the little-known Pietro Bianchi, and Borromini all contributed to its decoration. The mosaic celebrates the Immaculate Conception of Our Lady, while beneath the altar are some relics of St John Chrysostom. The body of this revered fourth-century theologian and Archbishop of Constantinople was seized by Crusaders in 1204, and taken to Rome, but Pope St John Paul II returned some of his bones to the Orthodox Church in 2004, a gesture much appreciated by the Orthodox: they are now enshrined in the Cathedral of St George in Istanbul.

Then you will come to the monument to Pope Innocent VIII, made by Antonio del Pollaiolo in 1498, the only monument transferred from Constantine's church. Pollaiolo was a Renaissance sculptor and artist who taught Botticelli. Next to the pope are the four cardinal virtues: Prudence, Justice, Fortitude and Temperance. The upper lunette displays the three theological virtues: Faith, Hope and Charity. Opposite is a statue of Pope St Pius X, whose body rests under the altar of the next chapel, the Chapel of the Presentation. He is the pope most associated with encouraging frequent Holy Communion and with the struggle against Modernism. On the right wall of the chapel a bronze memorial to Pope St John XXIII shows him visiting prisoners, children and the sick. Once on a visit to the Regina Coeli Prison in Rome, he told the inmates that since they couldn't come to see him, he had come to see them. To the left of the Altar of the Presentation a statue of Pope Benedict XV kneels on a tomb representing the First World War, which he described as a 'useless massacre'. The tomb is covered in olive branches of peace. In the relief behind the statue Mary presents Jesus, the Prince of Peace, to a world in flames.

Then there are two memorials of great interest to the English and Scots: the Stuart Monument, a neo-classical masterpiece by Canova, partly paid for by George III; and opposite, the monument to Maria Clementina Sobieska, James III's wife, which includes her portrait in mosaic. Beneath the Stuart Monument, in the crypt, are the bodies of the last members of the Royal House of Stuart: James III, the 'Old Pretender' to the English throne, and his two sons, Bonnie Prince Charlie, the 'Young

Pretender', and Henry Benedict, who became a Cardinal. There is more about their story on p. 132.

The last chapel of the left aisle is the Baptistery: it was designed by Carlo Fontana, who was apprenticed to Bernini for ten years, before branching out on his own. (He seems not to have been of the same family as Domenico Fontana.) The porphyry font is the inverted cover of the sarcophagus of Otto II, the Holy Roman Emperor who died in Rome in 983, but is Roman in origin and traditionally associated with the tomb of Emperor Hadrian in Castel Sant'Angelo. Fontana designed the superb gilded cover. All children in Rome have the right to be baptised in it, and the pope himself sometimes celebrates this Sacrament here.

As you cross the back of the Basilica notice the large purple porphyry disc (or *rota*) set into the marble pavement about thirty metres from the central west door. It came from Constantine's Basilica and may (or may not) be the one on which Charlemagne is said to have knelt to be crowned by Pope Leo III on Christmas night of the year 800—there were four such *rotae* in the old Basilica.

Michelangelo's *Pietà*, now shielded by bullet-proof glass because of an attack on it in 1972, always draws a crowd, so it is not easy to pray there. Michelangelo carved it from a single block of marble, and so perfect is it, and so young was he (only 24), that it was rumoured he was not the sculptor. He therefore came into the Basilica one night and across the bandolier chiselled, 'Michaela[n]gelus Bonarotus

Florentin[us] Faciebi[t]' (*Michelangelo Buonarotti of Florence made this*). He never needed to sign anything again.

You then pass the monument of a very reluctant pope, Leo XII, imparting his blessing during the Jubilee of 1825, and, opposite, Carlo Fontana's monument to Queen Christina of Sweden who in 1654 abdicated her throne and moved to Rome, converting to Catholicism en route in Brussels. She is depicted in profile on a gilded bronze medallion, and her abjuration of Protestanism is shown in the relief on the front of the sarcophagus.

The Chapel of St Sebastian is a popular place of prayer, because below the altar now dedicated to Pope St John Paul II, is his tomb. It fell to him to implement the teachings of the Second Vatican Council. He was pope for 26 years, the second-longest reigning pope after Pius IX and the most-travelled pope in history. He preached the Gospel to more people than anyone before him, and was one of the world's most influential figures in the twentieth century, facilitating the collapse of communism, beginning in his native Poland. He survived two attempts on his life, and inaugurated World Youth Days in 1986, which he enjoyed with millions of young people, to whom he was a hero and saint, and which continue to be held every two or three years in different cities around the world.

To right and left are statues of two twentieth-century popes. On the right is the seated figure of Pope Pius XI, a brilliant scholar, and author of thirty social encyclicals, who vigorously condemned Nazism before the outbreak of the Second World War. He was the first pope to use radio and, like St John Paul II, a keen mountaineer. His successor, Pope Pius XII, elected in 1939, is commemorated on the left with a stern-looking bronze statue by the well-regarded Francesco Messina. The pope's gesture is said to represent his saying, '*Nothing is lost in peace, all can be lost with war*'. Pius XII has been much maligned for not speaking out more publicly against the Nazis, yet on his election he made the unprecedented appointment of Jewish professors to certain Vatican Departments. He decided it was best to work secretly to save Jews, ordering the issue of false baptismal certificates to them, and requesting Religious Houses both of men and women all over Italy to hide them. In the tiny Vatican City itself he concealed thousands of Jews, despite Hitler's warnings that his troops would enter the City State. It is estimated that the efforts of Pope Pius XII saved 860,000 Jews from the death camps.

The monument to the devout and reforming Pope Innocent XII, flanked by the allegorical figures of Charity and Justice, is by the eighteenth-century neo-classical sculptor, Filippo della Valle. Robert Browning, in his poem, *The Ring and the Book*, tells the true story of the Pope's intervention in a notorious murder trial in Rome. Opposite you will see the monument, made by Bernini in 1635, to Matilda of Canossa, Margravine of Tuscany, a powerful ruler on whom, in 1111, the Holy Roman Emperor, Henry V, bestowed the title Imperial Vicar and Vice-Queen of Italy. Her remains were transferred here from Mantua, where she had been buried, by Pope Urban VIII.

The Blessed Sacrament Chapel you come to now is strictly guarded and you are only admitted to pray. An exceptionally heavy curtain hangs over the door, which effectively shuts out all sounds. It is an oasis of peace, and you can pray undisturbed there before Bernini's gilded bronze tabernacle and Pietro da Cortona's painting of the *Holy Trinity*. The Blessed Sacrament is perpetually exposed, and Benediction is given each day at 16:45.

The next monument is by Camillo Rusconi who, like Filippo della Valle, bridged the gap between the Baroque and the Neo-Classical. Made in 1723, it commemorates Pope Gregory XIII, who was active in the renewal of the Catholic Church, following the Reformation, and who in 1582 introduced the Gregorian calendar: in that year 4 October was followed by 15 October. The promulgation of the new calendar is shown in relief on the front of the sarcophagus. (Great Britain did not adopt the Gregorian calender until 1752, when 2 September was followed by 14 September.) Opposite, the funerary monument of Gregory XIV, who was pope for only a year, in 1590, is exceptionally simple, at his own request, consisting of a niche set into the wall with a plain sarcophagus below it.

Straight ahead is the Altar of St Jerome, easily located by the file of people praying before Pope St John XXIII, who rests beneath it. He convened the Second Vatican Council, and promoted ecumenism. He abolished much papal ceremony, paid pastoral visits to hospitals and prisons, and even occasionally went out alone late in the evening into the streets of Rome, meeting people, earning the nickname 'Johnny Walker'. Above the altar is an eighteenth-century mosaic copy of the famous painting by Domenichino, the *Viaticum of St Jerome*. The aged saint receives Holy Communion from St Ephraem in his monastery at Bethlehem. Kissing the hand of the dying saint is St Paula of Rome, one of the great Biblical scholar's favourite disciples. This chapel forms part of the area known as the Gregorian Chapel, begun by Michelangelo and completed by Giacomo della Porta. On the back wall is the altar of *Our Lady of Succour*, whose image (painted on wood), was formerly in Constantine's Basilica.

> O Mother of Perpetual Help, grant that I may ever invoke thy most powerful name, which is the safeguard of the living and the salvation of the dying. O Purest Mary, O Sweetest Mary, let thy name henceforth be ever on my lips. Delay not, O Blessed Lady, to help me whenever I call on thee, for, in all my needs, in all my temptations, I shall never cease to call on thee, ever repeating thy sacred name, Mary, Mary.

The remains of St Gregory of Nazianzus, who died in 390, one of the great Cappadocian theologians, are preserved in a porphyry urn beneath the altar. To the right is the monument of Gregory XVI, a monk of the Camaldolese Benedictines, who reigned from 1831 to 1846. One of the Church's most reactionary popes, he employed Austrian troops to crush uprisings in the Papal States, opposed Italian nationalism, freedom of conscience, freedom of the press, and the separation of Church and State. At the same time, he was a strong promoter of the missions, and in 1839 issued the strongest of condemnations of the slave trade, reiterating the anathemas of earlier popes, absolutely forbidding Catholics to have any part in it. He was the last Religious to be elected pope until the Jesuit Pope Francis in 2013.

On the left of the aisle into the south transept is the Altar of St Basil the Great, who composed the Rule for monks and nuns, still used, especially in the Orthodox Churches. The mosaic shows St Basil celebrating solemn Mass for Epiphany in 370.

So absorbed is he, that he is oblivious to the entry of his opponent, the Arian Byzantine Emperor Valens, with his retinue. Opposite, the monument to Benedict XIV represents the pope rising from his throne, his right hand raised in blessing, possibly for the Jubilee Year of 1750.

The right or south transept is reserved for Confessions, heard in many languages at all hours the Basilica is open. The altar on the right is dedicated to St Wenceslas, king and patron saint of Bohemia, and subject of the famous carol, who was martyred *c.*930. The central altar commemorates two Roman martyrs, St Processus and St Martinian: warders in the Mamertine prison, they were converted and baptised by the prisoners, possibly even by St Peter. Their relics are in the porphyry urn under the altar. The altar on the left is dedicated to St Erasmus, a martyr under Emperor Diocletian. As you walk up the aisle you will see one of the finest works of Canova, the monumental tomb of Clement XIII. The pope kneels in prayer with the tiara on the ground in front of him: below, the entrance to the tomb is flanked by two crouching lions, one sleeping (Meekness), the other vigilant (Strength). Much of his pontificate was taken up with combating the anti-Christian critiques of Voltaire and the Encyclopaedists, and their determination to have the Jesuits, whom they feared, suppressed. A brave and gentle pope, he instituted the Feast of the Sacred Heart. Opposite this monument is the Altar of the Navicella, deriving its name from the Gospel narrative of Jesus and Peter walking on the water (Matthew 14:22–33).

In front of you at the end of the aisle is the Altar of St Petronilla. Her relics, beneath the altar, were removed from the Catacomb of Domitilla in 750, and placed in the Chapel of the Kings of France in Constantine's Basilica. To this day, the French community in Rome gathers at this altar on 31 May to venerate her. A fanciful legend says she was the daughter of St Peter, but nothing is known of her apart from her martyrdom. The next altar to the left is of St Peter raising Tabitha, the woman of Jaffa (Acts 9:36–42), and opposite it a monument to Pope Clement X, elected reluctantly at the age of 80 in 1670. He was pope until his death in 1676. He generously assisted Poland against the Turks, and sought to encourage the kings of Europe to make peace, but perhaps he will be remembered most in Rome for commissioning Bernini to design the ten spectacular marble angels on Ponte Sant'Angelo over the Tiber, each of whom holds an instrument of Christ's passion.

In the floor in front of the monument to Clement X, under a simple tombstone, lie the remains of Popes Sixtus IV and Julius II. Sixtus IV, a Franciscan who was unexpectedly elected pope in 1471, is remembered for building the Sistine Chapel and for his patronage of the arts and science. Allegorical images of the arts and sciences decorate his magnificent bronze funerary monument by Antonio del Pollaiolo (which is in the Treasury). Sixtus gave his collection of several important Roman sculptures to what became the Capitoline Museums, and he refounded and enlarged the Vatican Library. He also successfully moderated the Spanish Inquisition. His nephew, Julius II, who was elected in 1503, ordered the demolition of old St Peter's and the construction of the new Basilica. His simple tombstone was not at all what he had in mind, as you will discover if you visit S. Pietro in Vincoli (p. 178). Like his uncle, Julius was a Franciscan and a patron of the arts; he commissioned his close friend Michelangelo to paint the ceiling of the Sistine Chapel, and spotted the talent of Raphael. But he also had the task of clearing up the mess left behind by Borgia Pope Alexander VI, including restoring the Papal States, which the Borgias had ruined; and fighting to prevent the French domination of Italy, which regarded him as its saviour.

After this tour around the Basilica you return to the portico at the front. It is often so crowded it is difficult to look at the doors. The great central bronze doors, salvaged from the old St Peter's, have detailed reliefs depicting the martyrdoms of St Peter and St Paul. Cast by Antonio Filarete, they took twelve years to make, and were finished in 1445 to commemorate the (short-lived) union between the Catholic and Orthodox Churches achieved at the Council of Florence. Every twenty-five years, and sometimes more often, there is a Holy Year, a Year of Jubilee, an idea taken from the Jewish Faith in which debts were remitted and quarrels made up (Leviticus 25:8–13). In a Holy Year the Holy Door (on the far right) is opened to recall the words of Jesus, *'I am the door. If anyone enters by Me, he will be saved, and will go in and out and find pasture'* (John 10:9). It is also known as the 'Door of the Great Pardon'. Replacing a wooden door, it was cast in bronze by Vico Consorti in 1950 and has panels portraying scenes from the Gospels of people receiving Christ's pardon, like the Prodigal Son. When Pope Francis opened the door in the Year of Mercy, 2015, he said: *'The Holy Door will become a Door of Mercy through which anyone who enters will experience the love of God who consoles, pardons, and instils hope'*. Facing the main doors is the *Navicella*, a mosaic designed by Giotto, from the old Basilica, of Jesus walking on water.

Dome

The entrance is on the right side of the portico of the Basilica, close to the facility for leaving bags. You can take a lift up as far as the roof, and from there enjoy views over the city and Vatican Gardens. If you do ascend by lift you may like to walk back down and see marble plaques of the names of the famous who have been there before you. To reach the dome you then have to climb up the 320 steps from the roof. It is worth doing to see how the dome is constructed; you walk at an angle between the inner and outer skins, interrupted by windows. There are toilets, coffee bar and a gift shop when you get down.

Crypt

The crypt of St Peter's is known as the Grottoes. Here, in a peaceful atmosphere of prayer, rest many popes, including Adrian IV, the only English pope (who died in 1159), as well as other notables. If you visit the *Scavi* (p. 51) your tour ends here: access from the Basilica is normally by the staircase beside the statue of St Andrew near the Papal Altar. On the way down you will pass columns and sculpture from Constantine's Basilica, including the lintel of its main doors. The centre of the crypt is the Clementine Chapel close to the tomb of St Peter. By peering through the grill you can see something of the discoveries made during the excavations. The block of marble with the red stripe of porphyry is the monument raised over the tomb by Constantine. Parts of the crypt are railed off, but if you ask an attendant he may point out the tombs of Adrian IV —a splendid pagan sarcophagus of Egyptian granite made in the third century AD—and the last three members of the Royal House of Stuart (p. 132), whose remains now lie together in a sarcophagus of polished travertine surmounted by a bronze crown which dates only from 1939. As well as the tomb of Pius VI, there is a fine kneeling statue by Canova of this pope who established the Vatican Museums, but whose condemnation of the French Revolution and France's invasion of Italy caused him to be seized by Napoleon and taken to France, where he died.

Depending on the time, you may like to visit the Divine Mercy **Church of S. Spirito in Sassia**, *especially on a pilgrimage. It is close to St Peter's. Out of the Square, instead of going down Via della Conciliazione, take the road to the right of it, Borgo S. Spirito, and you come to the church (Map p. 239). Alternatively, go a little way down Via della Conciliazione, and turn right along Via dei Cavalieri del S. Sepolcro.*

Santo Spirito in Sassia

Open: 7:15–12:00; 14:50–19:00.
Mass in English: Sunday 10:00.

Hard to believe it now, but the whole area near St Peter's was once crammed with narrow streets and little houses before Mussolini drove Via della Conciliazione through the lot of them. They went back to the eighth century, when the newly-converted tribes of Anglo-Saxons, Germans, Scandinavians and other northern Europeans made settlements close to Peter. Almost every street between the Castel Sant'Angelo and St Peter's is a *Borgo*: in English, 'Burgh' or 'Borough'; in German 'Burg'; and Scandinavian 'Borg'. The Sassia (Anglo-Saxons) were there first, where you are standing.

In 727, King Ina of Wessex founded a church, St Mary's, and a Hospice here, where lived a resident population of English priests and people, giving hospitality to visiting kings and queens and pilgrims, who came with their prayers to St Peter here in 'Peterborough'. A decline in pilgrimage in the eleventh century due to the Crusades, led Pope Innocent III, in 1200, to turn the Hospice into the Hospital of the Holy Spirit, which became one of the most famous hospitals in the world, caring especially for foundlings who could be left in a baby hatch, which you can still see in the wall to the left of the main gate. The church was rebuilt in the twelfth century, and in 1475 was enlarged, given a bell tower, and joined to the Hospital. After being damaged during the 1527 Sack of Rome the church was rebuilt by Antonio Sangallo, a pupil of Bramante, in the 1540s, and given an organ still in use. Finally, it was richly adorned by Pope Sixtus V in 1590, and is much as he left it.

In 1994 it became the official sanctuary of Divine Mercy, and there are devotions all day, especially a Holy Hour beginning with the Three o'clock Prayer. The third chapel on the right side contains the image of Jesus painted by P. Moskal in 1994, a statue of St Faustina Kowalska, the Apostle of Divine Mercy, and her reliquary donated by Pope St John Paul II after her canonization.

> At three o'clock implore my mercy, especially for sinners; and, if only for a brief moment, immerse yourself in my Passion, particularly in my abandonment at the moment of agony. This is the hour of great mercy for the whole world.
> Saint Faustina's Diary.

There are inexpensive sandwich bars and restaurants around St Peter's, especially in Borgo Pio, many offering a Menu Turistico. In the afternoon you may wish to buy souvenirs, and maybe visit Castel Sant'Angelo (p. 224) at the end of Via della Conciliazione, or continue your pilgrimage to the Basilica of St Paul's outside the Walls, to honour the apostle whose name is always remembered in Rome with St Peter.

You can get to St Paul's by metro or bus (Maps pp. 239 and 240). The quickest way is on the Red Linea A from Ottaviano San Pietro, changing at Termini to Blue Linea B to Basilica S. Paolo (direction Laurentina). Turning left out of the metro station, go to the main road intersection, look right and you will see the distinctive bell tower at the back of the Basilica.

Alternatively, from Piazza del Risorgimento or Piazza Pia, take the 23. Keep your eyes open through the windows on the left and eventually you will see the front of the Basilica. The stop is just past it.

Afternoon: Basilica of St Paul outside the Walls (San Paolo fuori le Mura)

Open: 7:00–18:30.

The most impressive way to enter the Basilica is from the front, so if you arrive by metro it is worth walking round to admire the beautiful nineteenth-century courtyard garden. The great Carrara marble statue of St Paul was sculpted by Giuseppe Obici (1807–78), and the vast portico designed by Guglielmo Calderini (1837–1916), an architect and professor whose many important buildings include the Palace of Justice in Rome. The mosaics on the façade, which shine brilliantly in the sun, were based on designs by Filippo Agricola and Nicola Consoni, both very skilled craftsmen.

Before entering the Basilica have a look at its enormous bronze doors, sculptured in 1930 by Antonio Maraini, an artist and a politician. Ten relief panels depict events from the lives of St Peter (left) and St Paul (right). Starting at the bottom, those on the right show Paul being welcomed as he reaches Rome in chains; Paul teaching in his lodgings; his own conversion, with a silvered figure of Christ; his conversion of the Roman centurion; and his beheading. The five reliefs of Peter show him baptising in a catacomb (at the bottom); founding the See of Rome; receiving the keys of the Kingdom from Christ (who is silvered); *Domine quo vadis* (*p. 83*); and his crucifixion.

On entering the church, but before moving up the nave look back to your right, to the 1070 Byzantine door. Now the Holy Door, it was formerly the main door of the Basilica, and a masterpiece of its era, depicting scenes from the life of Christ and the Apostles, along with martyrs, prophets, two eagles and two crosses.

When St Paul arrived in Rome in AD 61, according to the Acts of the Apostles (28:15–31), crowds came to meet him along the Appian Way, and for the first two years he lived in rented accommodation under house arrest. Nonetheless he was allowed visitors and preached to them about the Kingdom of God. The Acts of the Apostles ends here. A few years later, during the persecution of Nero, he was seized and beheaded. His body was buried in a necropolis owned by a Christian woman named Lucina, and the faithful would pray over his grave. Over it was erected a simple memorial stone. Then, in 324, Constantine raised a small basilica over his tomb. Fifty years later Emperor Valentinian II built a very large one.

Mosaics and other embellishments were added over the years, and it was probably at its most magnificent in the thirteenth century. You can see paintings of it in the Art Gallery and Museum, located in the sacristy and in two other rooms. A new high altar was added in 1600 and the Chapel of the Blessed

Sacrament was built in 1725. But in 1823 fire gutted this ancient church through the negligence of a workman who was repairing the lead roof. The news of this terrible disaster was kept from the gravely ill pope, Pius VII, whose favourite church this was. It was rebuilt with astonishing speed after a world-wide collection, and re-consecrated in 1854. Thanks to powerful architecture, rather than ornamentation, it faithfully reproduces the spacious grandeur of the early basilica, with its forest of eighty granite columns dividing the nave and four aisles. The principal architect entrusted with the work, Luigi Poletti, promised to rebuild it *as if the original builders had returned and ... had revisited the design and corrected its errors*.

During the rebuilding, the tomb of the apostle was unearthed, but there being little interest in archaeology in those days no one thought about providing access to it. They did, however, cast a

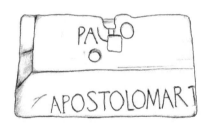

replica of the top of his tomb, crudely engraved with the words *Paulo Apostolo Mart*, and with holes in the top through which the faithful praying for healing had touched cloths to his body, as they did when he was alive (Acts 19:12). This replica hangs on a wall of the Museum. In 2006 the area around his tomb was exposed, and visitors can now see the end of his marble sarcophagus from the *confessio* before the high altar. Through the holes in the top of the sarcophagus they took fragments of bone for forensic examination, and in 2009 Pope Benedict XVI declared it *seems to confirm the unanimous and undisputed tradition that these are the mortal remains of the Apostle Paul*. They also found *traces of a precious linen cloth, purple in colour, laminated with pure gold, and a blue coloured textile with filaments of linen* similar to that wrapped round the bones of St Peter.

Above the columns are roundels containing mosaic portraits of all the popes from Peter, replacing the original frescoes, forty-one of which survived and can be seen in the Museum. They say that when the last blank frame is filled, the occupant will be the last pope, and it will be the end of the world. There isn't long to go!

Despite the fire, some great works of art, old and new, adorn the Basilica. The fifth-century mosaics in the apse depicting Christ with St Peter and St Andrew on his left, and St Paul and St Luke on his right, were saved and re-stored. The little kneeling figure in white by Christ's  right foot is Pope Honorius III, who commissioned the mosaics from Venetian craftsmen. The triumphal arch, also fifth-century, suffered severe damage in the fire but was faithfully replicated, and shows Christ, between two angels and the twenty-four elders of the Apocalypse, blessing the faithful. Below them are St Peter and St Paul: Paul pointing down towards his tomb. The precious thirteenth-century baldacchino, the earliest work of Arnolfo di Cambio, the great Florentine master of Italian gothic, was saved. The niches above its porphyry columns contain small statues of Saints Peter, Paul, Luke and Benedict. The spandrel on the right (as you face the apse) shows Abbot Bartholomew, abbot from 1282 to 1297, who commissioned the canopy, offering it to St Paul, on the left. Saved also was the superb twelfth-century pas-chal candlestick by Pietro Vassalletto who, like the Cosmati, be-longed to a family of wonderfully creative artists in marble, active in Rome between the twelfth and fourteenth centuries. It has eight segments containing plant and animal motifs, and scenes from the Easter Vigil; above them are eight monstrous figures, and lastly the holder containing the candle. There are also scenes of the Passion, Crucifixion, Resurrection and Ascension of Christ.

The Blessed Sacrament Chapel to the left of the high altar, rebuilt in the eighteenth century, mercifully survived, with its thirteenth-century mosaic and a fourteenth-century crucifix; and at the back a wooden statue of St Paul scratched by pilgrims taking splinters, now put out of reach. It was here, before the mosaic of Our Lady, that St Ignatius and his brothers made their first vows as Jesuits. To the left is St Stephen's Chapel, built with marble recycled from the fire. It recalls that St Paul witnessed and approved of Stephen's martyrdom. At the end of the left transept is the Chapel of St Paul's Conversion, with a painting of the scene above the altar by Vincenzo Camuccini, considered the greatest of the nineteenth century neo-classicists.

To the right of the high altar is the Chapel of St Lawrence, built by Carlo Maderno in 1619. Its paintings were lost in the fire, but the twentieth-century artist, Antonio Viligiardi, has decorated it with scenes from the saint's life. The choir stalls were designed by Calderini and it is in this chapel that Benedictine monks, who have served the Basilica since Pope Gregory II brought them here in the eighth century, pray their Offices and Mass each day. The monks used to have a special link with England: until the Reformation English monarchs were canons of St Paul's, and its Abbots were prelates of the Order of the Garter.

> Lord Jesus Christ, you converted Paul on the road to Damascus, and sent him out as the teacher of the Gentiles. Grant that following his teaching we may lead converted lives and grow in holiness.
> St Paul pray for the Church, pray for the world.

Next is St Benedict's Chapel, designed by Poletti. The twelve columns were found in 1912 during excavations in Veio, an Etruscan city north-west of Rome. The much-admired nineteenth-century sculptor Pietro Tenerani carved the statue of St Benedict. You have now reached the Baptistery, which has a font made in 1930 by Arnaldo Foschini decorated with malachite, lapis lazuli and mother of pearl. The frieze, by the renowned painter, Antonio del Massaro, features frescoes of the Evangelists, Doctors of the Church, and Saints Peter and Paul with God the Father, and is dated 1460–65. The little oratory of St Julian has repainted frescoes, probably going back to the end of the twelfth century.

You are now near the Museum which is well worth the small admission charge. It contains paintings of the old basilica, about forty works from the thirteenth to nineteenth centuries, some copies of rare documents, including an illustrated Carolingian Bible from the ninth century, various engravings of the fire of 1823, and the replica of St Paul's tomb. Among the exhibits is the *Praeceptum*, a large marble stone with an epigraph of Pope Gregory the Great and bearing his name.

Not to be missed are the wonderful cloisters built by the Vassalletto family, with thirteenth-century Cosmatesque work, perhaps the most beautiful in Rome, and undamaged in the fire. Interesting inscriptions and fragments of tombs, Christian and pagan, found beneath the floor of the old church, are displayed. You will find inscriptions not only in Latin, the language of the early Romans, but also in Greek, the *lingua franca* of the Roman Empire as it reached Alexander the Great's conquests of the eastern Mediterranean and Asia Minor. The New Testament was written in Greek and the Old Testament had been translated into Greek, and Greek was the language of the Church. Pope Damasus in the 380s began changing it to Latin in the West. *Kyrie eleison* is a Greek vestige that remains in the Mass. If you look carefully you will find some Latin inscriptions from the transitional period employing the Greek alphabet. On the way out there are toilets, a bookshop and the entrance to the excavations.

Naturally St Paul's is one of the Seven Pilgrimage Churches of Rome.

The easiest and quickest way back is by metro. Alternatively return on the 23 bus, though at rush hour it can be a long journey. The 23 stop is across the road at the back of the basilica.

3

FROM PERSECUTION TO FREEDOM AND BUILDING CHURCHES

Morning: Catacombs on the Appian Way

T he earliest Christians in Rome, like St Peter and St Paul, were buried in communal burial grounds but, from the second century, burial space was getting hard to come by and diggers, known as *fossors*, began tunnelling-out catacombs for Christians and Jews, both of whom chose burial rather than cremation, which was generally the pagans' preference. Burial within the city was forbidden, but wealthy individuals with property outside the city would allow catacombs to be dug on their land. There are six Jewish catacombs, two of which are open; and seventy known Christian catacombs, with perhaps more to be

discovered, along the Appian Way and other old roads out of the city. The ancient Appian Way (Via Appia Antica), which dates from 312 BC, was the most important of all the Roman trade routes; the remains of many monuments still line it.

Catacombs are passages cut in the soft tufa rock, branching out in all directions. In the walls of these passages are graves (*loculi*). The body was wrapped in linen, and sealed in the grave with a slab of marble or alabaster, inscribed with the name and other details of the deceased. There are also more elaborate arched recesses (*arcosoli*), and  chambers (*cubicula*) for families. Christian catacombs were called cemeteries, meaning 'places of rest', reflecting St Paul's phrase 'fallen asleep in Christ', awaiting the Resurrection, whereas the pagans used the word necropolis, 'city of the dead'. The first passages were honeycombed out as far as the boundary of the owned land, then a vertical shaft was dropped, and another level started, and so on. Some catacombs go down five levels. This means that the oldest graves are nearest the surface. There are estimated to be around 140 kilometres of passages beneath Rome, and up to a million people may have been buried there, many of them babies and children, when infant mortality was high. Some were martyrs in the persecutions; Christians would gather round their tombs to pray and remember them.

On the tombs of their loved ones Christians wrote many prayers and moving inscriptions: *Sweet Faustina may you live in God*; *Dear Cyriacus, sweetest son, may you live in the Holy Spirit*; *Leo, may you always live in God with all your family*; *Lord, preserve Calendion in your holy name*; *Januaria enjoy your happiness and pray for us; Marcellinus and Peter, intercede for Gallicanus the Christian.* A father wrote on the grave of his seven-year old son: *Your soul rests in God, pray for your sister.*

Five Christian catacombs in Rome are open to the public: those of S. Callisto, S. Sebastiano and Domitilla along the Appian Way; the Catacomb of Priscilla along the Salarian Way; and the Catacomb of S. Agnese on Via Nomentana. But you only see a small part of them. Others can be visited by special arrangement including the cost of a guide. Far from being gloomy and spooky the catacombs are enlivened by art. As in a pagan necropolis there are birds and flowers and trees, rich reds and blue, lines and designs, stucco and fresco. Pagan motifs are adopted and Christianised: for example, the well-known pagan myth of Orpheus who travelled to the underworld to bring back his wife Eurydice, because Jesus descended to Hell to bring salvation to the dead. Catacombs are filled with scenes from the Bible relating to salvation and the resurrection of the dead. Jonah is often depicted because he remained in the belly of the whale for three days, evoking Christ's burial and resurrection.

The most frequent painting in the catacombs is of a shepherd with a sheep across his shoulders. Adapted from pagan art, this was the picture of Jesus that had the deepest appeal; the Saviour who seeks and saves those who are lost, recalling the Psalm, *The Lord is my Shepherd . . . though I walk through the valley of the shadow of death, I will fear no evil.* Salvation is also depicted by Shadrach, Meshach, and Abednego, who were saved by God from the fiery furnace. Susanna features, saved from the false accusations of the elders. Noah is rescued from the flood, and Daniel was unharmed in the lions' den. There are New Testament healing miracles: of the blind man, the paralysed man, the hemorrhaging woman; and the raising from the dead of Lazarus, and of the daughter of Jairus, and the son of the widow of Nain. They also painted Sacraments: Moses striking the rock evokes baptism; a man being baptised in a river is fished out of the water by St Peter. There are various depictions of the Eucharist: sitting around a table, standing beside a small table, feeding the five thousand, and a dolphin with a basket containing bread and a flask of wine. Orantes figures pray with upraised arms. The Three Kings

offer their gifts to
the infant Jesus.
It is in the cat-
acombs we first
meet Christian

symbols: the Chi-Rho, the Greek initial letters of Christ; the

anchor for the cross; A (alpha)
and Ω (omega) for Christ; olive
and palm branches, doves, fish
and the phoenix (a mythical
bird, which rises from its ashes,
representing the resurrection). Many
artefacts have been found in the catacombs: terracotta lamps with images
of the Good Shepherd and Chi-Rho;
doves and other symbols; golden
glass tab-
lets with scenes that include the
Eucharist; and bottles filled with
perfume used when sealing the
tombs.

Around the graves of the deceased, Christians held ceremonial meals called *refrigeria*, a custom taken over from paganism.
Whether the earliest Christians celebrated the Eucharist in
the catacombs is not known, but it is certain they did so in the
fourth century, using the top of the tombs of the martyrs. In this
originates the custom of sealing relics of martyrs and saints in
altars today. The Edict of Milan in 313, which ended the persecutions and permitted Christians to build churches, meant that
burials in the catacombs began to come to an end. But as the
Western Empire fell under waves of invasions, the barbarians
sacked Rome, entered the catacombs, looted the graves, scattered
the bones, and destroyed priceless inscriptions and paintings.
Appalled by this sacrilege the popes ordered the remains of the
martyrs and faithful to be removed and placed in churches. And
so pilgrimages to the tombs of the martyrs were made to the
churches instead, and the catacombs were abandoned, forgotten
and lost.

It was St Philip Neri, the 'apostle of Rome', and the followers he gathered, who re-awakened interest in them. Philip would spend whole nights in prayer in the Catacomb of S. Sebastiano, the one catacomb that was never lost; experiencing there, in 1544, a spiritual conversion in which he found his vocation. The discovery, exploration and scientific study of the catacombs began in the early seventeenth century with Antonio Bosio, nicknamed the 'Columbus of Subterranean Rome', and in the nineteenth century a systematic exploration of the catacombs, in particular those of S. Callisto, was carried out by Giovanni Battista de Rossi (1822–94), who was instrumental in founding the *Pontifical Commission of Sacred Archaeology*, which is responsible for them. All the catacombs belong to the Church; they are sacred places looked after by Religious Communities, and any priest may book to celebrate Mass there.

All catacombs provide guided tours in English. You have to decide which one to visit. They are all much the same, but there are unique features in each. Priscilla is particularly rich in paintings. The ones below are on the Via Appia, which has a special charm. For the others see p. 195.

Getting to the Catacombs of S. Callisto and S. Sebastiano

You need to go to Piazza Venezia, Circo Massimo or S. Giovanni Laterano. For the latter take Metro Red Linea A to S. Giovanni, bus 85 from Termini, or 81 from Piazza del Risorgimento (Map p. 240.).

From Piazza Venezia (Map p. 241) or at Circo Massimo (Map p. 104) take the 118. On the journey you pass the immense ruins of the Baths of Caracalla, and further on go through the Porta S. Sebastiano. You are now on the old Via Appia, and it is not far. If you look at the stops (and buses may not stop unless requested), the next stop after Porta Sebastiano is Appia Antica Travicella. Then it is Appia Antica/ Domine Quo Vadis. Get off here and walk on to the little church on the left where the road forks. It is **Domine Quo Vadis**. *The lane in the middle that goes to Catacombe S. Callisto is well marked, offering a peaceful walk between cypress trees and olive groves, with sheep grazing. But if you wish to go straight to the catacomb stay on the bus,* past the next two stops Appia Antica/Caffarella and Appia Antica/ Scuola Agraria, and alight at Catacombe S. Callisto. For Catacombe S. Sebastiano stay on to the following stop.

From the little bus station at S. Giovanni Laterano (Map p. 89) use the 218. It goes alongside the Aurelian Wall (on your right) and then turns left at the Porta S. Sebastiano. Ignore the first stop, Appia Antica Travicella (the bus will not stop unless it is requested), and then get off at Appia Antica/Domine Quo Vadis, if you wish to visit this little church. If you don't want to go to the church, or if you miss the stop, the bus then takes the right fork, Via Ardeatina. The next stop is Ardeatina, but you get off at the following one, Fosse Ardeatine, where the road widens out. You will see the sign to S. Callisto. To visit the Catacomb of S. Sebastiano get off here and cross over to the old pilgrim road Vicolo delle Sette Chiese (not Via delle Sette Chiese). Near the road junction where you are standing, behind you to the right, is **Fosse Ardeatine**, a shrine and burial ground of 335 Italians killed there as a reprisal for the killing of thirty-two German soldiers by the resistance movement.

Getting to the Catacomb of Domitilla: Take the 218 from S. Giovanni and get off at Fosse Ardeatine (as above). Walk back the way the bus came, but instead of taking the right fork along Via Ardeatina, take the left fork, Via delle Sette Chiese (not to be confused with Vicolo delle Sette Chiese). You reach the catacomb on the left in a few minutes. If you come on the 118 get off at Catacombe S. Callisto. Walk through the parkland, past the entrance to S. Callisto, and down to Via Ardeatina and then Via delle Sette Chiese.

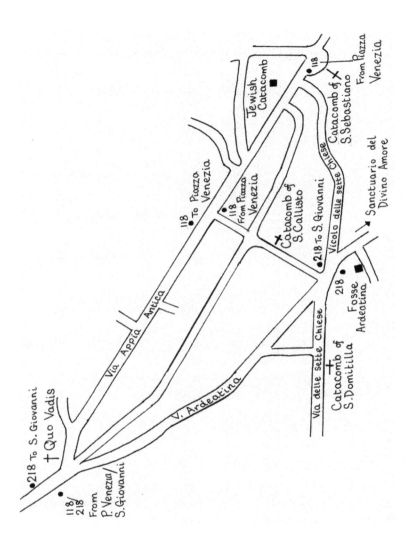

Church of Domine Quo Vadis

Open: 8:00–18:00.

The catacombs are busy and it is difficult to pray in them unless you are going to Mass. This church offers some peace. It commemorates a legend that on this spot St Peter, having been urged to escape persecution in Rome in order to survive and preach elsewhere, met Christ carrying his Cross. Peter asked, *'Domine Quo Vadis?'* (Where are you going, Lord?), Jesus told him he was going to Rome to be crucified again, so Peter went back into the city to face his martyrdom. The legend obviously derives from the words of Jesus:

> Jesus said to him, 'Feed my sheep. In all truth I tell you, when you were young you put on your own belt and walked where you liked; but when you grow old you will stretch out your hands, and somebody else will put a belt round you and take you where you would rather not go.' In these words he indicated the kind of death by which Peter would give glory to God. After this he said, 'Follow me.'
>
> John 21:18–19

Wall-paintings in the simple nave illustrate the story, while another shows Peter being crucified upside down. You will notice a marble slab with a footprint. Devotion tells us that the footprint (or rather the original, now in the Basilica of S. Sebastiano, for this is a copy) was left by Christ. The present church dates from 1637, but there was a church here in the ninth century.

Catacomb of San Callisto

Open: see page 6.

St Callixtus was a deacon in the early third century, entrusted with the care of the catacomb. In due course he was elected pope. One unique feature of this catacomb is the Crypt of the Popes, the burial place of nine popes who served between 230 and 283, most of whom were martyred. It also contains the graves of three African bishops who died on a visit to Rome. Pope Damasus (366–384) was responsible for the Latin verse on the tablet, honouring the martyrs:

> Here lies gathered, if you seek it, a host of holy people.
>
> The venerated tombs hold the bodies of the saints,
>
> The court of heaven has taken their sublime souls to itself.
>
> Here are the companions of Sixtus, who bore off the trophy from the enemy;
>
> Here is a group of popes who guard the altars of Christ;
>
> Here lies the bishop who lived long in peace;
>
> Here are the holy confessors that Greece sent;
>
> Here are the youths and children, old men and their chaste grandchildren
>
> Who preferred to keep their virginal purity.
>
> Here I, Damasus, confess I would have liked to be buried
>
> But that I feared to vex the holy ashes of the saints.

Another chapel once contained the body of the martyr St Cecilia. Her body was moved by Pope Paschal I to the newly-built church above her home in Trastevere. When the tomb was re-opened in 1599 her body was found to be intact. Pope Clement

VI summoned Stefano Maderno to view the body before it was reburied, in order to make a sculpture, and Maderno signed a document affirming that he had sculpted her as he found her. A copy of his statue lies in her original grave (for the original see p. 123). A number of second-century frescoes have survived in the Cubicle of the Sacraments, including depictions of the Eucharist and Baptism. There are Orantes figures, and Jonah, and frescoes of the Good Shepherd surrounded by his flock, as well as a lovely painting of Christ.

After your visit to S. Callisto, if you are going back to Circo Massimo, Piazza Venezia or Colosseum, turn right from the entrance and walk

along the roadway to Via Appia. When you reach it turn left and you come to the 118 bus stop on the other side of the road (Map p. 83).

If you intend to follow the afternoon programme, you need to catch the 218 bus to S. Giovanni Laterano. That means turning left from the catacomb and walking down the roadway to Via Ardeatina. You will see the 218 bus stop just to the left (Map p. 83). There is a bar to the right if you want a snack.

Catacomb of San Sebastiano

Open: see page 6.

This cemetery was originally called *ad catacumbas* (near the hollows), giving its name to all the underground cemeteries. There  are many inscriptions here of the Chi-Rho, the anchor and doves, and other paintings, but the main interest focuses on three finely-decorated mausoleums, though there is nothing to suggest they were Christian. During the persecutions waged by the Emperor Valerian in 258, the remains of St Peter and St Paul were taken from their respective graves and re-buried in this catacomb, probably because Christians were too afraid to gather at the tomb of St Peter, or there was a danger of desecration by barbarians. Six hundred graffiti asking for the prayers of Peter and Paul, one dated 260, have been found in the *Triclia*, a room reserved for their honour. Archaeologists have identified part of an *aedicule* there, as at St Peter's. Constantine raised a grand basilica over it, but no sooner was this completed than it was decided, presumably by Constantine and Pope Sylvester, to return the remains of the apostles to their original burial sites, and build basilicas there. So the basilica here was rededicated in honour of St Sebastian, a soldier-martyr, who was buried in the catacomb during the persecution of Diocletian at the end of the third century: little of it survives. The present church dates from the early seventeenth century, with a later façade, and has a beautiful seventeenth-century painted wooden ceiling show-ing Sebastian bound to a tree, with a Roman soldier carrying a quiver of the arrows with which he was martyred. The relics of the saint are in his chapel on the left; his statue is by Antonio Giorgetti, a pupil of Bernini. Bernini himself carved the huge bust of Christ (*Salvator Mundi*): it was his last work, and was moved into the church only a few years ago after being found in the monastery next door. The original stone with the reputed footprint of Christ is in the chapel on the right.

S. Sebastiano is one the Seven Pilgrimages Churches of Rome.

After your visit to S. Sebastiano, if you are going back to Circo Massimo, Piazza Venezia or Colosseum, turn left along the Via Appia, and after passing the roadway to S. Callisto you come to the 118 bus stop on the other side of the road (Map p. 83).

If you are ready for lunch there is a restaurant, the Cecilia Metella, across the road and up a pathway, and usually a refreshment van parked outside the basilica.

If you intend to follow the afternoon programme, you need to catch the 218 bus to S. Giovanni Laterano. That means going down Vicolo delle Sette Chiese beside the church to the 218 stop on Via Ardeatina (Map p. 83).

Catacomb of Domitilla

Open: see page 6.

The Catacomb of Domitilla is the longest. The passages run to fifteen kilometres on four levels, and it is known from an inscrip-tion that the land originally belonged to Flavia Domitilla. She was a niece of Emperor Domitian and married to Titus Flavius Clemens, a consul. We met them at S. Clemente. The distinc-tive feature of this catacomb is the impressive basilica that Pope Damasus built at the end of the fourth century, partly above ground, over the tomb of two martyrs, Nereus and Achilleus, who were soldiers of the Imperial Guard, and probably victims of the persecution raged by Emperor Diocletian in the year 303.

On a pillar near the altar is a remarkable sculpture depicting the execution of St Achilleus. The church is now wholly underground, damaged, it is thought, by an earthquake that struck Rome in 897. Along the walls of the basilica and the galleries of the catacomb are the usual Christian symbols. Some graves were undisturbed, with their marble slabs and inscriptions intact,

 and there is a good collection of lamps, shells, and glass objects around. You are shown a fine painting of St Peter and St Paul. Paintings of the Good Shepherd are found in many catacombs, but in Domitilla was discovered the oldest statue of this subject. It is now in the Vatican Museums, but there is a copy here. On the way out, beneath the arch in front of the exit stairway, on the right hand side, is a fragment of a sarcophagus depicting Our Lady with the Child Jesus in her arms and the Three Kings kneeling before them; and to the right, the miracle of Moses bringing water from the rock.

The 218 bus from Fosse Ardeatina (on the opposite side of the road to where you got off) goes back to S. Giovanni Laterano from where you can, if you wish, continue the day's tour.

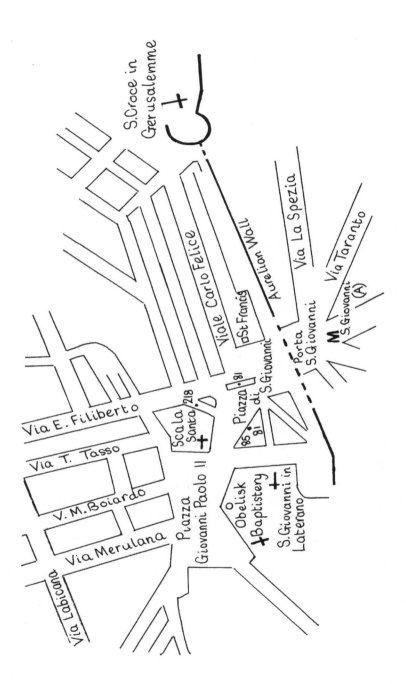

Afternoon: Basilica of St John Lateran (San Giovanni in Laterano)

Open: 7:00–18:30.

Christians must have gazed in utter amazement as they watched St John Lateran being built, plank by plank and stone by stone. They were the survivors of the very worst persecution the Empire had thrown at them. Emperor Diocletian was determined to destroy Christianity for ever: clergy and people were put to death; Holy Scriptures were burnt and sacred vessels of silver and gold were confiscated. Then suddenly Diocletian fell ill and resigned. A new emperor, Constantine, was proclaimed in 306, and in 313 he issued the Edict of Milan, permitting freedom of religion.

Almost at once this huge church began to take shape before their astonished eyes, built by Constantine as though to atone for the actions of his predecessors. Its dedication on 9 November 324 continues to be celebrated throughout the Catholic Church. It was the first great church to be built, and the mosaic of the

Saviour in the apse was the first image of Christ to be seen in a public place. It was, and remains the Cathedral of Rome and of the Pope as Bishop of Rome. A Latin inscription over the portico, with the Papal Tiara and a laurel wreath, translates: *Most Holy Church of the Lateran, Mother and Head of all the Churches in the City and the World.* Originally it was dedicated to Christ the Saviour; St John the Baptist was added to the dedication in the tenth century and St John the Evangelist in the twelfth.

The Church was now able to enter public life with an exciting confidence in the Gospel, and a new enthusiasm to spread the Faith and influence society. The faithful set about building churches all over the city and the empire, and the owners of some *tituli* allowed them to be demolished and replaced by a proper church on the same site, as we saw at S. Clemente. Constantine built St John Lateran on land that Nero had confiscated from the Laterani family. The barracks of the Imperial Guard occupied it: the Guard of Constantine's rival Maxentius, whom he had routed. Constantine had the barracks demolished for the basilica, and gave the imperial palace beside it to the pope, a palace that remained the papal residence for a thousand years.

Little remains of the original basilica except stone fragments and a papal throne in the cloisters, for this church has suffered from invaders, an earthquake, floods and fire. And when the papacy was in Avignon (p. 152) the basilica was abandoned and fell into disrepair, so that when the popes returned they lived first at S. Maria in Trastevere and finally in the Vatican. Nonetheless, after Pope Gregory XI returned from Avignon in 1376 he ordered its rebuilding. Martin V, who ended the Great Schism in 1417 (p. 154), embellished it. Pope Innocent X commissioned Francesco Borromini to undertake a major restoration in time for the Holy Year of 1650. Borromini was a contemporary, often described as a rival, of Bernini and Pietro da Cortona, and like them a leading figure in the emergence of Roman Baroque architecture in the seventeenth century. In the early eighteenth century Pope Clement XII held a competition to design a new entrance façade which was won by Alessandro Galilei, a native of Florence who made his name in England and Ireland (where he designed the front of Castletown House). His new neo-classical style façade was completed in 1735: criticised at the time, it was later much admired.

As you walk up to the church, glance to your right, to the tribune housing the **Scala Santa**, part of the old palace; you will see on the right a restored apsidal eighth-century mosaic of Jesus sending out the apostles to preach the Gospel, which once graced the pope's dining room.

Inside the narthex of the Basilica there is an ancient statue of Constantine. The great central bronze doors formerly hung at the Roman Senate House (*Curia Julia*) in the Forum; they were moved here in 1660. The last door on the right is the Holy Door. When Pope St John Paul II opened it in 2000 he said, *'We have entered through this Door, which represents Christ himself: in fact, he alone is the Saviour, sent by God the Father, who enables us to pass from sin to grace, bringing us into the full communion which unites him to the Father in the Holy Spirit.'*

The massive Basilica, like the original, has a nave and double side-aisles. Dynamic Baroque statues of the apostles guard it, the work of several sculptors; above them are scenes from the Old and New Testaments by Alessandro Algardi. The fourteenth-century baldacchino was made by the little-known Giovanni di Stefano, and relics of St Peter and St Paul are honoured behind a grill at the top. The altar encloses a wooden altar used for the Eucharist until the fourth century, a table from the house of the Roman senator, Pudens; a *titulus* where the early Christians worshipped, near the Church of S. Prassede. It is suggested that St Peter would have known the house and perhaps even celebrated the Eucharist on this table. The mosaic in the apse depicting Christ is a copy of the original from Constantine's Basilica; he  is surrounded by saints, who now include St Francis of Assisi and St Anthony of Padua. The floor is Cosmatesque, and the magnificent gilded wooden ceiling is ascribed to Giacomo della

Porta, who followed a design of his tutor, Michelangelo. St John Lateran is not specially noted for its artworks, but behind the first pillar on the right is a fresco, attributed to Giotto, of Pope Boniface VIII announcing the first Holy Year in 1300.

The first chapel on the left, the Corsini Chapel, was made by Galilei, and the red porphyry coffer on the left, beneath Clement XII's tomb, came from the Pantheon. The Blessed Sacrament Chapel, at the end of the left transept, usually quiet and prayerful, is richly adorned, and the four superb gilded-bronze Corinthian columns have an amazing history. The bronze came from the prows of Cleopatra's ships lost at the Battle of Actium in 31 BC, the final and decisive battle of the Roman Republic between the victorious Augustus and the combined forces of Mark Antony and Cleopatra. Recast, they were fashioned into pillars for the ancient Temple of Jupiter on the Capitoline Hill, before finding their way into this chapel in 1600. In the right transept is a splendid organ case dated 1598. Just below the left set of pipes is a sculpture of David playing the harp, and above him decoration that includes a pair of early trombones among other instruments. On 14 January 1707 Handel played the organ here, astonishing a large audience of cardinals, bishops and nobility with his virtuosity.

Six popes are buried in the Basilica: notably Martin V, kneeling in the *confessio*, who, as well as ending the Great Schism, lifted repressive laws against Jews, and excommunicated Christians who were slave dealers; in the left transept is Leo XIII, who wrote the first social encyclical *Rerum Novarum* in 1891, engaging with political and social thought.

> As pilgrims in the cathedral of Rome, we thank you Father for the diocese of Rome, for its people, religious, priests, deacons, and their bishop, the pope. Grant that they may be blessed and faithful, so that this Church which presides in love may strengthen all the Churches of the world, and help draw Christians into unity of Faith, through Jesus Christ our Lord.

On the left, near the transept, is the entrance to the early thirteenth-century cloister. Perhaps not so well-preserved as others in Rome, it was beautifully crafted by the Vassalletto and Cosmati families and incorporates a ninth-century well-head  in the centre. Don't miss the funerary monument of Cardinal Riccardo Annibaldi (d. 1276): the first major work in Rome of Arnolfo di Cambio, it established his reputation.

In the right transept is a small museum of vestments and treasures. You can leave the basilica by the nearby side door; as you do so notice the magnificent white façade with its twin bell-towers which Domenico Fontana imposed on the earlier façade in 1586.

St John Lateran is, of course, one of the Seven Pilgrimage Churches.

When you come out into the piazza turn left and you come to the octagonal baptistery. Beyond this is the entrance to the Pontifical Lateran University, founded in 1733.

Baptistery

The baptistery was built by Constantine in 315 and remodelled as an octagon in 440, making it the oldest surviving baptistery in the world. Although it now contains a green basalt bath-shaped font, a basin from one of the Roman baths, it was originally designed for the immersion of adults of whom there were thousands (a practice being revived in some Catholic churches). Five frescoes on the walls represent scenes from Constantine's life, including the apparition of the Holy Cross with the promise *in this sign you will conquer.* The eight porphyry columns are from Constantine's baptistery. The baptistery was extensively restored and altered during the seventeenth century when the roof, which was collapsing, was replaced.

The adjoining chapels were built at various times. Two were added by the martyred pope St Hilarius (461–8): that on the left, dedicated to St John the Evangelist, retains its original fifth-century mosaic in the vault, of the Lamb of God with birds and flowers; on the right, the Chapel of St John the Baptist still has its original entrance and doors decorated with shields made of an alloy of silver, gold and bronze, which 'sing' when opening. The chapel opposite the entrance dedicated to Saints Rufina and Secunda (or Saints Cyrian and Justina) was the original fifth-century entrance or narthex and has an apse at each end; in the left-hand apse is a fifth-century mosaic of green and gold tendrils against a blue background. The Chapel of Saints Venantius and Domione, reached though the passage on the left side, has seventh-century Byzantine-style mosaics that rival those in Ravenna.

The Lateran Obelisk

When you come out, make your way to the red granite obelisk in the former Piazza San Giovanni, renamed Piazza Giovanni Paolo II by Rome's mayor in 2013. Dated 1500 BC, it is 31 metres high and weighs over 230 tons, the largest Egyptian obelisk in the world and the oldest in the city. Constantius II, son of Emperor Constantine, brought it from the Temple of Amun at Karnak and had it erected in the Circus Maximus; Pope Sixtus V transferred it here in  1588 to commemorate the baptism of Constantine, as described in the inscription on the base. Sixtus, who only reigned five years, was a brilliant town planner: his work in Rome was featured in a short film, *Impact of an Idea*. He created open piazzas, and long vistas with straight avenues linked by ancient obelisks, focal points for pilgrims to follow. He and his trusted collaborator, Domenico Fontana, were responsible for new aqueducts bringing fresh water back to Rome, and with them the beautiful fountains we still appreciate today.

Make your way across the roads to the white building with its mosaic, which you saw when you were walking to the Basilica.

Scala Santa

Open: 6:00–14:00; 15:00–18:30 (19:00 in summer).

Constantine's mother, Helena, was a Christian, and while her son was building churches in Rome she was doing the same in the Holy Land, on the site of Christ's crucifixion and other places, and arranging for the shipment of some sacred relics to Rome. Amongst them was the marble staircase from Pilate's house in Jerusalem, down which Christ was brought after his condemnation. The twenty-eight steps are encased in wood and this building was made to receive them. You go up on your knees, praying on each step in recollection of Christ's Passion. At the top of the stairs (also accessible from the side staircases up which you can walk) is the Chapel of St Lawrence, the *Sancta Sanctorum*, the private chapel of the popes, when they lived here. You can only see it through a grill unless you have arranged a visit. Its special treasure is a fifth-century picture of Christ 'painted by angels'.

*When you leave the Scala Santa, look at the Aurelian Wall, begun by Emperor Aurelian in AD 271 when it was becoming evident that Rome might be attacked. To the right of the present openings (Porta S. Giovanni), between two massive towers and guardhouses, is the infamous **Asinarian Gate**, through which Totila the Ostrogoth entered to sack and pillage Rome in 546. The story is that after laying siege for a year, a soldier hid in a laundry cart entering the city, and at night overpowered the guards to let in the invaders. Cross over to the sculpture of St Francis and his companions.*

St Francis

Facing the Lateran Basilica is an impressive bronze group of St Francis and his followers on their visit to Rome in 1209, looking towards the Lateran, and beseeching Pope Innocent III to approve their new religious family and their rule. It is the work of the Italian sculptor Giuseppe Tonnini (1875–1954), who cast it in 1925 to celebrate the 700th anniversary of the saint's death. Pope Innocent initially had doubts, but following a dream in which he saw Francis holding up the Basilica of St John Lateran to prevent it from falling down, he gave his approval to this man, who did indeed restore and spiritually rebuild the Church. That was on 16 April 1210, the date still observed as the official founding of the Franciscan Order. At Assisi there is a delightful painting by Giotto in the upper church, showing the pope in bed dreaming of Francis, literally supporting the Lateran on his shoulder.

> It is not fitting, when one is in God's service, to have a gloomy face or a chilling look.
> St Francis

You need to decide where to go now (Map p. 89). The metro station is on the other side of the Aurelian Wall. If you wish to go to Piazza Venezia or Piazza del Risorgimento catch the 81 bus from the middle of the road in front of St Francis. The little electric bus 117 takes you to the Colosseum, the Spanish Steps, and Piazza del Popolo. Or, you may like to continue the tour to the Basilica of the Holy Cross, which is about 300 metres away along the little strip of park behind St Francis.

Santa Croce in Gerusalemme

Open 7:00–12:45; 15:30–19:30.

Under Constantine's instructions, his mother the Empress Helena directed excavations in Jerusalem for the building of the Church of the Holy Sepulchre on Mount Calvary, and there she found the cross on which Jesus died. She left part of it in Jerusalem, another part she sent to Constantinople, and in 327 she brought the rest, with other relics of the Passion, back to her house in Rome, the Sessorian Palace, where she turned several rooms into chapels to display them for prayer. You will see some walls of her palace on the right as you approach the church, and if you ask at the hotel next door you can see more of it. After Helena's death in c.330 at the age of 80, Constantine converted part of the palace into a church in her memory. She was buried in a mausoleum on Via Labicana, built by Constantine for himself, which he gave to her. It is now in ruins, but her grand sarcophagus is in the Vatican Museums.

The eighteenth-century façade, by the little-known Pietro Passalacqua and Domenico Gregorini, who always worked together and won prestigious awards, is elegant and gracious; the interior is more restrained, apart from the splendid frescoes in the apse by Antoniazzo Romano, an early Renaissance painter. They show St Helena finding the cross, and its recovery from the Persians by the Byzantine Emperor Heraclius: in the semi-dome above, the figure of Christ bestows his blessing. The baldacchino is charmingly rococo. The paintings in the vault of the nave of *The Virgin presenting St Helena and Constantine to the Trinity* and the *Apparition of the Cross* are by the eighteenth-century Italian Rococo painter Corrado Giaquinto. The campanile, added in 1144 when Constantine's church was rebuilt, was refashioned again in the eighteenth century.

The relics are on view for veneration and prayer in a room to which you ascend by passing a series of meditative texts and Stations on the left of the high altar. Among them is part of the Title from the Cross on which is written in Hebrew, Greek and Latin the words *'Jesus of Nazareth, King of the Jews'*. This was assumed to be a medieval forgery. But in 1884 the diary of the fourth-century Spanish pilgrim, Egeria, who travelled to the Holy Land, was discovered, and she describes the veneration of this Title relic, along with the Cross, on Good Friday in Jerusalem. It would seem that just as Helena left part of the Cross in Jerusalem so she left part of the Title too, and outside the chapel you will see a reconstruction of the full Title as it would have been. Further indication that it may not be a forgery is the fact that not only the Hebrew, but also the Latin and Greek, is written from right to left, suggesting that a Jew accustomed to writing in that direction, rather than a medieval Latin-speaker, wrote the inscription. The authenticity of some of some relics, like the finger of St Thomas, is understandably questioned. Copies of the nails were made in the Middle Ages, some of them containing filings from the original. Such relics are what we may call 'visual aids' to assist in devotion. What is unquestionable is their ability to speak to us still, perhaps more eloquently than words, of the horror of crucifixion and the death Jesus endured to save us with his triumph on the cross.

> O Saviour of the world, who by your cross and precious blood has redeemed us: save us and help us, we pray.

Down a flight of stairs to the right of the high altar you reach the oldest part of the Basilica, the Chapel of St Helena, one of the rooms of the Sessorian Palace which she turned into a chapel. It has a Roman-era statue of her holding the cross, a copy of the Vatican Juno: by giving her a cross, the pagan goddess has become a saint. Beneath the statue is a floor where you can see soil from the Holy Land brought back both out of devotion and as ballast for the ship. In the fifteenth-century mosaic are the first depictions in the West of birds native to South America: parrots and toucans.

S. Croce is one the Seven Pilgrimage Churches of Rome.

It is not easy to get useful public transport from S. Croce, so best retrace your steps to the metro station of S. Giovanni or to the buses.

4

THE FALL AND RENAISSANCE

OF ROME, AND A TRIP TO

TRASTEVERE

When the Western Roman Empire finally capitulated to barbarian invaders in AD 546, Rome fell into a state of devastation. The destruction of the aqueducts forced people to drink polluted water from the Tiber. Those who didn't succumb to disease fled to the hills. The population dropped to maybe 20,000 before climbing up catastrophically to 90,000 with refugees fleeing from the Lombard invaders in the north of Italy. There is a legend, significant though untrue, that for a moment no one remained living in Rome. Into this ghastly scenario enter Gregory, the son of a wealthy landowner and patrician. Born about 540, he witnessed for himself the invasion of the Goths and the desperation of the people. His education and upbringing destined him for public service, and at the age of 30 he found himself appointed Prefect of Rome, the highest office in the city, with the weight of the world on his shoulders. He lasted a year or so, and then abandoned everything to become a monk, turning his family home on the Caelian Hill into the Monastery of St Andrew, which is the first destination today.

Three years later, in 578, much against his personal wishes, he was ordained by Pope Benedict I as one of the deacons of Rome, in charge of the seventh district. Pope Fabian (236–250), had divided Rome into seven ecclesiastical districts, setting a deacon over each one, with responsibility to care for church widows and members who were poor, coupled with general administration in the Church. This was only the start. The Lombard threat led Pope Benedict to send Gregory with a delegation of monks to seek help from the Byzantine Emperor in Constantinople, where he remained for six unhappy years in the imperial court, trying to maintain his daily prayer and study of the scriptures. What became clear to him over these years was that no help would be forthcoming from the East, and that if Rome were to recover it would have to find its own resources.

With his mission in failure, he was relieved to be recalled to Rome in 586, and return to the monastery, where the monks soon elected him abbot. Under his leadership the abbey grew from strength to strength. One day, according to the English historian, the Venerable Bede, Gregory was walking through the slave market, when he was struck by some fair-haired youths for sale, and enquired where they came from. On being told 'England', he was reported to have quipped, 'Not angles, but angels, surely'. He made enquiries about the state of the Church in Britain and discovered that, like Italy, England had been invaded: worse still, the Faith had been all but obliterated. The conversion of barbarians was a priority for him, and he set off for England on a mission himself with some of his monks. As soon as the people of Rome heard that the man in whom they had put their hopes had gone, messengers were dispatched to bring him back by force. But by the time they caught up with him three days later, Gregory had sensed that it was not right to leave, and willingly returned.

In 589 the horrific situation in Rome deteriorated beyond belief. The Tiber burst its banks: farms and homes were swept away, and the corn granaries were lost. Plague followed famine, and Rome became a city of the dead; the only movement on the streets being wagons collecting bodies. And in the following year the pope, Pelagius II, died, adding to the despair and confusion. Unsurprisingly Gregory was chosen to succeed him. He contested it strongly, but in the end he had to say goodbye to his cloistered life, the first monk to be pope. He bemoaned it:

> At one moment I am forced to take part in certain civil
> affairs, next I must worry over the incursions of bar-
> barians ... now I must accept political responsibility in
> order to give support to those who uphold the rule of
> law ... when I try to concentrate and gather all my in-
> tellectual resources for preaching, how can I do justice
> to the sacred ministry of the Word? I am often com-
> pelled by the nature of my position to associate with
> men of the world and sometimes I relax the discipline
> of my speech.

It was under Pope Gregory the Great, as he became known, that the reconstruction, not only of the city but of the remnants of the Western Empire began. Gregory took over the civil responsibility of feeding all the people of Rome, and saved them from starvation, by opening more *diaconia* (welfare centres), and ordaining deacons to organise them. He set a personal example by having twelve poor people to dine with him each day. The title, *Servant of the Servants of God* ('servus servorum Dei') was coined by Gregory to explain the papal office. Gradually, not without setbacks, life in Rome improved. From his time, and for the next 1,300 years, the history of Rome became the history of the popes, and their spiritual, religious, architectural and cultural legacy is everywhere to be seen.

Meanwhile the invaders were being assimilated all over the West, and granted citizenship of the Empire, while their leaders ruled as exarchs of the Byzantine Emperor. Their conversion to Christianity went on apace. In the spring of 596 Pope Gregory realised his hopes of eventually re-evangelising England by sending forty of his monks there led by St Augustine, whom he appointed first Archbishop of Canterbury. The vision came to be the building of Christendom, with emperors and kings anointed, like popes and bishops, as God's chosen representatives. It was a shared responsibility, and inevitably gave rise to great conflicts between popes and emperors, bishops and kings, as for example between Archbishop Thomas Becket and King Henry II of England; but Gregory, the first medieval pope, laid the foundations in the West of a Christian civilisation of faith, life, learning and culture.

It is now time to visit Gregory's church.

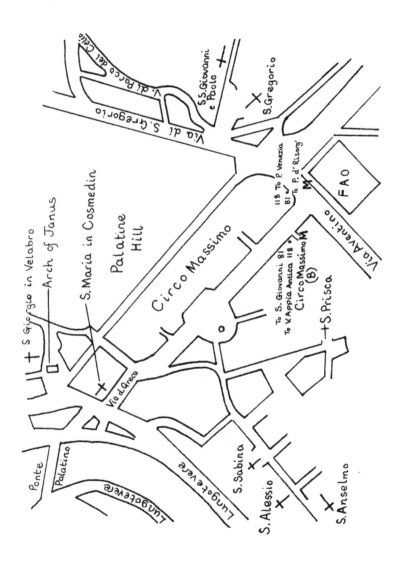

If you come by metro from the direction of Termini to Circo Massimo metro station you emerge by the large white building of the Food and Agriculture Department of the United Nations (FAO). Across the road is the end of the **Circus Maximus** *with the brick ruins of the Emperors' palaces towering above it on the Palatine Hill. If you arrive on the 81, 51, 60 or 80 bus, you run alongside the Circus Maximus, and alight just before the end. The stop is called Circo Massimo, and it is the one after Circo Massimo/Roseto Comunale.*

Follow the FAO building round the corner, going past its main entrance to the wide road and over the zebra crossing. Glancing to your left you will see the dome of St Peter's in the distance. After crossing the roads turn left and just before you reach the little rectangular building, the **Fons Mercurii** *(the source of a spring of water), go up Salita di S. Gregorio. You will pass the centre of the Missionaries of Charity, the sisters of Mother (Saint) Teresa of Calcutta, who look after homeless people. The anniversary of her death, 5 September, is designated by the United Nations as the International Day of Charity; and on 4 September 2016 she was canonised. You now reach the steps up to the church.*

St Gregory the Great (San Gregorio Magno al Celio)

Open: 9:00–12:00; 16:00–18:00.

As soon as you climb the impressive steps and enter the atrium, two monuments on the left will remind you of the most catastrophic conflict of all between a king and a pope. The first is of Sir Robert Peckham (d. 1569), an MP, who saw the execution of martyrs in England, the destruction of the monasteries, and the loss of the  Church he loved. So grieved was he, that he became an exile in Rome. His epitaph (in Latin) reveals the anguish of English people like him in the reign of Henry VIII.

> Here lies Robert Peckham, Englishman and Catholic, who after England's break with the Church, left England because he could not live in his country without the Faith and, having come to Rome, died there because he could not live without his country.

But he left his heart in England. In accordance with his wishes, his body was buried in Rome, and his heart in the Church of St Mary's, Denham in Buckinghamshire.

The second, and very stylish monument, is to Sir Edward Carne (d. 1561), who represented the English court at Rome, seeking unsuccessfully to obtain for Henry VIII a decree of nullity from his marriage to Katherine of Aragon. He ended his days as the Warden of the English Pilgrim Hospice in Rome, which is now the English College.

The walls of the original church and monastery are beneath the present, largely eighteenth-century church, and some remains of Gregory's cell are to be found off St Gregory's Chapel on the right-hand side, where his supposed 'sleeping place' or 'bed' is preserved behind a grill. At the entrance to the chapel you will also see a first-century chair which by tradition was his *cathedra*  from where he preached and celebrated Mass. Many of his sermons and writings have been preserved, including his *Rule of Pastoral Care*. Not only is this an unrivalled work for bishops and clergy, with its emphasis on service rather than control, but also, having been been 're-discovered', an invaluable handbook for leaders in business and politics.

The chapel is beautiful, with an altar incorporating three fine fifteenth-century reliefs of the saint celebrating Mass by Luigi Capponi, a little-known sculptor. The corresponding chapel on the other side is the Blessed Sacrament Chapel. The altarpiece, dated 1893, is by the German artist Alberto de Rohden, and has the title *Anglia Dos Mariae*, 'England, the Dowry of Mary', England's medieval title. It shows the Madonna and Child with Saints Joseph, Peter, Gregory and Augustine of Canterbury. Near this chapel is a door that leads to the Salviati Chapel, finished by Carlo Maderno in 1600. It has an ancient fresco of Our Lady who, according to tradition, spoke to St Gregory; and opposite a marble reredos by the early Renaissance artist Andrea Bregno and his pupils. This chapel is used by Romanian Catholics of the Byzantine Rite.

The ceiling of the church, by Placido Costanzi, depicts the *Triumph of St Gregory*: beneath your feet is a spectacular Cosmatesque marble floor, dating from the thirteenth century.

Three Archbishops of Westminster have been titulars of this church, Cardinals Manning, Vaughan and Godfrey.

To the left of the church is a door (open Tuesdays, Thursdays, Saturdays and Sundays from 9:30 to 12:30) into a garden with three chapels. St Andrew's, in the centre, dates from the eleventh or twelfth century. The altarpiece shows *Our Lady with St Andrew and St Gregory*, and the side walls have two large frescoes: on the right the *Flagellation of St Andrew* is by Domenichino who won many good commissions in Rome; Guido Reni, a deeply spiritual man, who similarly gained wealthy patrons, painted *St Peter and St Paul* on either side of the altar; as well as *St Andrew being taken to Martyrdom* on the left. The oratory on the right is early seventeenth century; dedicated to St Silvia, St Gregory's mother, it is probably located over her tomb. This oratory has frescoes of a *Concert of Angels* by Reni. The third chapel, St Barbara's, dates from the twelfth or thirteenth century: built on the foundations of Gregory's monastery it was restored in the seventeenth. The inscription on the doorway lintel is *Triclinio di San Gregorio*, for the chapel commemorates the feeding of twelve poor people by St Gregory every day. Much of the floor space is taken up with his *triclinio*, a massive third-century marble table on a granite column, its end supports carved with lion-headed griffins, where they ate.

Leave S. Gregorio, as you arrived, by the Salita di S. Gregorio, and cross the roads to the left side of the Circo Massimo.

Circus Maximus (Circo Massimo)

The Circus Maximus was a vast stadium, as you can see, Rome's largest public arena: hence its name. Livy said it was built by Rome's first kings in the sixth century BC, but the first certain date is 329 BC. Archaeology confirms extensive rebuilding in the first century AD and in the late second and early third centuries, by which time it could hold audiences of 385,000 in tiers as high as the Colosseum. Along the central spine were the obelisks now in Piazza del Popolo and beside St John Lateran. The arena was in regular use for chariot races, wild animal hunts, gladiatorial contests and other spectacles well into the fifth century; the last official games were organised by Totila the Ostrogoth in AD 549. The Emperors' palaces on the Palatine overlooked it, as you see, and the royal box was halfway along it. During the Middle Ages the site reverted to fields, and the little tower at the end belongs to this period. In the nineteenth century it was used for industrial purposes, including a gasworks, before being cleared in the 1930s to make a rather neglected public park. There are hopes it will be restored.

*Walk along the left side of the Circus and cross the road on the zebra when you see the statue of Giuseppe Mazzini, high and lifted up. He and Giuseppe Garibaldi were leaders in the long process that led to the unification of Italy in 1871. Walk round him to go through the gated Via di Valle Murcia. It passes through the **Roseto Comunale**, a garden of a thousand roses, open to the public from early May until late June, when they are in full bloom. Beneath the neatly arranged rose beds are the remains of hundreds, perhaps thousands, of Jews. In 1645, Pope Innocent X gave the city's Jews permission to build a cemetery, far more extensive than these gardens, which became known as **L'Orto degli Ebrei**, the Garden of the Jews. Undisturbed for more than 250 years, almost all the cemetery was shamefully destroyed between 1922 and 1934 with the rise of Fascism.*

*You reach the Aventine Hill; once crowded with temples, gardens, baths and houses, it is still an elegant residential area. On the left as you come out of the gates is a sign to the **Church of S. Prisca** (see p. 210). Unless you wish to go there keep straight on and you soon reach the famous Aventine churches of **S. Sabina**, **S. Alessio** and **S.***

__Anselmo__. First you will pass the __Parco Savello__ with its orange trees and spectacular view. From the park you also have the best view of S. Sabina, an early fifth-century church almost unchanged in appearance externally since it was built.

The years between 950 and 1300 were a period of remarkable spiritual growth, renewal and missionary work in the Church, following which came the beginning of the Renaissance, that great cultural revival of 'the grandeur that was classical Rome'; it began in Florence and brought to Rome wonderful architects and artists, like Michelangelo and Raphael. Ageing churches were restored and new ones were built, along with many public buildings, fountains and monuments, which transformed the city. To this period belongs the foundation of great Religious Orders and Lay Movements in the Church. The churches on the Aventine introduce you to some of them.

Santa Sabina

Open: 8:15–12:30; 15:30–18:00.

S. Sabina is the principal House of the Order of Preachers, the friars founded by St Dominic. It is a very old church but was restored in 824 and again in 1216, after which Pope Honorius III gave it to St Dominic. His Order includes friars, sisters and laypeople, and is respected for its intellectual tradition, producing many leading theologians and philosophers, including St Thomas Aquinas, who lived and taught here.

S. Sabina is one of the wonders of Rome. Enter, not by the door you see, but by the main door in the arcaded passage to the left, where there are fragments of sculpture with both pagan and Christian inscriptions. The door is exceptional, and by dropping a euro into a machine you will illuminate one of the world's earliest carved crucifixions at the top on the left, for this door of cypress wood is the

original door, contemporary with the church. Its carvings illustrate scenes from the Old and New Testaments.

An inscription over the door inside tells us that the church was built by a priest, Peter of Illyria, during the time of Pope Celestine I (422–432), and that he had a *'great fortune of which he kept nothing for himself'*. On each side are female figures who represent, on the left, the conversion of the Jews, and the on the right the conversion of the Gentiles. These are all that remain of the fifth-century mosaics which once covered the church, as they do the churches in Ravenna.

It is a wide and spacious basilica, supported by twenty-four columns of Proconnesian marble, re-used from Juno's Temple on the same site, with few seats and little decoration, an almost perfect example of a very early church. Sunshine illuminates the church through windows of selenite (a transparent mineral). The contemporary red porphyry and green serpentine motifs above the pillars represent the chalice and bread of the Eucharist. In a restoration that began in 1924 the work of Baroque architects, including Domenico Fontana and Borromini, was removed, except in the side chapels,

In the floor of the nave you will find the tomb, with its fine mosaic image, of the Spanish monk Fra Munio di Zamora, a Master General of the Dominicans, who died in 1300. Halfway down on the left is a chapel containing Sassoferrato's painting of *Our Lady giving the Rosary to St Dominic with St Catherine of Siena* (St Dominic is credited with popularising its use). Many consider this to be the artist's finest work. The beautifully sculptured walls of the choir are ninth century, and beneath the altar are the remains of several martyrs, including, of course, St Sabina. She was martyred under the Emperor Vespasian, or perhaps Hadrian, having been converted to Christianity by her Syrian servant, Seraphia, who was also martyred. Her home became a shrine and is believed to be beneath the church. Part of a pillar exhibited in the right aisle may have come from that house.

When you leave the church by the old door, look through the hole in the wall opposite and you will see an orange tree in the monastery garden, said to be descended from one that Dominic planted here from his native Spain. There is a bookshop outside the church where you may ask to visit St Dominic's room, now a chapel. Here he met with the founder of the other famous Order of friars, St Francis.

Sant'Alessio

Open: 8:30–12:30; 15:30–18:30 (20:00 in summer).

While the West was recovering from its disasters, the Byzantine Empire came under fearsome threat. During the lifetime of Pope Gregory, Mohammed was born, and within a few years of his death in 632 Islamic armies swept with breathtaking speed across western Asia, North Africa and into Europe, conquering Mesopotamia, Persia, Egypt, Syria, the Holy Land and Jerusalem. By 715 they occupied much of Spain and southern France. In 1067 they conquered Armenia. Constantinople was repeatedly attacked, and the relentless conquest of the Byzantine Empire went on. Many Byzantine Christians sought refuge in Rome. The Byzantine Emperor appealed to the Pope for help, and after long deliberation on how to respond, the First Crusade was launched in 1096. It was against the background of Islamic threat that this fourth-century church emerged into history in 977, when Pope Benedict VII gave it to Archbishop Sergius, a refugee from Muslim persecution in Damascus in Syria. He established a community of both Latin and Byzantine monks, and the monastery very quickly became famous as a missionary centre. Among the monks was St Adalbert of Prague, who set out from here in 995 on his mission with the Gospel to Hungary, Poland and Prussia (where he was martyred in 997).

In due course, Benedictines from Cluny Abbey replaced them, and after them, Premonstratensian canons in 1231. In 1426 the Premonstratensians gave way to the Hermits of St Jerome, a new enclosed Spanish Order. To celebrate the Holy Year of 1750, they turned the church into the Baroque edifice it is now. They left in 1846, and the Somaschi Fathers, who have a particular ministry to the poor, were installed and are still there. Nothing much earlier than the eighteenth century remains apart from the Cosmatesque floor, and Cosmati work around the door and on two pillars behind the altar (it is said that Napoleon looted the rest); the thirteenth-century campanile, a tenth-century icon of Our Lady in the Blessed Sacrament Chapel to the right of the high altar, and a lovely tabernacle, also survived. If you see one of the Somaschi Fathers he may open the crypt, where you can venerate a relic of St Thomas Becket. Before you leave, go to S. Alessio's Chapel on the right of the door. You saw his story in S. Clemente. Here he is again, dressed as a pilgrim, dying under the stairs. As you pass through the courtyard you may like to give something in his memory to the church people who run the soup-kitchen on the left. There are beggars all over Rome, many refugees from the Middle East; you soon run out of coins if you try and give to them all, but here you can make an offering knowing it will really help.

Piazza dei Cavalieri di Malta

There is always a queue waiting to peep through a keyhole in a green door at No. 3. What you see is a secret, so have a look. The doorway was designed in 1765 by Giovanni Battista Piranesi, an Italian artist noted for his engravings of Rome, who also laid out the piazza. Behind the door is the garden of the Villa of the Knights of Malta, one of the last surviving Orders of Knights left over from the Crusades, whose heroism in defeating the in-vading Moslems in the great siege of Malta in 1565 went down in military history. Though no longer fighting, they are no less heroic today, quietly bringing aid and relief to people in countries that include Iraq, Syria, Bulgaria and Cambodia, and assisting prisoners and their families in the USA.

Sant'Anselmo

Open: 6:30–19:30.

Most guidebooks scarcely mention S. Anselmo because it is a modern church. Designed in 1900 by its exceptionally gifted first abbots, Hildebrand de Hemptinne and Fidelis von Stotzingen, it faithfully reproduces the classic basilica style. As the Benedictine Primatial Abbey, the residence of the Order's senior abbot (the Abbot Primate), and as an international university offering courses in philosophy, theology, liturgy, music, monastic studies, languages and history, S. Anselmo is hugely important.

As you pass through the pleasant garden you see a late-twentieth-century bronze statue of St Anselm (1033–1109), the scholarly Benedictine Archbishop of Canterbury, to whom the monastery is dedi-cated. The interior is simple, with three naves separated by granite pillars, and a choir planned for the monastic liturgy for which the church is renowned. The paschal candlestick is in Cosmatesque style. The crypt can be visited through a door by the Altar of the Blessed Sacrament. Behind this altar is a statue of St Benedict, his arms raised in prayer, the posture in which he died. Monks sing Gregorian chant on Sundays: 6:50 Lauds; 9:00 Solemn Mass; 19:15 Vespers. And on weekdays: 6:20 Lauds and Mass; 19:15 Vespers. It is useful to know there is a toilet in the grounds, along with a shop and drinks dispenser.

*Retrace your steps, going not through the Rose Garden, but keeping left down Clivo dei Publicii. When you reach Via della Greca cross to the other side, and turn left to the big intersection. Then you will come to the **Church of S. Maria in Cosmedin.***

Santa Maria in Cosmedin

Open: 09:30–17:50.

You have better things to do than wait in a queue to put your hand into *La Bocca della Verità* (the Mouth of Truth), but if you can't resist it, take comfort: people were doing this in the Middle Ages too. It is only an old drain cover with a god's face on it, perhaps Faunus, or Hercules, protector of the olive trade. But be sure you have never told a lie, or your hand will be bitten off. The queue

is for the drain cover, not the church. This area was the *Forum Boarium*, the Cattle Market, close to the Tiber, which brought Greek traders to settle here in Rome's early Republican days. They had their own cults, notably Hercules, and in the crypt of the church (entrance to the left of the choir) you can see part of the Altar of Hercules they built in 495 BC (on the right at the bottom of the stairs). Adjacent to it was the Temple of Ceres. In AD 4 this was closed and turned into a grain distribution centre. Some of its huge columns survive inside the church entrance and sacristy. After the barbarian invasions, when the Church took over the responsibility of feeding the people, Pope Gregory the Great turned the centre into a *diaconia*, with a small chapel, part of which survives in the crypt. In the eighth century, fugitives escaping the Iconoclasm Controversy in Constantinople found a generous welcome in Rome, with gifts of churches and monasteries. Pope Adrian I gave them the chapel, and enlarged it by demolishing the Temple of Ceres. They called it *in Cosmedin*, meaning 'well-adorned', because of its beauty.

The old church was badly damaged in an earthquake, but well-adorned it still was after being rebuilt in 860, with frescoes on the triumphal arch and on the right and central naves, that are now almost completely lost. The other frescoes you see are all rather fine nineteenth-century paintings in the style of the twelfth century. The classical doorway was carved in the eleventh-century. Sacking by the Normans necessitated further restorations in 1118 and in 1124. In due course the Cosmati brothers laid the magnificent floor, and the choir, ambos and chair were added. The slender campanile belongs to this restoration. In the portico is the tomb of Camerlengo Alfano, who directed the 1124 restorations, and to whom we largely owe the present appearance of the church. The altar canopy and paschal candlestick were made in 1300. In 1718, after some neglect, the church was given a new façade and the interior made over in Baroque style, but, as in S. Sabina, these accretions were cleared away at the end of the nineteenth century, restoring the former appearance of this most pleasing church. It is used today, as it was under the Greeks, for the Byzantine Rite; now by the Melkite Catholic community, consisting mainly of Syrians and Iraqis.

Interesting objects, at each side of the central door, are two spherical black basalt Roman steelyard weights from the Temple of Ceres. Temples had the care of these official weights, and the Byzantine Emperor Justinian asked churches to take over this responsibility. Another treasure to see is on the wall of the bookshop. It is part of a mosaic of the *Adoration of the Magi* from the old St Peter's Basilica, dated 706. The shop sells good Rome guides, icons and cards.

Turn right from S. Maria in Cosmedin and cross Via dei Cerchi, where there are always parked cars; on your right you will see the **Arch of Janus**, *the most neglected of Rome's ancient ruins, framing the* **Church of S. Giorgio in Velabro**.

Arch of Janus (Arco di Giano)

Built in the reign of Constantine, this massive arch is the only surviving example in Rome to have a gateway on each of its four sides—a type known as quadriferous from the Latin for four fronts. It was a meeting point and shelter from the rain and midday sun for merchants in the *Forum Boarium*. Through the Forum passed the important trade route to the Mediterranean. The temples across the road were part of this busy commercial centre. On the keystones of the arch are small figures of the goddesses Roma, Juno, Ceres and Minerva. It came to be called after Janus, the Roman god of gateways, whose name gives us January, because his head, like the month, looks forwards and backwards. No doubt merchants too had to watch their backs as well! Its proportions were changed, and not for the better, when a substantial top storey was removed in 1830.

San Giorgio in Velabro

Open: 8:00–18.30.

Mass in English: Monday to Friday 7.30. In winter Mass is celebrated in the convent. Please ring the bell at Via del Velabro 19.

In this valley, known as *Velabrum*, close to the Tiber and still prone to flooding (a high-level water mark of 1870 can be seen in the portico), was the swamp where Romulus and Remus were said to have been suckled by the she-wolf. There was a church here in the fourth century and, as he did at S. Maria in Cosmedin, Pope Gregory the Great made it a *diaconia* from which the deacons distributed food. The church was enlarged in the seventh century, making use of antique columns, to much as you see it today, one of the most atmospheric in Rome. (Later accretions were stripped away in the 1920s.) Originally dedicated to St Sebastian, the dedication to St George, patron saint of Greece, was added by Pope Zachary (741–752) for the sake of all the Greek-speakers who lived around here. Of Greek origin himself, the pope placed a relic of St George under the altar, where it is still. The apse was decorated with frescoes by Pietro Cavallini, a

Roman artist, who moved away from the Byzantine style and was an important influence on Giotto. The altar canopy, as well as the campanile, façade and portico were added in the thirteenth century. If you look carefully from the back you will think your eyes are playing tricks because the walls are not parallel; the plan is in fact slightly trapezoidal as a result of the additions made to the building. St John Henry Newman was a Cardinal Deacon here, and on the right wall you will see a tablet commemorating him.

> Praise to the Holiest in the height
> And in the depth be praise:
> In all His words most wonderful;
> Most sure in all His ways!
> St John Henry Newman.

In July 1993 a car bomb blew the portico apart and what you now see is a perfect reconstruction.

Before you retrace your steps examine the ancient remains to which the church is attached, the *Arcus Argentariorum*, Arch of Silversmiths, a little, originally free-standing arch erected by the money changers and cattle dealers to honour their emperor, Septimius Severus, and dedicated in AD 204. Inside, on the right, you will see a relief of the emperor (with his toga drawn up over his head) pouring a libation, and his wife, Julia Domna, beside him. The church was built into the arch, thus saving it from destruction,

*Turn left out of the church, go up the hill and turn left into Via di S. Teodoro. On the left is the Hotel Kolbe, named after **St Maximilian Kolbe, OFM Conv.**, the Auschwitz martyr. He lived next door, at No. 42, and you may ring the bell and ask to see his cell. It is a prayerful place with some of his possessions, including his habit, and an exhibition about his life and the Crusade of Mary Immaculate which he founded here.*

Retrace your steps to S. Maria in Cosmedin and cross the road to the temples and the fountain.

Temple of Hercules Victor and the Temple of Portunus

The lovely round temple is often called the Temple of Vesta, because it is similar to that in the Forum, but it was dedicated to Hercules. Dating from the second century BC, it is the earliest surviving marble building in  Rome, and we know that it was designed by a Greek architect, Hermodorus of Salamis. The nearby rectangular Temple of Portunus, protector of seafarers and harbours, dates from the first century BC, replacing an earlier building. Both temples were converted to Christian churches (now closed), which explains why they are so well preserved. The nearby Fountain of the Tritons was completed in 1715 by the architect Francesco Carlo Bizzaccheri, a pupil of Carlo Fontana.

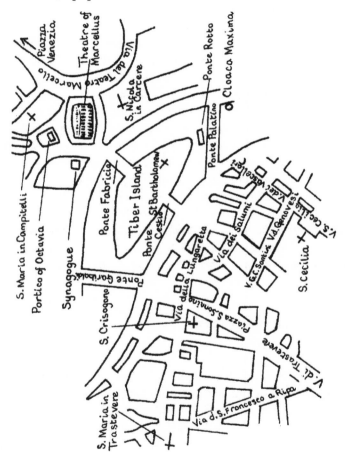

*Walk up the shallow steps to the right of the Temple of Hercules, and cross to the bridge, **Ponte Palatino**. Look down on the left side and you will see the outlet of the Cloaca Maxima. Cross to the right side and you will see the remains of **Pons Aemilius**, a bridge built in the second century BC, and known the **Ponte Rotto** ('Broken Bridge').*

Having walked across Ponte Palatino you have a choice as you cross the road and enter Trastevere, with its narrow cobbled streets of small shops and workshops, restaurants and beckoning waiters. You may wish to visit the **Church of St Cecilia** *and the excavations of the saint's house beneath it. But remember this church closes 13:00–16:00. For St Cecilia, cross the road and go towards the petrol station on the left where you will find Via dei Vascellari. Go down Vascellari—noting No. 61, now a hotel, where S. Francesca Romana worked and died in 1440—this soon becomes Via S. Cecilia, which opens out into a piazza with a white arch on the right admitting you to the courtyard and garden in front of the church (p. 123).*

Instead, you may opt for an extended lunch in one of the many good but not necessarily expensive restaurants on the way to **S. Maria in Trastevere**, *which does not close for siesta. Cross the road from Ponte Palatino, but bear right; go through the parked cars, and you will see Via della Lungaretta. Before long it takes you to Piazza Sidney Sonnino with its wide road, Viale Trastevere, where the No. 8 tram stops. Cross over, pass the various stalls, noticing on your left the attractive porticoed façade and campanile of* **S. Crisogono**. *Via della Lungaretta becomes Largo S. Giovanni and then Via della Lungaretta again. In a short while it opens up into Piazza di S. Maria in Trastevere.*

Santa Maria in Trastevere

Open: 7:30–19:00.

This lovely church, with its beautiful façade and twelfth-century mosaics of bridesmaids with their oil lamps burning, is linked to a strange story. One day in 38 BC oil gushed out from the ground and ran in a stream to the Tiber. The mystery led to many magical and esoteric explanations, and two centuries later Christians in the district considered it a prophecy about the Gospel spreading like soothing oil all over the world. So they wanted a church there. On the site was the *Taberna Meritoria*, a tavern or hospice for wounded soldiers, which became involved in a legal dispute with other tavern owners. Christians in the locality put in a bid for the site and (this was before Constantine) the open-minded

Emperor Severus Alexander (who greatly respected Christians and Jews) ruled in favour of the Christians against the taverners: *'I prefer that it should belong to those who honour God, whatever their form of worship'*. The Pope, St Callixtus, (he who had been super-intendent of the catacomb) paid for the victory dearly. He was lynch-mobbed and drowned close by. The church they built in 222, the *Titulus Calixti*, has, of course, been altered many times, and what you see now is substantially Pope Innocent II's rebuild-ing of 1139, with later additions. The remains of St Callixtus are under the altar. Nearby is a grill with the words *Fons Olei* (mean-ing 'source of oil'), connecting it to this curious story.

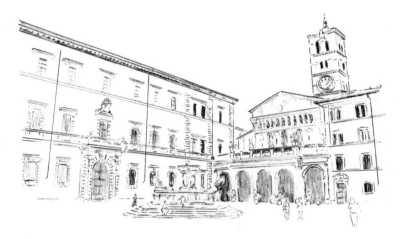

The portico, re-fashioned in 1702 by Carlo Fontana, contains many pieces of early sculpture from the catacombs and from ear-lier churches, as well as a fifteenth-century *Annunciation*. The nave is divided by twenty-two granite columns, with (mostly) Ionic capitals decorated with the heads of Egyptian gods, clearly re-cycled from a Temple of Isis or maybe the Baths of Caracalla. The Cosmati floor is superb; Domenichino designed the richly-gilded ceiling with its painting of the *Assumption*. As ever, the eye is drawn to the twelfth-century Byzantine-style mosaics on the triumphal arch and in the apse. The former show Isaiah, Jeremiah and symbols of the Evangelists. In the apse Christ and Our Lady are flanked by Saints Callixtus and Lawrence, and Pope Innocent

II (offering his church to Our Lady), and, on the right, by Saints Peter, Cornelius, Julius and Calepodius. Above Christ's head is the Hand of God. In the band below are twelve lambs, symbolising the apostles, coming from the cities of Bethlehem and Jerusalem, with the Lamb of God at the centre (similar to those you have already seen similar in S. Clemente and SS. Cosma e Damiano). The exceptional mosaics below these, between the windows and continuing round onto the walls below the triumphal arch, are by Pietro Cavallini (whom you met in S. Giorgio in Velabro). They depict scenes from

the life of Our Lady, including the Presentation of Jesus in the Temple, illustrated here.

By the foot of the steps at the end of the right aisle, in a niche, there are three Roman weights like those in S. Maria in Cosmedin. Above the door at the end of this aisle you will be astonished to see the British Royal Arms. They are in their Stuart configuration, for the chapel here was restored by Henry Stuart, Cardinal Duke of York, younger son of James, the 'Old Pretender', and brother of Bonnie Prince Charlie (p. 134). As you leave, note on the left wall a large fifteenth-century aumbry containing the holy oils. To the left of the apse is the Altemps Chapel, with frescoes by Pasquale Cati, a follower of Michelangelo, which include the *Council of Trent* with its ranks of bishops; above the altar is a sixth-century icon of the *Madonna of Clemency and Peace*. In the left aisle, between the Chapels of the Sacred Heart and St Francis, is the tomb of Innocent II, whose body was moved here in the early fifteenth century from St John Lateran: it was made in 1869 by order of Pope Pius IX.

Any evening at 20:30 you can join members of the **Sant'Egidio Community**, mainly young people who fill the church with praise and prayer. Founded in 1968, its 60,000 members in more than 70 countries centre their lives around prayer and Bible reading, and on many projects helping refugees and the poor around the world; in spreading the Gospel to help people make sense of their life; and engaging in dialogue with members of other Faiths and non-believers.

> O God, you renew the Church in every age by raising up men and women, outstanding in holiness, living witnesses of your saving love: bless the Sant'Egidio Community and all the new Movements of your Church, so that your holy name may be glorified and the people of our time may see Jesus, the Way, the Truth and the Life. Amen.

Outside the church on warm evenings young people love to congregate around the fountain, the work of Bramante with later additions by Bernini and Carlo Fontana.

If you now decide to go to St Cecilia, make your way back to Piazza Sidney Sonnino, cross Viale Trastevere, and head right, past Via della VII Coorte on your left, and on to Via Giulio Caesare Santini. In a short while this becomes Via dei Genovesi. A little further and you reach Via S. Cecilia on your right, which leads into Piazza S. Cecilia and the arch through which you enter the courtyard in front of the church.

If you are going to the Tiber Island follow the same route; cross Viale Trastevere and keep straight on Via della Lungaretta. On the left you will spot Via della Gensola. Going up there you will see some pillars set in a building and steps beside a small grassy area. The steps will lead you to **Ponte Cestio** *(Pons Cestius), built in 46 BC, and onto the Tiber Island.*

Or, if your afternoon is over, take the No. 8 tram from Viale Trastevere to Piazza Venezia.

Santa Cecilia in Trastevere

Open: 9:30–12:30; 16:00–18:30. Convent 10:15–12:15.

You met St Cecilia if you went into the Catacomb of S. Callisto. Her body was taken from there by Pope Paschal I in 820 to this church, which he built above the house where it was thought her family had lived. Excavations, which you can visit from the entrance located near the end of the left hand aisle, have revealed two Roman houses with mosaic pavements; a small museum has been created. St Cecilia converted her husband, Valerian, and her brother, Tiburtius, both of whom were martyred, probably during the reign of Marcus Aurelius around 177. Shortly afterwards, she was condemned too. Their house became the first *titulus* church here, but only its baptistery has been discovered.

You approach the church through a garden, especially lovely when the flowers are in bloom, with a fountain in the middle for washing your hands (the origin of holy water stoups in churches). The campanile, and portico with its strip of mosaic work above the capitals, were erected in 1120. The façade of the church was built in 1725 by Ferdinando Fuga, who worked a lot in Naples as well as in Rome, and the interior is mainly eighteenth century. The brick walls of Pascal's church remain intact, and were unfortunately encased in the nineteenth century, but the small chapel at the back on the right, near the Blessed Sacrament Chapel, through a passage, has not changed much. It is said to be the *caldarium*, the hot bath, still with its steam conduits, in which her torturers tried to suffocate the young saint, before beheading her. The *Beheading of St Cecilia* is by Guido Reni, and in the passage are landscapes by the Flemish artist, Paul Bril. Other chapels were added in the fifteenth century.

Ninth-century mosaics adorn the apse, with the figures of St Paul, St Cecilia and Pope Paschal (his square halo indicating he was still living) on Christ's right and, on his left, St Peter, St Valerian and St Agatha. The thirteenth-century baldacchino is the work of Arnolfo di Cambio. Below the altar is the lovely sculpture of the saint by Stefano Maderno, clearly showing the cut made by the axe in her neck: in front of it on the pavement, engraved on a large round red-marble tablet, is his statement made on oath that this is how he found her when her tomb in the catacombs was opened in 1599 (p. 85). At the end of the right aisle is the entrance to the decorated crypt, though it is often locked. Here are the tombs of Cecilia, Valerian, Tibertius, Maximus, and Popes Urban I (d. 230) and Lucius I (d. 254). This is a church in which to pray for all those who are being martyred for their Faith in the world today, even beheaded, like St Cecilia.

You might also pray for musicians, for Cecilia is the patroness of music. She is often depicted playing an organ, and even credited with being its inventor: unlikely as this is. In Rome, the National Academy of St Cecilia, founded by Pope Sixtus V in 1585 and one of the oldest and most prestigious musical institutions in the world, is named after her.

Before you leave, note on the left of the central door a tomb with the carved arms of England; it is that of the medieval English Cardinal, Adam Easton, who died in Rome in 1397 (though the date on the tomb is 1398). The son of Norfolk peasants, he became one of the greatest scholars and most influential churchmen of his day, and perhaps the spiritual director of Julian of Norwich.

To the left of the façade is the entrance to the convent, where the sisters weave the *pallia* (p. 56). It is only open in the morning and you have to go through the convent (escorted by a sister) if you wish to see Pietro Cavallini's famous *Last Judgement*, which although on the back wall of the church, is hidden by the enclosed gallery of the sisters' choir.

For the Tiber Island go back along Via S. Cecilia, which becomes Via dei Vascellari. Cross to the riverside and go left along it until you reach Ponte Cestio onto the Tiber Island.

To go to S. Maria in Trastevere turn left out of S. Cecilia along Via S. Cecilia; turn left into Via dei Genovesi, and into Piazza Sidney Sonnino. Cross Viale Trastevere, by S. Crisogono, and go along Via della Lungaretta, which becomes Largo S. Giovanni and then Via della Lungaretta again, taking you to S. Maria in Trastevere.

*Alternatively, you could make a short diversion to **S. Francesco a Ripa**, or maybe save it for another day. Turn right from the church and leave Piazza S. Cecilia by Via di S. Michele. Turn right into Via della Madonna dell'Orto, then left on to Via Anicia, which brings you into Piazza di S. Francesco d'Assisi.*

San Francesco a Ripa

Open: 7:00–13:00; 15:00–19:00.

On this site there was once the Hospice of S. Biagio (St Blaise) run by Benedictines, where St Francis used to stay on his visits to Rome. Through the sacristy (guided tours) you can see the room where he spent time with leprosy sufferers. Here also he enjoyed over a long period a spiritual friendship with the Trasteveran noblewoman and widow, Jacoba de Settesoli, who at his request was present with him when he died in Assisi in 1226. He wanted to taste one last time the almond pastry she made, and she brought some with her. After his death she continued her work in Rome amongst the poor, and persuaded the Benedictines to give the Hospice to the Franciscans. She died in Assisi in 1239, and is buried near St Francis in the crypt of the Basilica there. Her epitaph calls her 'Brother Jacoba', the name the brothers affectionately gave her, and she is credited with founding the Third Order Franciscans.

The church was built in 1231 and has always been a place where the people of Trastevere have found friendship and comfort. In 1906 it became a parish, and since 2011 the Friars Minor (Frati Minori) have been sharing it with homeless brothers and sisters. It is, perhaps, a church that beckons us to pray more than admire its art. But it does have some. In the last chapel on the left is a remarkable sculpture by Bernini of *Blessed Ludovica Albertoni*, a contemporary of Michelangelo, who devoted much of her time to caring for the poor. The first chapel on the right was furnished by Carlo Fontana. The seventeenth-century Franciscan sculptor, Diego da Careri, carved three fine statues for this church: *St Francis in Ecstasy* (over the high altar); *St Anthony of Padua* (above the altar at the end of the left aisle); and *St Hyacinth Mariscotti* (above the altar at the end of the right aisle). Even as a nun St Hyacinth lived a life of luxury, until eventually she made public confession of her faults and adopted a life of poverty.

> The friars who live here today greet you with the words of St Francis: 'The Lord give you peace'.

To get from S. Francesco to S. Maria in Trastevere, cross the square to the far right corner and go up Via di S. Francesco a Ripa, cross the tree-lined Viale Trastevere, and straight on until you reach Piazza S. Maria in Trastevere.

If your afternoon is over follow the route above to Viale Trastevere, turn right as soon you come to it, to the stop Trastevere/Mastai, for the No. 8 tram to Piazza Venezia.

For the Tiber Island go back to S. Cecilia and follow the directions on p. 125.

Tiber Island (Isola Tiberina)

Back in the third century BC, when a plague was raging, a devoted band set sail for Greece to seek the aid of Aesculapius, the Graeco-Roman god of healing and medicine. His emblem was a snake, and his snake-entwined rod remains a symbol of medicine today. When the ship returned and docked, a snake slithered off the boat onto the Tiber Island. This good omen led to a Temple of Aesculapius being built there, which became a centre of healing with a hospital. Walls were wrapped around the island to make it resemble a ship, with an obelisk in the middle for its mast. Faint vestiges of Aesculapius's rod with an entwining snake are still visible on the 'prow'. You can go on to the platform by the river to see it and for a good view of the Roman bridges.

San Bartolomeo all'Isola

Open: 9:30–13:30; 15:30–17:30.

The first church was built over the ruins of the temple in 998, to honour the martyred missionary, St Adalbert, whom you met at S. Alessio. In 1113 Pope Paschal II built the campanile and improved the church to house the relics of St Bartholomew, who was added to its dedication. His reliquary under the main altar is a beautiful porphyry cistern with lion's heads from the Baths of Caracalla. In the centre of the chancel steps is a unique marble well-head from the first church, above a spring thought to be associated with the cult of Aesculapius. Fourteen antique Roman columns and two lion supports remain from the first church. Half the church was carried away by a flood in 1557, but the relics were saved, and the church was reconstructed in 1624, with a new Baroque façade by Orazio Torriani, who also made the sensational staircase for the church of the Pontifical University of the Angelicum. Further restorations were undertaken in 1852.

In 1993 the church was entrusted to the care of the Community of Sant'Egidio. University and high school students gather in the church for liturgy and prayer on Tuesdays at 20:00, and from Wednesday to Friday at 20:30, using the surrounding halls and rooms for their activities assisting the poor. After the Holy Year 2000, Pope St John Paul II asked that the memory of twentieth-century Christian martyrs of all denominations should be recalled in this church, and, after much research, dossiers on 12,000 martyrs were produced, and a large icon was placed on the high altar, depicting their personal stories. Objects belonging to some of these martyrs are placed in the small side chapels.

> The souls of the saints are rejoicing in heaven, the saints who followed the footsteps of Christ, and since for love of him they shed their blood, they now exult with him for ever.

The tradition of healing never really left the island, and when the Church took over the site another hospital was built and gradually expanded. One famous pilgrim nursed here was Rahere, an Anglo-Norman priest and close friend of Henry I of England. While in Rome he contracted malaria, and vowed that if he recovered he would build a priory and hospital dedicated to St Bartholomew in London as a thank-offering. That is how, in 1123, the still-prestigious 'Bart's' came to be founded, with Rahere as its first prior and master. The brothers of the Order of St John of God came in 1584, and are still here, keeping to their original mandate of giving free help to the very poor. The hospital sheltered and saved Jews during the War by diagnosing them with a fictitious disease called 'Syndrome K'. In 1882 the medical tradition of the island was enhanced with the establishment of a Jewish Hospital in a former convent.

The four-sided monument in front of the church commemorates the First Vatican Council (1869–70); there was formerly a standing cross here which had replaced the temple obelisk.

*Leave the island by **Ponte Fabricio** (Pons Fabricius); built in 62 BC, it is the oldest bridge in Rome still in use. At the end of it you can see two herms (pillars with heads) with four faces. If you are exhausted there is a small bus terminus across to the right, Monte Savello. 810 and 63 will take you to Piazza Venezia: 63 goes on to Piazza Barberini (see p. 159), where there is a metro station. But if you still have a little energy then walk past the large **Rome Synagogue** with its square dome on your left, to the Portico of Octavia. The Chief Rabbi at this synagogue, Eugenio Zolli, became a Catholic after the war. He knew of all that Pope Pius XII was doing to save the lives of Jews in Italy, and while presiding over the religious service in the synagogue on the holy day of Yom Kippur in 1944, he experienced a vision of Jesus.*

The Portico of Octavia

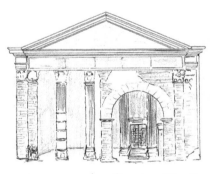

This portico, for many years under heavy restoration but now largely clear of scaffolding in front, was part of an impressive marble-lined passageway over a hundred metres long, built in 146 BC, and reconstructed by Augustus in honour of his sister, Octavia. It was an entrance to the *Campus Martius*, ('Field of Mars'), an area of ancient Rome about two square kilometres in extent, full of temples and public buildings. Little remains, but you can see many fragments of fine capitals and architraves all around, some embedded in surrounding houses. In the Middle Ages this was the most populous area of Rome and, as you may realise from the name of the road, Via del Foro Piscario, there was a fish market, which remained until the end of the nineteenth century. There is even a church, Sant'Angelo in Pescheria (the Holy Angel in the Fish Market), which you can see through the ruins.

*Go down the metal ramp alongside the excavations and make your way past bits of pillars and capitals, and the three re-erected pillars of the **Temple of Apollo**; on your right is what you may at first think is the Colosseum, but is in fact the Theatre of Marcellus.*

Theatre of Marcellus

It looks like a small Colosseum, and indeed Vespasian's architects must have studied it when they built the Colosseum. But it was completed over eighty years earlier, in 13 BC, and inaugurated the following year by Emperor Augustus. He dedicated it to his nephew, Marcellus, who died before building work was finished. Estimates suggest it was capable of holding 20,500 people, but here, unlike the Colosseum, the audiences watched performances of drama and song, and the plan was D-shaped not oval. Christopher Wren acknowledged that his design for Oxford's Sheldonian Theatre was influenced by Serlio's engraving of this building (Wren himself never visited Italy). The surroundings are used today for small summer concerts.

The theatre fell out of use in the early fourth century and, like the Forum, served as a stone quarry. It was saved from total destruction by being turned into a fortress, and in the early sixteenth century the Savelli family built a palace on the top which was later taken over and added to by the Orsini family. The Palazzo Orsini has some magnificent frescoed state rooms and a garden with fountains and orange trees: in 2012 it was on the market for €33m.

This brings us to the end of the day. Turn left from the theatre, and you will quickly reach Piazza Venezia and its buses (Map p. 241). If you are ready for an evening meal why not return to Trastevere on the No. 8 tram? Or you could see an interesting church, **Santa Maria in Campitelli**, *only a minute or two away. If you can be there at 18:30 on Saturday and stay for Mass, even better. On leaving the pathway from the Theatre of Marcellus turn left down Via Montanara into Piazza Campitelli.*

Santa Maria in Campitelli

Open: 7:00–19:00.

This church is of special interest to English and Scottish people because in 1747 Henry Stuart, Duke of York, the younger grandson of King James II, became its Cardinal Deacon. He and his father endowed it to have prayers said each Saturday for the return of England to the Catholic Faith. Prayers for unity are still offered after the 18:30 Saturday Mass by the little Italian congregation, who are always thrilled when English people join them. They will pray with you in English if you ask the priest before Mass.

> Most Holy Virgin … hear the prayer which we earnestly make to you for the whole Church of Christ and in particular, for our brethren of the Anglican Communion … Mother, may that day soon come in which all of us, in harmony, may form a single flock under one Shepherd. Amen.

Above the altar is enshrined a tiny eleventh-century enamel copy of an ancient icon of Our Lady. Pope Gregory the Great carried the original icon in the procession that stopped the plague of 590 (p. 225), and it was venerated highly in S. Maria in

Portico, a church long since demolished. This copy was carried during the plague of 1656, and to thank God for its cessation this worthy church was designed especially for it in 1662 by Carlo Rainaldi: it is regarded as his masterpiece. Like the façade with its detached columns, the interior is a forest of pillars, drawing the eye to the *Gloria*, a dramatization of light around the icon above the high altar, which was designed less than a year after Bernini's in St Peter's.

If you have few minutes (and there are always extra things to see or do in Rome) turn left out of the church and walk along Via dei Funari (passing the recently restored but rarely open **S. Caterina** on your right) and you soon come to the tiny Piazza Mattei and one of the love- 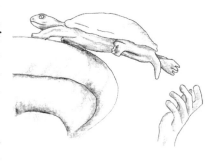 liest fountains you will ever see. The **Fountain of Tortoises** (Fontana delle Tartarughe) was designed by Giacomo della Porta in 1584, but the delightful tortoises, which give the fountain its name, were added, possibly by Bernini, during a restoration in 1658–9.

To return simply retrace your steps and turn left to Piazza Venezia (Map p. 24).

The Stuarts in Rome

James II, King of England and Ireland from 1685 until 1688, (known in Scotland as James VII), was the last Catholic monarch to reign over the Kingdoms of England, Scotland and Ireland. When his son James Francis Edward was born in 1688 and the Catholic succession seemed assured, the anti-Catholic nobles and bishops deposed James, and set his elder daughter, Mary, and her husband William of Orange, both Protestants, on the throne. James, with his wife and young son, fled to France in exile.

On the death of James in 1701, his son proclaimed himself King James III, and attempted to regain the throne. The price of this was to renounce his Catholic Faith, which he refused. In 1715 he appealed to Pope Clement XI to support a 'Jacobite' rising in Britain, and in September the standard of 'King James VIII and III' was raised in Scotland. James went himself in December, but the dwindling Jacobite army was no match for the government forces and he left in early February, never to return. No longer welcome in France, he settled in Rome, and, to the alarm of King George I, decided to marry. George feared that any sons would have a strong claim to the throne. The chosen bride was the sixteen year-old Polish Princess Maria Clementina Sobieski, and George I persuaded the Emperor Charles VI to have her kidnapped on her way from Poland. She was imprisoned in Innsbruck Castle from where four intrepid Irishmen, led by Sir Charles Wogan, supplied with passports by the Pope, rescued her one dark snowy night. The drama rapidly turned into pantomime. You couldn't make it up. A maid of one of the conspirators, a tall girl called Jeanetton, was supposed to change clothes with the diminutive Clementina, but at first she refused to hand over her high heels to make Clementina taller. The Stuart succession was nearly lost through a pair of shoes. The tantrum over, Clementina left the castle with two parcels, one containing clothes, and the other some of the Crown Jewels of England, including the Stuart Sapphire, given her by James as an engagement gift. Wogan took her to the Black Eagle Inn, where a coach was waiting to carry them over the Alps. Dawn was breaking when Clementina realised she had left the Crown Jewels behind, and conspirator Captain Lucius O'Toole was sent back to the inn through the thickening snow to recover them, fearful that if they had been found by the innkeeper there would already be a hue and cry, and a posse on the way to apprehend them. Fortunately he found the jewels still in her room and the party set off again, before becoming very sick through eating some cold chicken which Wogan had cooked. By now Clementina had been missed, and officers were sent out with dispatches ordering her arrest. One caught up with them, but the Irishman O'Toole easily dealt with him, plying him with wine and brandy, and relieving him of his dispatch when he was under the table. The horses were tiring, then, as they approached the Italian border, the carriage axle broke, and the grand-daughter of the King of Poland, cousin of the Emperor and of the Queen of Spain, ended up walking and then being carried into Italy on a small cart.

James and Clementina were married in 1719, and Pope Clement XI acknowledged them as King and Queen of England, Scotland and Ireland and generously provided them with the Muti Palace in Piazza SS. Apostoli as their residence in Rome. The couple produced two sons, Charles Edward (Bonnie Prince Charlie, the 'Young Pretender'—his father was the 'Old Pretender') and Henry Benedict, who became a priest. But Clementina suffered deep depression after Henry's birth and suddenly was up and off to the convent of St Cecilia in Trastevere. Rome was scandalised, and her husband distraught. All over Europe James was traduced as a wicked man whose evil ways had driven his poor wife into a nunnery. However, after two years she returned, as suddenly as she fled, now, it was said, more religious than the pope: James and his sons welcomed her back with joy. When she died in 1735, aged only thirty-two, the family was heartbroken. She was buried in St Peter's with full royal honours on the orders of Pope Clement XII, but her sad heart was interred in her beloved parish church, SS. Dodici Apostoli (p. 200), in the same square as the palace where she had spent half her short life. James prayed beside her heart every day of his remaining thirty-one years, and in this church his own body lay in State for five days, in royal robes with crown and sceptre, before burial in St Peter's.

The 'crown' was inherited by Scotland's hero, the dissipated Bonnie Prince Charlie, who led the last Jacobite rebellion and was finally defeated at the Battle of Culloden in 1746. After his death, his devout brother, Henry Benedict, Duke of York, by now the Cardinal Bishop of Frascati, and head of the College of Cardinals, proclaimed himself King Henry IX of England. The pope did not recognise him, but this did not stop him riding around Rome in a fine carriage emblazoned with the Royal Arms of Great Britain and footmen in court livery. He was greatly loved in Frascati for his generosity, his care for his diocese, for the hospital and seminary he built, and for other charitable works. In Frascati he was a King, and addressed as 'Your Majesty', not quite the usual style for cardinals. When Napoleon invaded Rome, Henry gave all his money to help the pope and was left penniless. King George III persuaded him to accept a pension of £4,000 a year, and his son the Prince Regent (later George IV) contributed to Canova's handsome Stuart monument in St Peter's, which Elizabeth, the late Queen Mother, paid to have restored. As for the Stuart Sapphire, the impecunious Cardinal sold it to George III and later Queen Victoria had it set in the new Imperial State Crown.

Just inside the entrance to the Muti Palace there is a plaque (high up on the left) which records the residence here of Henry Benedict and, with his death, the extinction of the direct Stuart line. If the doorway is open the porter will usually let you in to see the plaque.

5

WITH THE POPE, AND A STROLL
ROUND BAROQUE ROME

Morning: The Papal Audience

Every Wednesday morning when he is in Rome the Pope holds an audience in St Peter's Square, or in the Pope St Paul VI Audience Hall during the winter. It is an opportunity for him to greet pilgrims from all over the world, Catholics and people of all faiths and none. (p. 5).

Groups of people are greeted by name, and choirs and music groups sometimes sing and play so the morning can be very entertaining and joyful. It is also a spiritual time, with the Pope offering a brief reflection and readings mainly in Italian but also in English, French, German, Spanish, Polish, Portuguese and sometimes other languages depending on groups visiting.

The Pope invites everyone to pray with him, if they wish; the *Our Father* is prayed in Latin (printed on the back of the free Audience Ticket). He then imparts his Apostolic Blessing upon the crowd which also extends to loved ones who are sick and suffering, and he blesses any religious articles such as rosaries that people have with them. Finally he is usually driven around in the Square, often stopping to meet people.

After the audience there are many places for lunch around St Peter's, including sandwich vans. If you are going on the afternoon stroll it would save time and your legs to make your way to Borgo Pio and eat there (Map p. 239). After lunch you need to head off down Borgo Pio or Via della Conciliazione towards Castel Sant'Angelo.

Afternoon: From Castel Sant'Angelo to the Spanish Steps

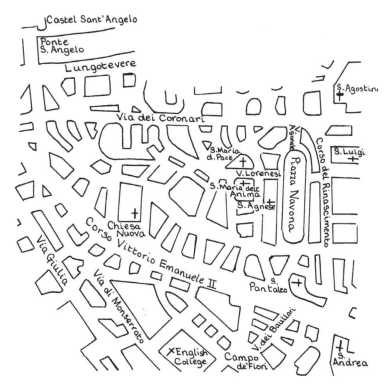

Just before you reach Castel Sant'Angelo, at the end of Via della Conciliazione, you will pass a garden containing a beautiful white marble memorial to St Catherine of Siena, whom you will meet later in the afternoon. She and St Francis of Assisi were proclaimed patron saints of Italy in 1939. The monument was designed in 1961 by Francesco Messina, one of the best classicist Italian sculptors of the twentieth century—you may have seen his statue of Pope Pius XII in St Peter's. Four relief panels depict scenes from the saint's life, and when you meet her later you will then discover why in one of them she appears to be wagging her finger at the pope!

Castel Sant'Angelo is the tomb of Emperor Hadrian, later converted into a fortress for the pope (p. 224). Cross **Ponte Sant'Angelo**, built by Hadrian in AD 134 to enable people to reach his tomb. Later it was called St Peter's Bridge, because pilgrims used it to reach the tomb of St Peter. In 1667 Bernini designed the ten flying angels, each holding one of the instruments of the Passion so that pilgrims should recall the penitential nature of pilgrimage and the price Jesus paid for our redemption. You are really crossing in the wrong direction, for at the end you will see the entry to the bridge is guarded by the apostles Peter and Paul.

Cross the embankment and move towards the left, going down Via di Panico and into Piazza dei Coronari, leaving it by the narrow Via dei Coronari (street of the Rosary-makers). Not so many rosaries-makers now, for they are found around St Peter's, but still full of little shops and workshops, and, on your right, at No. 65/66, the Gelateria del Teatro, thought by many to sell the best ice cream in Rome. Via dei Coronari eventually brings you to Piazza delle Cinque Lune. Keep straight on and through the arch of Via di S. Agostino and into the piazza in front of the church

Sant'Agostino

Open: 7:45–12:00; 16:00–20:00.

People visit this church to see the famous Caravaggio in the first chapel on the left, dedicated to Our Lady of Loreto, which shows Our Lady with her Son welcoming two peasants as pilgrims to her house. Their dirty feet in a holy picture caused quite a stir in 1605. Caravaggio's ability to capture a dramatic moment and his use of light and dark were admired, but contemporaries did not appreciate his realism as we do.

The pilgrim is drawn to the tomb of St Monica, the mother of one of the greatest theologians in the history of the Church, St

Augustine, who lived from 354 to 430. This devout woman from Carthage died suddenly at Ostia in 387 (p. 233), a few weeks after experiencing the joy of her son's baptism in Milan, after all her prayers and tears for him. There was a convent oratory on this site, but in 1296 Boniface VIII ordered it to be replaced by a new church in honour of St Augustine. Although the church was not completed until 1446, St Monica's body, in its original sarcophagus, was brought from Ostia in 1430 and placed in the chapel on the left of the choir, the Blessed Sacrament Chapel. During nineteenth-century restorations it was decided to lay her beneath the altar, but the sarcophagus remains against the wall to the left, with a beautiful fifteenth-century figure of the saint on it.

In 1483 the little-known architects Giacomo di Pietrasanta and Sebastiano Fiorentino, who always worked together, were entrusted with enlarging the church. That was not the end of the matter, for it was greatly altered by Borromini in 1662, and has been much changed since. It was once thought that Bernini designed the high altar, but this is now known to be the work of Leon Battista Alberti. Bernini is, however, thought to be responsible for the Chapel of the Crucifixion, the fifth on the right, where St Philip Neri liked to pray. The first chapel on the right contains paintings by Marcello Venusti, a close friend of Michelangelo, who along with other friends was given designs by the master to follow. Michelangelo was godfather to Venusti's son, also named Michelangelo; and Venusti looked after Michelangelo in his old age. The walls of the nave above the twelve arcades have episodes from the life of Our Lady, and between the windows are six women from the Old Testament. On the pillars are five prophets, that on the third pillar on the left being Isaiah, painted by Raphael. When Giovanni Coricio, who commissioned the fresco, complained to Michelangelo he had paid Raphael too much for it, Michelangelo replied, '*The knee alone was worth it*'.

Other great artworks in the church are the *Madonna and Child with St Anne* (below the Raphael) by Andrea Sansovino, the architect and sculptor who did much work in Florence and Venice, and the *Madonna del Parto* (of childbirth), just inside the door, by Jacopo Sansovino (Andrea's pupil who adopted his master's name): the latter is so popular her foot is worn away with prayerful touching.

Glance back at the plain façade as you leave, one of the earliest in Renaissance style; the travertine stone of which it is built is said to have come from the ruins of the Colosseum.

> Late have I loved you, O Beauty ever ancient, ever new, late have I loved you! You were within me, but I was outside, and it was there that I searched for you. In my unloveliness I plunged into the lovely things which you created. You were with me, but I was not with you … You called, you shouted, and you broke through my deafness. You were radiant, you shone, and you dispelled my blindness. You breathed your fragrance on me; I drew in breath and now I pant for youI have tasted you, now I hunger and thirst for more. You touched me, and I burned for your peace ….
>
> You made us for yourself, O Lord, and our heart is restless until it finds its rest in you.
>
> St Augustine of Hippo.

*Walk back to Piazza delle Cinque Lune and on the left is a small road, Via Agonale, which leads into Piazza Navona. Before going along it, walk on a few metres and you will see (on the left) some of the subterranean ruins of **Domitian's Stadium**.*

Piazza Navona

This now fashionable square occupies the site of a stadium holding 30,000 people, built by Domitian in AD 86 for athletic and cultural competitions: the Circus Agonalis, from the Latin meaning 'games'. The form of the stadium dictated the shape of the square, which is not square but rectangular with rounded ends. All year round artists seek to sell their wares or paint your portrait; it is a lovely place to hang around and perhaps have a cup of (rather expensive) coffee. At Christmastime it used to be full of cribs and toys, with shepherds from the Abruzzi Mountains playing bagpipes; and in the evening on Epiphany a kindly old crone called the *Befana*, arrived at about 5pm to distribute presents. In recent years this once popular Christmas Market has declined and the programme is now uncertain, but it is worth being in Via della Conciliazione on Epiphany morning to join thousands of families, many dressed as the Magi and the *Befana*, processing to St Peter's. New Year is something too, with fireworks going off on balconies all over the city at midnight.

It is Pope Innocent X we have to thank for this beautiful space: his family owned the Palazzo Pamphilj (now the Brazilian Embassy) here, and he poured money into restoring the square, and especially the fountain at the centre, for the Holy Year 1650. You will need to stay here until nearly 14:30 if you are going to S. Luigi. This should not be difficult if you heed the words of Pope Innocent's inscription on the north side of the central fountain offering 'healthy pleasure to those who pass by, drink for those who thirst, and an incentive for those who wish to meditate'.

The first fountain you see on entering the square from Via Agonale is the **Fountain of Neptune**, designed by Giacomo della Porta, and finally completed in 1878 by Antonio della Bitta, who added the imposing sculpture of Neptune fighting with an octopus. The large central fountain and the centrepiece of the piazza is the wonderful **Fountain of the Four Rivers** designed by Bernini: the four rivers are the Danube, Nile, Ganges and the Plate, representing the four continents (Australia had not yet been discovered). Cleverly, Bernini created gesticulating statues sitting on piles of rocks to support an obelisk brought to Rome by Domitian. The statue representing the Plate, with his arm raised almost defensively towards the façade of S. Agnese, is popularly supposed to be shielding his eyes from the architecture of Bernini's rival, Borromini: in reality the church's façade was not built until a few years later. The covered head of the Nile alludes to fact that the river's source was then still unknown.  At the south end of the piazza, the **Fountain of the Moor**, with its dolphin and four Tritons was made by Giacomo della Porta in 1556: Bernini added the statue of the Moor in 1653. During a restoration in 1874 the original statues were removed to the Villa Borghese, to be replaced with copies. From the time of Pope Innocent until 1867 the fountains were allowed to overflow and turn the piazza into a lake on Sundays in July and August, with parties and entertainment. Among those who enjoyed this spectacle were James Stuart, the 'Old Pretender', and his wife, and the young Bonnie Prince Charlie, aged only seven, who was once spotted throwing coins into the water for the street urchins.

Sant'Agnese in Agone

Open: 9:00–12:30; 15:30–19:00. Closed Monday.

This church stands above a Roman brothel, part of the stadium complex, to which a young girl, Agnes, was dragged, stripped and imprisoned, before being executed at the age of twelve or thirteen in the year 304 during the reign of Emperor Domitian. Her crime had been to turn her nose up at a suitor, who promptly denounced her as a Christian. Her parents buried her in the catacomb beneath the church that bears her name in Via

Nomentana (p. 195), though her skull is here, in a chapel reached through a door on the left of the high altar.

> Christ made my soul beautiful with the jewels of grace and virtue. I belong to Him whom the angels serve.
> St Agnes.

The present church replaces an original eighth-century oratory, which survives beneath it, and some later churches. It is a jewel of Baroque architecture despite much travail in designing it. Pope Innocent X commissioned Girolamo Rainaldi and his son Carlo in 1652, but after a year they were replaced by Borromini, who designed the splendid concave façade before falling out of favour with Innocent's successor Alexander VII, who brought back the younger Rainaldi. After nine years of no progress, Bernini was sent for to complete it, and the church was finally consecrated in 1672. Above the seven altars, instead of paintings there are statues and bas-reliefs made by Alessandro Algardi's followers. Inside the door to the left is S. Alessio again. Here in white plaster you see the dying hermit under the staircase, with his distraught parents holding the paper which confirmed his identity. S. Francesca Romana (whose church you may have seen) was baptised in the font. Above the main entrance is the tomb monument to Pope Innocent X, his right hand raised in blessing to the crowds who didn't much care for him, despite his being a kindly and compassionate man. His famous portrait by Velázquez hangs in the Palazzo Doria-Pamphilj art gallery (p. 189).

If you have time you may like to make a short diversion. Opposite the first fountain you saw on entering the piazza, is a narrow street, Via dei Lorenesi, which takes you to the **Church of S. Maria dell'Anima**, *with its pretty green and yellow spire. To the right of this church is Vicolo della Pace. Go left at the end of it and on your right is the* **Church of S. Maria della Pace**.

Santa Maria dell'Anima

Open: 9:00–12:45; 15:00–19:00 (entrance sometimes at the back of the church).

This unusual church, the German Church, began in 1350 as a hospice and chapel for pilgrims from the Holy Roman Empire and the Rhineland: it was replaced by the present building between 1499 and 1523. The designer is unknown: Sansovino has been suggested, and Bramante's influence has been detected in the windows. Giuliano da Sangallo, from Florence, was credited with the façade, but this attribution has now been questioned. The building is an example of a *Hallenkirche* or 'hall church', in which the nave and side aisles are of equal height, sometimes (but not here) under a single ceiling. In the last chapel on the right is a close copy of Michelangelo's *Pietà* by Lorenzetto. Of special interest in the sanctuary is the *Holy Family and Saints* by Giulio Romano, Raphael's favoured pupil: on the right is the tomb of the Dutch pope, Adrian VI, who died in 1523 having reigned for less than two years, the last non-Italian pope before St John Paul II. An intellectual, he tried in vain to reform the Church at the time of Luther but lacked support. The Latin inscription, 'Quantum refert in quae tempora vel optimi cuiusq' (*'How important, even for the best of men, are the times in which he finds himself'*) was often quoted by Adrian himself.

Santa Maria della Pace

Open usually 10:00–16:00 Monday and Friday; other days 9:00–12:00. Closed Saturday and Sunday. Note, the opening hours of this church seem to change quite frequently

Pope Sixtus IV vowed to build a church in Rome dedicated to Our Lady of Peace if a bloody feud in Florence was settled. When it was, in 1480, he built this unusual church, with its short and narrow two-bay nave and four side chapels, and a domed octagonal transept. Above the chancel arch is the inscription, *et in terra pax*, 'and on earth peace'. The lovely semi-circular entrance portico of six columns was added by Pietro da Cortona in the seventeenth century.

An earlier church on the site, demolished for the present building, had housed a popular image of Our Lady, which was said to have bled when struck by a knife thrown by a drunken soldier. This image is now enshrined above the high altar, designed by Carlo Maderno. Above the arch of the first chapel on the right, the Chigi Chapel, are famous frescoes by Raphael of saints and prophets, and four Sibyls similar to those he had seen in the Sistine Chapel. It was widely believed in the Middle Ages that the Sibylline Prophecies contained prophecies of Christ. A Sybil had shown Augustus the Virgin and Child. And in Virgil a Sybil foretells the coming of a Saviour, whom Christians identified as Christ. Opposite is the Ponzetti Chapel with lovely frescoes and an altarpiece of *St Bridget and St Catherine of Alexandria venerating Our Lady* by Baldassare Peruzzi, who worked with Raphael in the Vatican Palace. You may also like to see, in the second chapel on the left, Marcello Venusti's altarpiece, *Our Lady with Saints Jerome and Ubaldo*, which his friend Michelangelo designed for him.

To the left of the church is a delicate two-storey cloister built by Donato Bramante and one of his first works in Rome (1504). It must have made a great impression, for Bramante was chosen as the first architect of the new St Peter's. A restoration of the church and cloister was completed in 2012, and the cloister is now an arts exhibition centre.

Return to Piazza Navona and leave by the Corsia Agonale, about half-way down the opposite side, between the enticing shop, L'Artigianato, and the restaurant. It brings you out on Corso del Rinascimento opposite the **Palazzo Madama**, *built by the Medici family in the early* *sixteenth century. Difficult as this is to believe, the façade dates from the mid-1650s. It was the seat of papal government in the nineteenth-century and now houses the Italian Senate. Turn left along Corso del Rinascimento, cross the road, then turn right into Via del Salvatore (with the farmacia on your left) which brings you to the piazza in front of* **S. Luigi dei Francesi***; the entrance to the church is on your left. Alternatively with a detour of no more than three minutes, turn right from Corsia Agonale into Corso del Rinascimento, cross the road and turn left into Via degli Staderari. Then you will see (on the right) the captivating* **Fountain of the Books** *on the side of what used to be Sapienza University, founded in 1303 by Pope Boniface VIII. It is one of a number of fountains designed by Pietro Lombardi in 1927. Continue along Via degli Staderari and turn left into Via della Dogana Vecchia, which brings you to San Luigi dei Francesi.*

San Luigi dei Francesi (St Louis of France)

Open: 9:30–12:45; 14:30–18:30.

This is the church of the French community in Rome, opened in 1589 as a pilgrim church. The façade, which has the salamander emblem of King Francis I, was designed by Giacomo della Porta, with whom you are now familiar. The interior has become rather cluttered over the years: one chapel that escaped is the Polet Chapel, near the entrance on the left, which was delicately fres-coed by Domenichino between 1612 and 1615 with *Scenes from the Life of St Cecilia*. On the right Cecilia gives away her riches, on the left she is martyred, while on the ceiling she and her husband are being crowned by an angel. The glorious *Apothesis of St Louis* in the nave ceiling is by Paris-trained artist Charles-Joseph Natoire (1700–77).

The main reason visitors come here, however, is to see three masterpieces by Caravaggio of *Scenes from the Life of St Matthew* in the Contarelli Chapel at the end of the left aisle. They can be il-luminated by inserting a coin into the machine. On the left is the calling of Matthew: Jesus enters the counting room with Peter, and extends his finger towards Matthew who is sitting with four other tax-collectors. (Peter, depicted as an older, grey-haired man, partly obscures the figure of Jesus whose head and right arm are dramatically highlighted.) The bearded Matthew points to himself, as though asking with incredulity, 'Me?' In front of you Matthew is writing his Gospel. On the right wall is the saint's martyrdom: Matthew's right hand reaches out towards the martyr's palm, held by an angel, while his wrist is simultaneously grasped by the nearly naked executioner: spectators look on in horror and awe.

> Jesus looked at Matthew with the eyes of mercy. He looked at him as no one had looked at him before. This look unlocked his heart. It set him free, it healed him, it gave him new hope, a new life, just as Jesus's merciful gaze gives new life to men and women today.
>
> Pope Francis.

Coming out of the church turn half right, cross the piazza and turn left into Via Giustiniani—where you will pass a good gelateria on your left. A bit further on the road opens into Piazza Rotondo and to your right is the Pantheon. The fountain, you will not be surprised to know by now, was designed by Giacomo della Porta, in 1575. The obelisk, which came from Heliopolis, was added in 1711 by Filippo Barigioni.

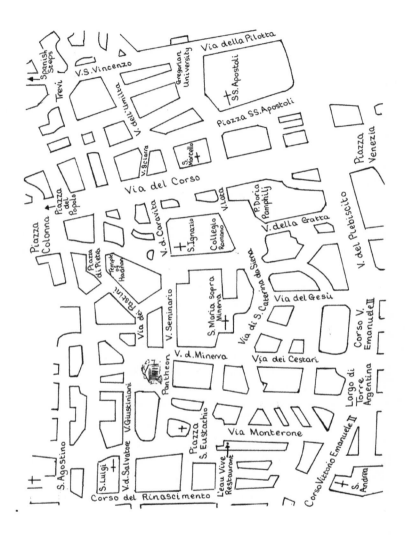

The Pantheon

Open: 8:30–19:15 (in winter closing times are earlier).

The Pantheon is the best-preserved and greatest architectural survivor of ancient Rome. The original structure was erected in 27 BC by Marcus Agrippa, a senator and architect, who greatly assisted Augustus with his building projects, including the aqueducts to give all citizens fresh drinking water and baths. The present building goes back to  Hadrian in AD 120, the first Pantheon having been badly damaged by fires. The dome, slightly larger than St Peter's, in this cavernous, windowless space, would form a perfect sphere were it touching the floor. Light streams from the large circular hole in the roof: rain too, which still drains away through Hadrian's channel. The roof was formerly covered in tiles of gilded bronze, a blazing beacon in the sun. Hadrian wrote:

> *My intentions had been that this sanctuary of all gods should reproduce the likeness of the terrestrial globe and of the stellar sphere ... The cupola ... revealed the sky through a great hole at the centre, showing alternately dark and blue ... the disk of daylight would rest suspended there like a shield of gold; rain would form its clear pool on the pavement below, prayers would rise like smoke toward that void where we place the gods.*

Abandoned after the fall of Rome, the Pantheon was saved by Byzantine Emperor Phocas, who in 608 gave it to Pope Boniface IV. He turned it into a church dedicated to St Mary and the Martyrs, enshrining relics from the catacombs. Its dedication on November 1 is the origin of the Feast of All Saints. In 667 the gilded-bronze roof tiles were removed by Byzantine Emperor Constans II and taken to Constantinople. The Pantheon was greatly treasured in medieval Rome: later the Barberini Pope Urban VIII allowed Bernini to add two incongruous bell-towers, nick-named 'ass-ears' (now fortunately removed), and also to strip much of the bronze from the portico (but not the ancient doors) for his baldacchino in St Peter's. The bronze left over made eighty cannon for Castel Sant'Angelo. Pope Urban's ruthless pillaging of this bronze, and the marble from many ancient monuments, led to a famous pasquinade being placed on a **Talking Statue:** 'Quod non fecerunt barbari, fecerunt Barberini'—*What the Barbarians did not do, the Barberini did.*

Here it is architecture more than art that excites wonder. Yet, there is a seventh-century icon of the *Virgin and Child* over the altar, a lovely fifteenth-century fresco of the *Annunciation* in the first chapel on the right, and a fourteenth-century fresco of the *Virgin and Child with John the Baptist and St Francis* in the next. Otherwise there is little of note except for the tombs of Raphael and of the first two kings of united Italy, Victor Emmanuel II (1820–78), and his son, Umberto I (1844–1900). Raphael's epitaph translates: *Here lies Raphael. While he lived Mother Nature feared to be outdone. When he died she feared to die with him.*

Leave the Pantheon and turn right, alongside it, and you will come to Piazza della Minerva, with its obelisk mounted on the back of a little elephant in front of the Church of S. Maria sopra Minerva. If you would like to look in the window of Gammarelli, ecclesiastical outfitters to the popes since 1798, walk on past the shop selling antiques prints and engravings and turn right at the corner into the little Piazza di S. Chiara; Gammerelli is at No.38. Here you can buy yourself a pair of red socks, but they may draw the line at a white cassock. Then retrace your steps to the little elephant.

The Minerva Obelisk

According to its inscription this red-granite obelisk was erected by Pharaoh Hophra at Sais in Lower Egypt in about 587 BC: Hophra is mentioned in the Book of Jeremiah (44:30). It was brought to Rome in the imperial era, and erected in a Temple of Isis on the *Campus Martius.* Lost in the mists of time, it was unearthed near here in 1665, in the grounds of a Dominican monastery. When Pope Alexander VII heard about it he decided it should stand

in the piazza of their church, and entrusted Bernini with making something of it. This charming and whimsical work is the result.

Santa Maria sopra Minerva

Open: 7:00–19:00.

Standing on the site of an eighth-century oratory built over the ruins of a Temple to Minerva, the church was built in 1280 in the gothic style, a rarity in Rome, by Dominicans who modelled it on their church in Florence, S. Maria Novella. The chancel was rebuilt in the seventeenth century, but the nineteenth century made the greatest impact with new rose windows and vault, and the striking azure blue that pervades the interior.

This may be the place to sit and reflect on a little more history, and perhaps pray for the Pope in his world-wide ministry. Pope Gregory the Great's acceptance of the papacy, for the sake of Rome's desperate people, inevitably led him and his successors into the wider remit of protecting them from invaders. Pope Stephen II in 756 invited Pepin, King of the Franks, to drive back the Lombards from Ravenna. Pepin did so and formally presented Ravenna to the pope, which effectively gave him the 'Papal States'. Popes were gradually drawn into international politics and alliances. Different countries now had a serious interest in who was elected pope. When Benedict XI died in 1304 the conclave to elect his successor was deadlocked for a year between supporters of a French cardinal and his opponents. Eventually, the Archbishop of Bordeaux was elected as Pope Clement V. Having been a close collaborator with the French king he was persuaded to live temporarily in Avignon, in a region which was technically Papal territory. However, determined French influence ensured that the next seven popes were French and they lived in Avignon until 1376, in what became known as the 'Babylonian Captivity' of the Church.

Now we come to the diminutive nun, whose effigy is under the high altar of this church, St Catherine of Siena, who became the adviser and confidante of popes, bishops and kings. When Pope Gregory XI was elected in 1370 his inclination to live in

Rome was bolstered by St Catherine, who urged him to *'attend to things spiritual, appointing good shepherds and good rulers in the cities under your jurisdiction … Above all, delay no longer in returning to Rome'.* When he did so (arriving in January 1377) he found the city in a shocking state, deprived as it had been of all leadership for more than seventy years.

At the age of 20 Catherine had joined the Third Order of the Dominicans. The secret of her influence was her intense spiritual life, which led her to open a convent in Siena. Her last years were spent in Rome, where she died in April 1380 in a room in the neighbouring convent. The walls of this room were reassembled and converted into a chapel which you can sometimes visit: go through the sacristy on the left. She generally spent most of the day in prayer, often in St Peter's. In 1939 she was proclaimed patron saint of Italy, and in 1999 Pope St John Paul II named her one of the six patron saints of Europe.

As you approach the high altar to venerate the saint you will see on the left of the sanctuary a statue of *Christ the Redeemer* by Michelangelo, holding the Cross and instruments of his Passion as precious things as though to show he laid down his life of his own accord. Michelangelo abandoned his first effort when he discovered a black vein in the white marble. Rushing to complete the commission with a new block, one of his assistants damaged it and another rescued it; but it did win wide acclaim from contemporaries. In both versions Christ was naked, to show his perfect and innocent manhood—the bronze loin cloth was added later. The original statue was lost, but in 2000 it was recognised in the sacristy of the Church of S. Vincenzo Martire, at Bassano Romano, near Viterbo, the black vein clearly visible on Christ's left cheek.

In the 'Vestibule' to the left is the tomb slab of the Dominican artist Beato Fra' Angelico (d. 1455), famed for his frescoes in the convent of S. Marco in Florence. The adjacent Frangipane Chapel has a fifteenth-century Renaissance tomb on the wall, and above that, unexpectedly, a Roman sculpture of Hercules struggling with the Nemean lion. There are many other tombs around the church, including those of two popes who did not respond well to the need for reform. They face each across the sanctuary behind the high altar: on the left Leo X, who allowed indulgences to be sold for St Peter's, and on the right Clement VII, who was confined in the Castel Sant'Angelo during the 1527 Sack of Rome.

On the other side of the sanctuary, in the right transept, do not miss the wonderful Carafa Chapel (also called the Chapel of the Annunciation), with frescoes painted between 1488 and 1493 by Filippino Lippi, another Florentine of the Renaissance. Over the altar is the *Annunciation*, with St Thomas Aquinas presenting Cardinal Carafa to Our Lady, and on the wall above the *Assumption*. The other frescoes honour St Thomas. Carlo Maderno designed the chapel further down on the right, and the painting commemorates the Confraternity of the Annunciation, which provided dowries to enable poor girls to marry.

> Lord, raise up shepherds after the pattern of your Son, to feed and strengthen your Church throughout the world: faithful bishops, priests, deacons and ministers of the Gospel. Grant to all lay people the grace to encourage them, and a desire to be in full communion and unity with them, for the sake of Jesus Christ, who prayed for us all to be one. Amen.

Turn left as you leave the church and go round it along Via di S. Caterina da Siena. Soon on your right you come to Via del Gesù, so if you missed it before, you could go to the Gesù now, especially if it is approaching 17:30 when the macchina barocca springs to life (p. 46). Otherwise continue along Via Piè di Marmo and don't miss the huge Roman foot on the corner of Via di S. Stefano del Cacco. You enter Piazza del Collegio Romano, and could, if you wish, go down Via di S. Ignazio on the left of the college to the **Church of St Ignatius** *(p. 205).*

Here, beside the **Collegio Romano,** you may like to take up some history again. The end of the Avignon papacy did not end the woes of the Church. Rival claimants made it uncertain who was elected pope, thus precipitating the Great Schism, during which three men claimed to be the true pope: this lasted from 1378 to 1417, until the Council of Constance resolved the crisis. It laid down strict rules for conclaves, requiring the cardinal electors to be isolated from all outside influences (nowadays banning mobile phones and other digital devices) and to remain in prayer and discussion until a name emerges with a two-thirds majority. Pope Martin V was chosen, and with his election the Schism ended.

The Great Schism was symptomatic of the ills that had befallen the Church. Yet *'the gates of Hell will not prevail against [his Church]'*, Jesus had promised (Matthew 16:18); and so by God's grace it always will be renewed, slow and unresponsive though it sometimes may be. Martin Luther, a German Augustinian friar and Professor of Theology, articulated what many had been saying for a century, especially in the Religious Orders, where renewal was well underway. Luther's writings were closely examined and deemed mistaken as he moved from what had begun in 1517 as a protest against the sale of indulgences to build St Peter's, and the doctrine of Justification this implied, to his opinion that the pope was the anti-Christ.

Tragically, the Reformation unleashed wars of religion in Europe in 1524. Reference has been made to the Sack of Rome in 1527; this was Rome's fall-out from the Reformation conflict. The heroic Swiss Guards were no match for 34,000 mutinous troops of Emperor Charles V, descending on Rome and running amok, turned rabid by Luther's invective against the pope. Inside the Vatican they scrawled Luther's name on Raphael's priceless paintings, but they did not catch the pope. Clement VII had fled into the Castel Sant'Angelo. As many as 12,000 inhabitants were massacred, and even the sick in the Hospital of the Holy Spirit were slaughtered. So many buildings and churches were damaged and looted that four-fifths of the city was left uninhabitable, and the population dropped from 55,000 to 10,000.

After this terrible setback to the renewal of the Church it eventually got underway (and is sometimes called the Counter-Reformation in English histories). Saints like Ignatius of Loyola, Teresa of Avila, John of the Cross, Francis de Sales, Charles Borromeo and Philip Neri were among the spiritual giants raised up by God to restore the vitality and spirituality of the Catholic Church. Old Religious Orders were renewed and new ones were founded; notably the Society of Jesus (the Jesuits) by St Ignatius in 1540, missionaries of the Gospel to lands where it had never been preached before: many were martyred all over the world, including England. Further delayed by a war between Charles V and France, the Council of Trent was eventually convened by Pope Paul III in 1545. It made huge reforms, gave new direction to the Church, and revitalised the education and life of priests. Pope Gregory XIII founded the **Gregorian University** to educate priests, and he promoted good liturgy and music in church.

Collegio Romano

The College was opened in rented accommodation by St Ignatius in 1551 to provide education from elementary to university level in the humanities, science and Christian doctrine. So successful did it prove that the huge building here was provided by Pope Gregory XIII in 1585. At one time there was an Observatory on its roof, one of the oldest in the world (now at Castel Gandolfo), and learned debates took place there between the illustrious Jesuit mathematician, physicist and inventor, Athanasius Kircher, and Galileo. The Gregorian calendar was developed here by the Jesuit Professor Christopher Clavius. Jesuit students of the English College, and other Jesuit missionaries, studied here. The training of priests was transferred to a different site in 1850, but part of the building has continued in use as a high school. Admitting girls in 1890, it became one of the first co-educational schools in Europe. Other parts of the building are now occupied by the Ministry of Heritage and Culture.

> Almighty God, creator of Heaven and earth, and of all things visible and invisible, guide the work of scientists as they discover the wonders of creation and unravel the mysteries of the universe for the benefit of mankind. Grant that as there is but one truth we may all seek it in humility, through Jesus Christ our Lord.

*At the end of the piazza is the **Palazzo Doria-Pamphilj** (p. 189) home to a remarkable art gallery and the **Anglican Centre** (p. 189).*

Leave Piazza del Collegio Romano by the far left corner, along Via Lata. Note the amusing little fountain on the left near the end,

Il Facchino (the Porter), one of the **Talking Statues**. *The Renaissance sculptor (some think it was Michelangelo) took as his model a water carrier with a reputation for drunkenness, who is now obliged to make do with water till the end of time.*

Look right down the Corso as you leave Via Lata; in the distance is the dominating monument to Victor Emmanuel II in Piazza Venezia. Immediately to your right **S. Maria in Via Lata** *stands over the site where St Paul is traditionally said to have spent two years under house arrest (Acts 28, 30–31). You can visit the crypt, also associated with St Peter and St Luke. If you are running out of time walk to Piazza Venezia for a bus (p. 241). Otherwise you may like to visit the* **Trevi Fountain**. *The most interesting route is to turn left, cross the Corso by the farmacia and turn down Vicolo Sciarra. In the Corso you will have noticed the magnificent façade of* **S. Marcello al Corso**, *designed by Carlo Fontana: inside is a monument to the English cardinal, Thomas Weld (1773–1837) of Lulworth in Dorset, whose titular church this was (3rd chapel on right). Vicolo Sciarra turns right and left by the restaurant before bringing you into Piazza dell'Oratorio. Pass the church (**Oratorio del SS. Crocifisso**), turn left beside it and you will come into the* **Galleria Sciarra**, *a glass-roofed arcade built in the late 1880s as a fashionable shopping centre. Worth stopping to look up and admire; the enchanting paintings and decorations in the Liberty style are a superb example of the influence of English pre-Raphaelite art on Italian artists, mixing Renaissance decoration with images of contemporary women. Painted above one of entrances are the words 'To the English Fashion'. The role of women in middle-class society is at the heart of the frescoes. Go straight on, passing McDonald's, and turn right into Via delle Muratte. This takes you to the Trevi.*

Trevi Fountain

No visit to Rome is complete without a visit to the Trevi Fountain, so it is always packed with tourists (and pickpockets), daytime and evening (when it is floodlit). You reach the small square and suddenly see and hear it above the hubbub. Presided over by Neptune in his shell chariot drawn by two prancing sea-horses held in check by a couple of tritons, the water cascading over

the rocks is *Aqua Virgo*, the purest in Rome, though here it is stored in a tank in the palace behind, and replaced only once a week. Agrippa built the aqueduct in 19 BC, and there was a fountain then, but like the all the aqueducts it was destroyed by invaders. Renaissance popes built new aqueducts which still bring plentiful water to the city today. Bernini designed a Trevi Fountain for Urban VIII in 1664, but the pope died that year, and it was abandoned because his successor, Innocent X, disliked Bernini. In 1730 Pope Clement XII held a competition which was won by Nicola Salvi, because his was the cheapest design, but the poor man died of pneumonia brought on by the wet conditions before the fountain was completed. Eventually it was inaugurated in 1762. If you throw a coin in you are guaranteed to return to Rome, and *Caritas* will benefit.

*As the afternoon draws to a close, you have a choice: **A** to Piazza Venezia and buses back. Or **B** to the **Spanish Steps** (10 minutes). The Spanish Steps is a lovely venue in the evening, and is close by Spagna metro station.*

***A**. Leave the Trevi by Via S. Vincenzo, which, as you face the fountain, is behind you over your right shoulder, beside the church across the corner, **SS. Vincenzo e Anastasio**. Continue on this road, crossing Largo Pietro di Brazza where, if you glance left, you will see the highest of Rome's seven hills, the Quirinal, on which stands the **Quirinal Palace**, the official residence of the President (p. 188). Continue and you reach Piazza della Pilotta, where you will see the **Pontificia Università Gregoriana**, (the Gregorian University), one of the seven Pontifical universities in Rome, founded to train priests. The 'Greg' began as the Collegio Romano, which you have just seen. This building was opened in 1930 and has the largest Philosophy and Theology Faculties in the world, with nearly four thousand* *students. Keep on Via della Pilotta with its elegant bridges linking the Colonna Palace on the right to its gardens on the left: this brings you into Via IV Novembre. Turn right and you will find the 40 and 64 buses going towards St Peter's, and across the road these and other buses going to Termini (Map p. 24).*

*If you have time for something more, then after turning right into Via IV Novembre take the next right into Piazza SS. Apostoli: the church is worth seeing (p. 200). The ochre-coloured building at the end (No. 59) is the **Palazzo Muti**, which Pope Clement XI gave to the Stuart kings in their exile (p. 134).*

***B.** For the Spanish Steps, leave the Trevi by Via della Stamperia on the far right corner of the fountain as you look at it. It veers right till you reach the wide Via del Tritone, which you cross and go up. When this widens into Largo del Tritone turn left into Via dei Due Macelli, which takes you to the bottom of the Spanish Steps. Alternatively, longer but worthwhile, keep on Via del Tritone until you cross Via Sistina and reach Piazza Barberini. Here you will see the **Fountain of the Triton**, a masterpiece of Bernini, and the last commission from his patron, Pope Urban VIII, who died in 1644. The tiara of this Barberini pope features his family's bees. Four dolphins support two giant scallop shells on which kneels Triton, an ancient sea-god, his head held back blowing into a conch spurting water. Go back to Via Sistina which will take you to the top of the Spanish Steps. There is a metro station in Piazza Barberini and another near the Spanish Steps.*

*A yet longer way to the Spanish Steps is by Via Vittorio Veneto— usually shortened to Via Veneto—one of Rome's most fashionable and expensive streets, with five-star hotels and renowned cafés, including **Harry's Bar**, featured in Federico Fellini's classic 1960 film,* La Dolce Vita. *While sipping cocktails there, you may meet stars and celebrities, but Harry's Bar, at No. 150, is a long walk. If you want a little walk up Via Veneto start where it begins, about half way along the left side of Piazza Barberini: Bernini's pretty **Fountain of the Bees** stands on one corner. Three bees at the base of a large shell squirt water into the basin. To reach the Spanish Steps turn left off Via Veneto down Via Ludovisi, then left into Via Francesco Crispi and right along Via Sistina. If you get as far as Harry's Bar you need to go back down again and turn right on Via Lazio, then left when you* *reach Via di Porta Pinciana which brings you back to Via Francesco Crispi.*

The Spanish Steps

Called Spanish on account of the proximity of the Spanish Embassy, this could be said to be a bit of England, though France has the best claim. The church at the top of the steps, **Trinità dei Monti**, was built by French kings (p. 220), as was the adjoining convent for the Franciscan Order of Minims. In 1821 the friars were succeeded by Sisters of the Sacred Heart who ran a school until 2006, when the Fraternités Monastiques de Jérusalem replaced them. One of the new Catholic Orders, they were founded in 1975 to live the monastic life in the heart of modern cities. The church, convent and much of the surrounding area, including the Villa Medici (home of Académie de France à Rome) are still the property of the French State. The elegant Spanish Steps, connecting the church with Piazza di Spagna below, were built by the French in 1723-6 because the way up from the piazza was so muddy. They were designed by the little-known Roman architect Francesco de Sanctis.

In the spring the Steps are glorious with azaleas; models in fashion parades prance up and down them in the summer; at

Christmas they form a backdrop to a remarkable crib; while all year round, and especially on warm evenings, they make a lovely (if crowded) spot to linger. To the left of the Steps as you face them are **Babington's Tea Rooms**, founded in 1893 by Miss Anne Marie Babington, an English woman, and Miss Isabel Cargill, a New Zealander. It was the third teashop they opened in Rome, catering for its many English residents at a time when tea in Italy could only be bought in pharmacies. Ironically, Miss Babington was a descendent of Anthony Babington, the Catholic, hung, drawn and quartered by Queen Elizabeth for the Plot that bore his name to install Mary Queen of Scots on the English throne; while an ancestor of Miss Cargill, Donald Cargill, was a Covenanter, executed for denouncing the pro-Catholic King Charles II. Babington's is a genteel rendezvous for writers, actors, artists and politicians, or anyone wanting a properly brewed cuppa.

On the right is the **Keats-Shelley House**, where the 25-year-old John Keats died in 1821. It is now a museum dedicated to English Romantic poets enamoured of the Eternal City. There is a library of seven thousand volumes, a priceless collection of manuscripts, letters, and mementoes of the lives of Keats, Shelley, Byron, and Leigh Hunt. Keats and Shelley, along with artists, ambassadors, and many unremembered residents and visitors to Rome, rest in the beautiful **Testaccio Cemetery** often, but inaccurately, called the Protestant or English Cemetery, where non-Catholic foreigners were buried (p. 233). *'It might make one in love with death, to think that one should be buried in so sweet a place'*, wrote Shelley, not long before he drowned. At the foot of the Steps is the **Fountain of the Sunken Boat** (Fontana della Barcaccia), created by Pietro Bernini (assisted by his son Gian Lorenzo) to recall the time when the Tiber flooded, obliging Pope Urban VIII to reach the piazza by boat. It is below ground level in order to get sufficient water pressure. You will see the Barberini bees on it.

To the right as you face the Steps is the twelve-metre-high **Column of the Immaculate Conception**. It was dedicated on 8 December 1857 in celebration of the recently-defined dogma of the Immaculate Conception. The Corinthian column, sculpted in ancient Rome, was discovered in 1777. At the base are statues (by four different sculptors) of four Hebrew prophets, Moses, David, Isaiah and Ezekiel, who spoke of the coming of the Messiah. The bronze statue of Our Lady on the top is by Giuseppe Obici, whose statue of St Paul you saw at St Paul's outside the Walls. The Rome Fire Service raised the column, and each year on the Feast of the Immaculate Conception (8 December) firemen place a bouquet around Our Lady's right arm during a ceremony attended by the pope.

*The streets around here form the 'Trident', an exclusive and expensive shopping area. Via dei Condotti, opposite the Steps, is full of silver and goldsmiths, and top names, and it leads to Via del Corso, which you crossed on the way to the Trevi. At No. 86 is the **Antico Caffè Greco** (or just Caffè Greco) which opened in 1760, the oldest bar in Rome. Its décor is of considerable interest, and it houses a nineteenth-century art collection. Byron, Goethe, Ibsen, Keats, Mendelssohn and Wagner are among the many luminaries to have taken refreshment there.*

You can leave the Spanish Steps by metro (Spagna). For a bus go down Via dei Condotti. Turn towards the right when you reach Via del Corso, and on the other side there is a stop for the small electric bus 117, which will take you to Piazza Venezia, the Colosseum and St John Lateran.

*Alternatively, if you wish to explore more, go down Via del Babuino—on the left as you face the Steps. It goes to Piazza del Popolo. Via del Babuino was formerly full of antique shops now largely superseded by smart fashion and cosmetic outlets: on the left side, just before the Greek Catholic Church of **Sant'Atanasio**, is the **Talking Statue** of **Silenus**, the perpetually drunk companion of the Greek god, Dionysus. Nicknamed 'Babuino' (baboon), he gave his name to the street. If you fancy a coffee or good meal in the presence of a life-size Pope Leo XIII, or even an emperor, pop into the unique **Canova-Tadolini**, the former studio of Canova's pupil Adamo Tadolini, whose plaster casts are everywhere. Further along is the Anglican Church of **All Saints**, an attractive building designed by George Edmund Street (1824–81), a pupil of Sir George Gilbert Scott and architect of many good churches in England, which opened on Easter Day 1887. Previously Anglicans in Rome had been served by smaller chaplaincies and chapels. Street also built the American*

*Anglican Church of **St Paul within the Walls**, on the corner of Via Nazionale and Via Napoli, in the same neo-gothic style. It contains some very fine mosaics, the largest work of the Pre-Raphaelite artist Edward Burne-Jones, and engraved glass doors commemorating the visit of Archbishop Michael Ramsey to Pope St Paul VI in 1966.*

Piazza del Popolo

If you leave this visit to another day, get here by the electric bus 117 on the route from St John Lateran, via the Colosseum and the top of the Spanish Steps. It enters Piazza del Popolo before stopping round the corner in Via del Corso. Alternatively use metro Red Linea A to Flaminio and walk through the Porta del Popolo.

In front of you (if you arrive by bus) is the **Porta del Popolo**, successor to the ancient **Flaminian Gate**, the imposing entrance to Rome from the north. Built in the early 1560s, the inner face was later modified by Bernini and includes an inscription com-memorating the arrival in Rome, through this gate, of Queen Christina of Sweden in December 1655. The piazza dates from 1538, but was remodelled by Valadier in 1823 around the three churches and obelisk to impress the traveller arriving in Rome. (Less impressive was the guillotine erected here by the French in 1813 to deter opponents of Napoleon's occupation.) The piazza is now a space where people love to congregate. The Egyptian obelisk from Heliopolis, inscribed with a prayer to the sun, was set up in the Circo Massimo by Emperor Augustus: Pope Sixtus V raised it here in 1589. Around it four lions spout water in the **Fountain of the Obelisk** built in 1823. On the side of the piazza below the Pincian Hill (on which are the Borghese Gardens) is the **Fountain of Mars,** with personifications of the Tiber and its tributary, the Anio; on the opposite side of the piazza is **Neptune with two Tritons.** But your eye is inescapably caught by the two domed churches of **S. Maria di Montesanto** and **S. Maria dei Miracoli,** separated by Via del Corso which runs between them.

Santa Maria di Montesanto

Open: Monday–Friday 10:00–12:00; 17:00–20:00. Sunday, Artists' Mass 12:00.

Santa Maria dei Miracoli

Open: 7:00–13:00; 16:00–19:30.

These twin (but not identical) churches are the work of Carlo Rainaldi, who designed them for Pope Alexander VII in 1662, thereby creating a lovely balance in the piazza, though S. Maria dei Miracoli (on the right with your back to the gate) is slightly larger. Rainaldi was one of the leading architects in Rome during the seventeenth century and in the course of a long career he contributed to the restoration of St Mary Major and more than fifteen churches. Bernini revised the designs for S. Maria di Montesanto, the first to be built, in 1662–75 with further additions in 1679. It replaced an earlier Carmelite church, and the icon over the high altar came from that church. Handel composed his *Vespers of Our Lady of Mount Carmel* for this community and they were sung here on 17 July 1707 with Handel himself directing the music. On 10 August 1904, Angelo Giuseppe Roncalli, Pope St John XXIII, was ordained to the priesthood here. Each Sunday artists gather for Mass, at which one of them reads a lesson, and at the end a prayer for artists is said.

The icon above the altar of S. Maria dei Miracoli (built 1675–81) is older than the church. A woman whose baby had fallen into the Tiber was praying before this image when her child was miraculously found alive, and a church was built to enshrine it in thanksgiving: hence its name. In the Chapel of S. Antonio, on the left, are the relics of St Candida, who was martyred during the persecutions of Diocletian.

Apart from the fine architecture there are no notable artworks to attract art lovers to these churches, and both are usually quiet and prayerful.

Santa Maria del Popolo

Open: 7:15–12:30; 16:00–19:00; Friday and Saturday 7:30–19:00.

By contrast, this older Renaissance church just inside the gate is an 'art gallery'. It was built because Nero's mausoleum was here, and people were frightened by his ghost and by evil spirits in the form of crows. Pope Paschal II shared their anxiety, so in 1099 the mausoleum was destroyed, Nero's ashes were dumped in the Tiber, and the site was sanctified by a church financed by the people, hence *'del Popolo'*. The pope personally chopped down a walnut tree on the site to get rid of the crows, and this is depicted on the triumphal arch inside. The original church was enlarged and embellished over the years, but this present church, designed by Florentine architects, was built in 1477. The apsed choir behind the high altar was added by Bramante for Pope Julius II in the early sixteenth century; and, most unusually for Rome, stained-glass windows were installed, made by a French artist, Guillaume de Marcillat. The elegant tombs in the apse of Cardinals Ascanio Sforza (d. 1505) and Girolamo Basso della Rovere (d. 1507) are by Andrea Sansovino.

These are not the only 'greats'. Pinturicchio painted the superb *Nativity* above the altar in the Della Rovere Chapel (first on the right), and the painted decoration on the frame and flanking pilasters was inspired by what he had seen in Nero's recently discovered Domus Aurea (p. 226). Note little touches like the ox's expression, the goat and the lamb, and the lion peeking out from behind St Jerome (on the left). Under the vault are scenes from the life of St Jerome. The third chapel on the right (Capella Bassa della Rovere) has a lovely Pinturicchio altarpiece, *Madonna and Child enthroned with Four Saints*, and good frescoes in the vault lunettes as well as monochrome scenes at the base of the walls attributed to his collaborators. Pinturicchio himself spent six years working in this church, and his last paintings are on the vault in the choir. In the centre is an octagonal panel of the *Coronation of the Virgin*, surrounded by medallions of the Four Evangelists. The spaces between are filled by reclining figures of the Four Sibyls. Then, in the corners, there are the Four Doctors: Augustine, Gregory the Great, Jerome, and Ambrose, enthroned in *aediculae*; their finest depictions anywhere.

Caravaggio painted the *Martyrdom of St Peter* and the *Conversion of St Paul* in the Cerasi Chapel, to the left of the high altar. Over the altar is a very fine work by Annibale Carracci, who also designed the frescoes in the vault above. They were commissioned together and form a unity. On the left Peter witnesses to the Risen Christ by his martyrdom; on the right Paul sees a vision of the Risen Christ; and in between the same two saints are witnessing Our Lady being raised into heaven as the first fruits of her Son's resurrection. To the left is the sad but beautiful nineteenth-century tomb of a young mother, Theresa Stephanie, who died in childbirth, with her son.

In the dome of the Chigi Chapel (second on left) are eight mosaic panels designed by Raphael and executed by Venetian craftsmen. They depict the sun, the moon, the starry sky, and the six known planets as pagan deities, accompanied by angels and the signs of the zodiac. The statues of Jonah and Elijah were carved by Lorenzetto, who belonged to Raphael's circle. Bernini later added the sculptures of Habakkuk and the Angel, and Daniel and the Lion. He had been called in when the church was in need of restoration, but his work here was restrained, and apart from these sculptures, the façade and other bits of decoration, S. Maria remains very much an early Renaissance church.

Augustinians have looked after the church since 1250. During his visit to Rome in 1510–11, a zealous young Augustinian called Martin Luther celebrated Mass here and preached a sermon denouncing the corruptions of Rome and the papal court, as his ideas for reform were beginning to ferment. Ironically, Lutheran troops in the 1527 Sack of Rome destroyed the monastery and damaged the church.

Between the twin churches, on Via del Corso, is the stop for the little electric bus 117. This will take you to Piazza Venezia, where there are many buses, and on to the Colosseum and St John Lateran (Maps pp. 241, 9 and 89). Or go through the Porta del Popolo to the metro.

It is possible you may be ready to eat: you are very close to PizzaRé which has a great reputation for good and inexpensive pizzas, and is open until midnight. Go down Via di Ripetta, which runs alongside S. Maria dei Miracoli, and in one minute you will see it on the left, No. 14.

6

WITH OUR LADY AND THE

SAINTS

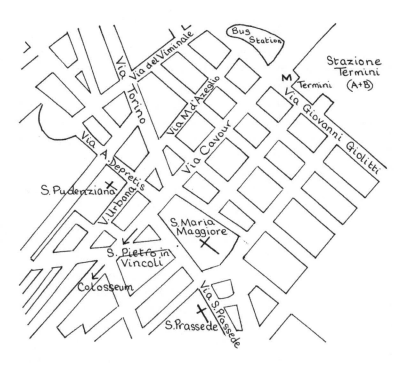

This morning's visits are around Stazione Termini. Go down Via Cavour. It leads you to the Esquiline Hill on which stands the **Basilica of St Mary Major** *(S. Maria Maggiore). Instead of going in, turn right, through the trees, and then left into Via Urbana, where you will soon see* **S. Pudenziana** *on your right.*

Santa Pudenziana

Open: 8:30–12:00; 15:00–18:00.

Pudens was a Roman senator, whose home was used for worship, reputably the oldest place of Christian worship in Rome. It is likely he was the Prudens mentioned by St Paul in a letter from Rome (2 Timothy 4:21). Next to him he mentions Linus, thought to be Peter's associate and successor, perhaps affirming the tradition linking St Peter with this house. It is impossible to sort out the facts, but it would seem the house was demolished in the second century AD for a substantial complex of Roman baths to be built on the site. In the fourth century the entrance and main room of the baths were turned into a church with an apse, from which most of the original fine mosaics have survived, the oldest Christian mosaics in Rome. It was called *Titulus Pudentis* or *Ecclesia Pudentiana*, the church of Pudens. Some think that by a linguistic accident *Pudentiana* was taken to be a woman, St Pudenziana, and that she had a sister, Prassede, the daughters of Pudens. Whatever the case, their names were removed from the Catholic Church's calendar of saints in 1969 as part of a pruning to remove those about whom nothing reliable is known. What we do know is that two very beautiful churches bear their names.

The below-street level of the church indicates its antiquity, but it has been embellished over the years. The architrave of the eleventh-century portal has a marble frieze, a significant work of medieval sculpture, that depicts (from left to right) Pastore (the first owner of the church), Pudenziana, Prassede and their father Pudens. The façade is a nineteenth-century rebuild. The columns in the nave were part of the original structure, but the aisles were added in the eighth century, the campanile in the twelfth and, in a substantial rebuilding, the elliptical dome in 1589. The Caetani Chapel off the left aisle, with its rich inlaid marble and a notable *Adoration of the Magi* by Paolo Olivieri over the altar, was completed by Carlo Maderno.

What immediately catches the eye, however, are the mosaics in the apse, so different and earlier than any you have seen in Rome. The lively figures from around 390 pre-date Byzantine influence, and if you have been to Pompeii they will remind you of those naturalist Roman paintings with their brilliant colours. The lower part of the mosaic has been destroyed, but what remains is wonderful. In a blue sky with an orange sunset stands the sign of Christ's triumph,

a large jewelled Cross on Golgotha, which is flanked by the symbols of the Four Evangelists: the angel (Matthew), the lion (Mark), the bull (Luke) and the eagle (John). These are the oldest surviving representations of the Evangelists' symbols anywhere. Below them are the roofs and domes of the heavenly Jerusalem (or perhaps the churches built by St Helena in Jerusalem). Christ, his right arm raised in teaching, wears an imperial robe and sits on a purple cushion: his apostles wear senatorial togas (from which the chasuble evolved). It has been noted how the seated figures of Christ and his apostles are echoed synchronously when the bishop flanked by his priests concelebrates Mass.

> Take care to do all things in harmony with God, with the bishop presiding in the place of God, and with the presbyters in the place of the council of the apostles, and with the deacons, who are most dear to me.
>
> St Ignatius, Bishop of Antioch.

Behind the apse is a passage leading to an altar containing part of a table on which, it is said, St Peter may have celebrated Mass (the remainder is inside the Papal Altar of St John Lateran). The statue of Jesus giving St Peter his keys of authority is by Giacomo della Porta (1549).

As you approach St Mary Major's you see a Roman imitation of an Egyptian obelisk, known as the Esquiline obelisk. This, and a similar one, once flanked the Mausoleum of Augustus (p. 226), but

subsequently disappeared under a covering of silt. In 1519 this one
was discovered in four pieces and Pope Sixtus V had it repaired and
erected here in 1587. Its twin is on the Quirinal. The top of the obelisk
is decorated with the three mountains and the star of Sixtus V.

The entrance to St Mary Major's is not at this apsidal end. The
grand façade here, uniting the old apse of the Basilica with the chapels
of Sixtus V and Paul V, was Carlo Rainaldi's last important work.
Make your way alongside the Basilica to the other end.

The Basilica of St Mary Major (Santa Maria Maggiore)

Open: 7:00–19:00.

It rarely snows in Rome, particularly during the hot summers, but there is tradition that in 358 Pope Liberius and a patrician called John had visions of Our Lady, requesting them to build a church on the Esquiline Hill, and to their amazement a blanket of snow fell during a summer night marking the exact spot. This freak event is depicted in thirteenth-century mosaics in the loggia over the portico: they can be glimpsed from the piazza, but you get a much better view by joining the guided visit, which also includes a museum. The snowfall is commemorated each year on 5 August, the Dedication Festival of the Basilica: at the conclusion of Solemn Mass thousands of white petals are dropped from the dome of the Lady Chapel. At sunset an artificial snowfall is staged as a tourist attraction in the piazza outside. An early name for the Basilica was Our Lady of the Snows, and it is one of the Seven Pilgrimage Churches.

Liberius's church did not last long, and may not have been on exactly this site; recent excavations, which you can visit, discovered no trace of it, though remains were found of a large first-century Roman house containing a rare frescoed calendar with agricultural scenes. In the fifth century Pope Sixtus III replaced the early church with this Basilica to commemorate the Council of Ephesus in 431, when the ancient title of Our Lady, *Theotokos* (Mother of God)—as in St Luke's Gospel, *'Mother of my Lord [God]'*—was confirmed to counter the Nestorian heresy, which had claimed that Jesus, at his birth, was not God. Inside, the original fifth-century mosaics on the triumphal arch depict the *Annunciation to Mary*. She is robed as an empress; the maid from Nazareth is exalted, as she prophesied: *'He that is mighty has magnified me ... all generations shall call me blessed'* (Luke 1:48–49). There is also the *Annunciation to Joseph*, the *Adoration of the Magi* and the *Massacre of the Innocents*. The nave is a visual Bible of Old and New Testament scenes in brilliant fifth-century mosaics.

The mosaics in the apse were made in the thirteenth-century by Jacopo Torriti. The theme is the *Coronation of the Virgin* surrounded by angels and saints, among whom are Pope Nicolas IV, who ordered the work, and Cardinal Colonna, who paid for it. On the altar in the *confessio* is a silver and crystal reliquary, shaped like a crib, containing pieces of ancient wood said to be part of the manger in which the new-born Jesus was laid to rest. Whatever the authenticity of the relic, it is a place of stillness and prayer, and Pope Pius IX, whose devotion led him to commission this chapel, sets an example by kneeling here before it. On the right side of the sanctuary, though they did little work here, you will see on a step the discreet tomb of the Bernini family, including Gian Lorenzo, the master sculptor, whose work you have been admiring all over Rome. His father, Pietro, made the high relief of the *Assumption* above the altar in the baptistery.

> Hail Mary, full of grace, the Lord is with thee, blessed art thou amongst women, and blessed is the fruit of thy womb, Jesus.
>
> Holy Mary, Mother of God, pray for us sinners, now and at the hour of our death. Amen.

The magnificent interior still resembles the Basilica of Pope Sixtus III, and perhaps more than in any other Roman church the later additions seem to harmonise well with it. These includes the Cosmati floor, and beautiful coffered ceiling designed by Giuliano da Sangallo—the gold used in its decoration is said to be the earliest gold brought from the Americas by Christopher Columbus in 1500, which the Spanish monarchs Ferdinand and Isabella presented to the Spanish Pope Alexander VI. Ferdinando Fuga, the eighteenth-century architect who designed the entrance façade of the Basilica, was also responsible for the baldacchino, which is supported on four antique porphyry columns from Hadrian's Villa at Tivoli.

The transept is formed by two large chapels opposite one another, the Borghese Chapel on the left, and the Sistine Chapel on the right, named after Pope Sixtus V who commissioned it in 1587. The Sistine Chapel, designed by Domenico Fontana, is the Blessed Sacrament Chapel. It has its own *confessio*, intended to invoke the cave of the Nativity in Bethlehem. The altar here was originally beneath the high altar, and St Ignatius of Loyola celebrated his first Mass there on Christmas night 1538. The statue of St Cajetan holding the infant Jesus was sculpted by Bernini. Two popes are buried in this chapel: St Pius V, who did so much to renew the Church at the time of the Council of

Trent, and Sixtus V, the great reformer of the Church, many of whose building works you have seen.

The sumptuous Borghese Chapel, also known as the Pauline Chapel, after Pope Paul V, was built in 1611 by Flaminio Ponzio, and has an incomparably rich altar, set with lapis lazuli, agate, amethyst and jasper. Enshrined over the altar is the large popular icon of *Salus Populi Romani*, the 'Protectress of the People of Rome', surrounded by angels of gilded bronze, one of the oldest Marian images in Rome. Above it is a relief of Pope Liberius tracing the outline of his Basilica in the snow. The relatively unadorned Sforza Chapel next door, reserved for prayer, is now recognised as the work of Michelangelo, a year before he died. At the age of 87 he invented the complex vaulting which Borromini came here to study.

Before leaving the Basilica pause in the portico. The Holy Door, which unusually is on the left side, is new and was blessed by Pope St John Paul II on 8 December 2001. Commissioned by the Order of the Knights of the Holy Sepulchre in Jerusalem, it was completed by the sculptor Luigi Mattei. The right panel shows the Risen Christ, modelled after the image on the Shroud of Turin, appearing to Mary, who is here represented as *Salus Populi Romani*. In the upper left corner is the *Annunciation at the Well*, a story taken from an apocryphal Gospel, and on the right an image of Pentecost. The lower corners show the Council of Ephesus which proclaimed Mary as Mother of God (left), and the Second Vatican Council which declared her *Mater Ecclesiae* or Mother of the Church (right).

The seventy-five-metre tall campanile, the highest in Rome, was built in 1377, shortly after the popes returned from Avignon, and the pyramidal spire was added in the early sixteenth century. To the right of the façade a memorial in the form of an up-ended cannon barrel, topped with a cross, was erected by Pope Clement VIII to celebrate the end of the French Wars of Religion in 1598. In the piazza in front of the entrance is a column that came from the Basilica of Maxentius: Carlo Maderno placed it here in 1614 to support a statue of Our Lady by the French sculptor, Guillaume Berthélot. Maderno also designed the fountain.

*Cross from the fountain to the far right corner of Via Merulana. The first turning on the right is the narrow Via S. Giovanni Gualberto, which leads to the side entrance of **S. Prassede**.*

Santa Prassede

Open: 7:00–12:00; 15:00–18:30.

Once again you are visiting a *titulus*, this one owned by a lady called Prassede, taken, as we have seen, to be the daughter of Pudens. The *titulus* became a church, but was abandoned, and this church was built near to it by Pope Paschal I (817–24). If you visited S. Cecilia you will be immediately struck by the similarity of the apse mosaics which Pope Paschal also commissioned there. St Peter and St Paul, with fatherly arms around them, are presenting respectively S. Pudenziana and S. Prassede to Christ; to the left, Pope Paschal with his square halo, offers his church; S. Zeno stands on the right. On each side of the apsidal arch are twelve martyrs holding wreaths of victory, welcoming souls into heaven. Above them, flanking the central roundel of the Lamb on his throne, are symbols of the Four Evangelists and four censing angels. The scene on the triumphal arch is based on the Book of the Apocalypse (Revelation), and depicts the walled city, heavenly Jerusalem, populated with Christ lifted up, surrounded by saints, and, at the ends Moses (left) holding up the Law, and (right) Elijah stretching out his arms, beneath his cloak, to Christ. Outside the walls the 144,000 saints, martyrs with their palms, and others crowd to be admitted. Part of the mosaic was lost in the sixteenth century when the small balconies were built to display the martyrs' relics.

Pope Paschal's entrance façade to St Zeno's Chapel is spectacular. The lintel of the doorway has a dedicatory inscription in Latin which translates: *The beautiful work of the prelate Paschal, gleaming as a divine dwelling; the devout oaths which he made, he took care to discharge to the Lord.* Sensational mosaics adorn the chapel, which Paschal built as a mausoleum for his mother, Theodora. It is worth using the coin-operated light to see them. You will spot his mother with a blue halo and the inscription *Theodora episcopa* (which some have mistakenly taken to mean his mother was a woman bishop!). It is not certain who St Zeno was, but he may have been one of thousands of slaves who built the Baths of Diocletian and were thought to have been martyred. A church is dedicated to their honour at Tre Fontane (p. 218). If you are interested in studying the mosaics you will need the detailed guidebook from the bookshop by the chapel.

According to a stone tablet on the pillar nearest the sanctuary in the right-hand aisle, part of the reason Pope Paschal built the new church was to enshrine no fewer than 2,300 relics from the catacombs. You can venerate these martyrs by going down steps (of rare Egyptian red marble) in the sanctuary to the ancient sarcophagi in the *confessio*. The relics of S. Prassede and S. Pudenziana are in one of them (note the inscription on the rim). Carved on another is a fine relief of Christ as the Good Shepherd, and Jonah resting on the beach after his encounter with the whale (or sea monster). A sign of Christ's resurrection, Jonah is also depicted at the entrance to the crypt on the lintel above the doorway.

The church has been heavily restored down the centuries, but much of the later work was stripped away in twentieth-century restorations. The floor was laid in 1916, in successful imitation of the Cosmati style. The eighteenth-century sanctuary was retained. Of particular note is the Chapel of St Charles Borromeo, the second chapel on the left side. This was his titular church when he became Cardinal Archbishop of Milan in 1564, and he took a great personal interest in it. As well as laying out money on embellishments, he would spend whole nights in prayer here on his visits to Rome. He retained rooms in the monastery, and distributed alms to poor people from the porch, using the table preserved here as a relic. The chapel was built to his honour in

1735. Pope Paschal founded a monastery for Byzantine monks to serve the church: these were replaced in the ninth century by Benedictines, and in 1198 by the reformed Benedictine congregation of Vallombrosa, who are still here.

If you have time when you leave it is worth turning right from the entrance and then first right into Via S. Martino ai Monti to view the original portico or main entrance gateway.

*There are plenty of places for lunch around here, and if it is your last day perhaps you will feel you have left the best till last. But if you wish to see more there are two possibilities nearby. **A** is to go to **S. Pietro in Vincoli** with its famous statue of Moses by Michelangelo. **B** is to return to the Termini area and see the unusual astronomical device on the floor of **S. Maria degli Angeli**, and perhaps visit the **Roman Baths and National Museum**.*

__A.__ If you went to see the original entrance of S. Prassede go back again to the side door, pass the Basilica, and turn left down Via Cavour (you can cut the corner by going left along Via di S. Maria Maggiore); after 10 minutes, you reach, on the left, Salita dei Borgia with its steps and tunnel that take you into the piazza in front of S. Pietro in Vincoli.

San Pietro in Vincoli (St Peter in Chains)

Open: 8:00–12:30; 14:00–18:00 (19:00 in summer).

Remains of Nero's vast Domus Aurea have been located beneath the church, and the first documentary evidence of a church here is in 431, a *titulus*. Substantially the church is from this date, especially the large apse, but during the Avignon papacy it deteriorated badly, and after a shaky start was restored in 1510. The portico was erected in 1475. Francesco Fontana, the son of Carlo, was responsible for the ceiling and much of the decoration in about 1690. Its central panel is a fresco of *The Miracle of the Chains* painted in 1706 by the Genoese artist Giovanni Battista Parodi, his only work in Rome. A further reordering took place in 1877 when the *confessio* was made by order of Pius IX. The dedication of the church refers to the chains with which St Peter was said to have been shackled in the Mamertine Prison, and the chains from his imprisonment in Jerusalem (Acts 12:6): one story says they were miraculously joined together. You can see them in a reliquary below the altar. On top is an angel, recalling the angel who led Peter to freedom in Jerusalem. You can light a candle there and perhaps pray for prisoners and their families.

It has to be said that most people come here, not for the chains, but to see Michelangelo's powerful statue of Moses on the monument to Pope Julius II at end of the right aisle. It had been intended for a grandiose, freestanding tomb—with forty life-sized statues—which Julius (who commissioned the rebuilding of St Peter's) had planned for himself in the new Basilica. But to Michelangelo's great disappointment, the tomb was never built. Instead, Julius lies beneath a simple marble tombstone in his Basilica, and the sculpture was brought  here in 1545. The curious horns on Moses's head are thought to represent beams of light, an iconographical oddity due to the Hebrew words for 'beams of light' and 'horns' being confusing similar (Exodus 34:29–30).

The third altar in the left aisle has a seventh-century mosaic of *St Sebastian*, relating to a plague in Pavia, in northern Italy, which ceased when the saint's relics were taken there.

If you feel your tour is over you can walk or return to Termini on the metro from Cavour station, which you have passed. Or you could re-visit ancient Rome by continuing down Via Cavour to the Colosseum area.

B. *S. Maria degli Angeli is in Piazza della Repubblica, just beyond the bus station outside Termini.*

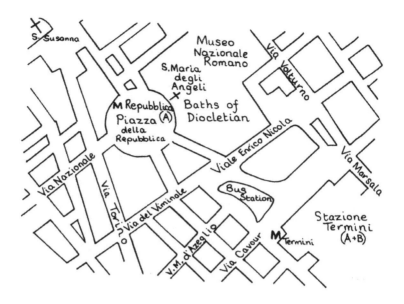

Santa Maria degli Angeli e dei Martiri

Open 07:00–19:30.

This unique church was designed by Michelangelo in 1561, when he was 86, but it is not clear how much of a hand he had in its building. Inevitably the centuries since have made their contributions, even to turning it through 90° in 1749. You enter through the concave wall of an apsidal recess in what had been the hot bath (*caldarium*) of the Baths of Diocletian, the largest in the city. Much of the Baths' massive structure still remains, but Pope Pius IV, who is buried here, turned this small part of it into a church dedicated to all the martyrs through the persistence of a Sicilian priest who saw a vision of angels over the Baths and kept pleading for a church there. New bronze doors were fashioned by Polish sculptor Igor Mitoraj in 2006.

The entrance opens into a vestibule which was the warm room (*tepidarium*). As you continue you pass a huge statue of St Bruno, the founder of the Carthusian Order, for into the Baths was later built a Carthusian monastery or Charterhouse, designed by Jacopo del Duca and Michelangelo. Shockingly, at the unification of Italy in 1870, the Carthusians were evicted and their monastery turned into military barracks. The church is now served by diocesan clergy. The transept or main body of the church was the cold bath (*frigidarium*), still substantially a wide and lofty fourth-century building, though the floor level has been raised. The cross-vaulting and eight massive pillars with shafts of pink Egyptian granite are as Diocletian built them (apart from the bases). The eight in the vestibules are replicas of brick and plaster. In the church note the *Martyrdom of St Sebastian* by Domenichino on the right wall of the chancel. Most of the paintings are eighteenth-century canvases from St Peter's, where they were copied in mosaic. Notable amongst them is *St Basil celebrating Mass before Emperor Valens* by the French artist Pierre-Hubert Subleyras. The Emperor is so overcome that he has fainted. Above the altar is a deeply venerated picture of *Our Lady being adored by Angels* by an unknown sixteenth-century Venetian artist.

The biggest surprise in the church is the bronze Meridian Line (*Meridiana*) laid in yellow-white marble which runs across the floor from the south transept to the chancel, a distance of 45 metres. Commissioned by Pope Clement XI for the Holy Year of 1700, it was made by the astronomer and mathematician Francesco Bianchini and completed in 1703 with the help of the astronomer Giacomo Filippo Maraldi. It was used to check the accuracy of the Gregorian Calendar and calculate the date of Easter. For almost 150 years Rome's clocks were set by it, and it still works, as you will see if the sun shines. On the right side of the transept wall part of the cornice has been cut away for the sun's rays, and there are holes in the ceiling through which, with the aid of a telescope, the passage of the stars can be observed. On the floor around the meridian line are the signs of the zodiac. As a promoter of science the Church staged an exhibition here in the Year of Astronomy, 2010, and a five-metre-high bronze statue of Galileo's *Divine Man*, designed by the 1957 Nobel physics laureate Tsung-Dao Lee, was unveiled: you can see it in the courtyard on the right.

The side chapels were entrances to plunge pools, as is the sacristy, which houses an exhibition on the history of the baths and church. Through a door you can see remains of the vast Baths complex, open to the sky. The rest of the Baths form part of the National Museum (**Museo Nazionale Romano**). It is well worth a visit, if only to see the Michelangelo's wonderful cloister with its small Carthusian cells. S. Maria degli Angeli is the official state church of Italy, and is used for many ceremonies, including the funerals of soldiers killed abroad. In the south transept are the tombs of three First World War heroes.

If you wish to visit the Baths, turn left out of the church, cut through the little park, keep left along Viale Enrico de Nicola and you reach the entrance.

The Baths of Diocletian and National Museum

One ticket takes you into the Baths, the Museum, the Palazzo Altemps and the Crypta Balbi.

Roman Baths were extravagant social centres which make our gyms, spas and sports complexes seem decidedly spartan. As well as baths and gyms, there were swimming pools, parks, fountains and gardens, libraries and reading rooms, lecture halls, theatres for plays and concerts, large halls for parties, restaurants, shops (especially perfumeries) and sleeping quarters. Poets, politicians and philosophers held court, jugglers and acrobats entertained. Business took place, combined with pleasure. Many baths were built on hot springs providing healing and relaxation. The best ones—and Diocletian's, completed in AD 307, was the grandest of them all—were magnificently decorated with bright mosaics and marble, stuccoed walls and ceilings, statuary, and expensive furniture. You still get a fair indication of its sheer immensity and grandeur: in its heyday it could accommodate perhaps three thousand people in various pursuits. Entrance was free, the Romans loved them and many went every day. Depending on local customs men and women sometimes bathed together, and some baths teemed with prostitutes. Christians generally kept away, calling them 'cathedrals of flesh', and indeed some Romans shared their contempt for the same reason.

> Gold-plated chairs, and silver ones, too, and ten thousand vessels of gold and silver, some for drinking, some for eating, some for bathing ... for they have arrived at such a pitch of self-indulgence, that they sup and get drunk while bathing ... The baths are opened promiscuously to men and women; and there they strip for licentious indulgence ... as if their modesty had been washed away in the bath.
>
> St Clement of Alexandria.

Turning Diocletian's Baths into a Charterhouse of holy monks must have seemed like a startling change of use (though the destruction of the aqueducts had sealed the baths' fate centuries earlier). The buildings now hold one of the world's most important collections of ancient Roman documents and inscriptions. The vast halls, peaceful garden, beautiful cloisters, cells, and chapels of the monks make a visit worthwhile, even if you have had enough of sculptures and inscriptions.

The National Museum entrance is through the small park on the Termini side.

The **Palazzo Massimo** of the Museum houses one of the world's greatest collections of classical art. Four hundred sculptures from ancient Greece and Rome include the *Boxer at Rest*, the *Discus Thrower* (a first-century AD marble copy of Myron's famous bronze), the *Sleeping Hermaphrodite*, the *Maiden of Antium*, and the *Dying Niobid*. There is the magnificent sarcophagus of Portonaccio, decorated with  a battle scene between Romans and barbarians, and there are carvings that decorated the Ships of Nemi. On the second floor are wall-paintings and luxurious mosaics from Roman houses and imperial villas. In the basement is Italy's largest collection of ancient coins.

The rest of the National Museum is located in different parts of the city:

The **Palazzo Altemps,** in Piazza di Sant'Apollinare 46, houses an extensive collection of antique Greek and Roman sculptures formerly owned noble Roman families.

You could visit when you are around Piazza Navona. From the piazza go along Via Agonale (Map p. 138) and straight across the road into Piazza di Sant'Apollinare.

The **Crypta Balbi,** in Via delle Botteghe Oscure 31, a few minutes from Piazza Venezia, is also part of the National Museum. Follow the route of the tramlines from stop C (Map p. 241). It traces the history of the site from Roman times, when it was part of the *Campus Martius,* through the medieval period to the present.

*Further along you reach Largo di Torre Argentina with its ruins of four Republican-period temples and lots of cats: the eastern end of **Pompey's Theatre**, where Julius Caesar was assassinated on the Ides of March in 44 BC, was here. There are several useful buses from Torre Argentina (p. 47).*

7

MORE PLACES TO SEE

Museums, Art Galleries, Gardens and Palaces

Borghese Gardens

Vastly more extensive than Vatican City, this huge park in the middle of Rome provides shade from the heat in its long leafy walks, and is home to the famous **Villa Borghese**, the **National Gallery of Modern and Contemporary Art**, the **Etruscan Museum of the Villa Giulia**, the **British School** (designed by Sir Edward Lutyens), an open-air theatre, and even a reconstruction of London's **Globe Theatre**. You can hire cycles and self-balancing electric scooters; and, on the lake, boats to the island with its 'Greek' Temple of Aesculapius.

You can easily get into the Gardens from the top of the Spanish Steps or from Piazza del Popolo. From Spagna metro station you can follow the signed route by way of escalators and pedestrian tunnels excavated into the hillside. Eventually you emerge by the Aurelian Wall, from where a walk to the right brings you to the entrance.

However, by using these routes you are a long way from the Villa Borghese Art Gallery. To get to the villa itself a taxi is easiest, but you can go by public transport using the following routes:

From Termini go by 92, 223, 360 or 910 (Map p. 238). Get off at Pinciana/Museo Borghese (the previous stop is Puccini). Walk back the way the bus has come, and into the Gardens near the Villa.

From Piazza del Risorgimento (Map p. 240), walk along Via Ottaviano towards the metro station. Cross over Viale Giulio Cesare to the other side, which is Via Barletta, with a 490 stop in the direction of Tiburtina. Get off at S. Paolo del Brasile (the previous stop is Victor Hugo) and in the park walk along Viale del Museo Borghese to the villa. Alternatively, in Piazza del Risorgimento, catch the No. 19 tram to the Museo Etrusco for the Villa Giulia (the stop after Belle Arti); or the next, Arte Moderna, for that gallery. You could get off here and follow signs to the Globe Theatre and Villa Borghese. Or stay on to Bioparco (the one after the next, Aldrovandi); walk through the park gates and turn left by the Zoo, along Viale dell'Uccelliera to Villa Borghese.

From Piazza Venezia (Map p. 241) the 160 goes to S. Paolo del Brasile, and 63 goes to Pinciana/Museo Borghese, just a step through the Gardens.

Villa Borghese

Open: 8:30–19:30. Closed Mondays. Advance booking is obligatory (p. 8).

The villa was built in the early seventeenth century by Cardinal Scipione Borghese, and in the following century the family employed Jacob More from Edinburgh to design the gardens, where Romans and tourists alike love to sunbathe and relax.

The **Museo Borghese** is on the ground floor of the villa and houses mainly sculpture, while the upper floor, the **Galleria Borghese,** is the picture gallery. Both collections rank among the finest in the world. Cardinal Borghese was Bernini's first patron and some of the works he commissioned are here; as are six of his Caravaggios.

The must-see sculptures in the Museo are: Room I, Canova's wonderfully sensuous *Paolina Borghese*, Napoleon's sister, posing as Venus, whose husband kept it locked up. Room II has Bernini's *David* caught seconds before he slings the stone that kills Goliath: the face is a self-portrait of the sculptor. In Room III you will find Bernini's most famous work, *Apollo and Daphne*, capturing the moment when Apollo catches up with his beloved, who by her father's spell is turning into a laurel tree. *The Rape of Persephone* in Room IV, another of Bernini's greatest works, carved when he was only 23, is astonishing for its movement and anguish. Here also you will find *Cupid Riding an Eagle*, attributed to Bernini's father, Pietro. In Room V is the *Sleeping Hermaphrodite*, a Roman marble copy, dated about 150 BC, of a Greek original: it was restored by Bernini who added the mattress. In Room VI is Bernini's first large commission, *Aeneas and Anchises*, carved when he was 15, with help from his father. In Room VIII, still on the ground floor, are the six Caravaggios: *Boy with a Basket of Fruit*; the *Madonna of the Palafrenieri*; *St Jerome*; *Boy Crowned with Ivy*, an early self-portrait; the young *John the Baptist*, possibly his last work; and *David with the Head of Goliath*, in which it seems the young Caravaggio is both David and the head of Goliath, revealing his tortured soul, and maybe representing a plea for mercy over a murder he had committed, or his longing for lost innocence.

In the gallery upstairs, Room IX houses three beautiful paintings by Raphael: his *Deposition*, also called *The Entombment*; *Portrait of a Man*; and *Young Woman with a Unicorn*. In Room X look out for Cranach's *Venus and Cupid*, and Correggio's *Danaë*. Room XIV has paintings and sculptures by Bernini, including two busts of Cardinal Borghese, one damaged as he chiselled it, his *Portrait of a Boy*, and what is probably his earliest work, *The Goat Amalthea with the Infant Jupiter and a Faun*. In Room XVIII is a very fine *Deposition* by Rubens, and in Room XIX are two works by Domenichino, the *Hunt of Diana* and the *Cumaean Sybil*. Titian visited Rome but twice in his life, and in Room XX is an early masterpiece, *Sacred and Profane Love*, as well as his *Venus Blinding Cupid*, *St Dominic* and the *Scourging of Christ*.

To return to Termini, turn left out of the gates and back to the stop where you alighted. Walk (left) to the next one (Pinciana/Allegri), and soon after take the right fork, Via Ruggero Giovannelli, where you will find on the right side the stop, Tartini, and the 910 bus.

For Piazza del Risorgimento, turn right from the villa and enjoy a pleasant walk along Viale dell'Uccelliera. Turn right by the elegant entrance to the Zoo, and go through all the parked cars to the gate. Through the gate go straight across the road to Viale Gioacchino Rossini and on its left side you will quickly find the No. 19 tram stop, Bioparco, in the direction of Risorgimento S. Pietro. If you wish to visit the Galleria Nationale d'Arte Moderna you could get off at the next but one stop, or at the third stop should you wish to go to the Museo Nazionale Etrusco di Villa Giulia.

Palazzo del Quirinale

Open: 9:30–16:00. Closed Monday and Thursday and in August. The gardens are only open to the public on the afternoon of Republic Day, 2 June.

Go to Piazza Venezia (Map p. 24). The first turning on the right after Via del Corso is Via del Mancino, beside Antico Caffè Castellino, then Piazza SS. Apostoli (where you find the Church of SS. Dodici Apostoli and the Muti Palace). A little further on turn left into Via della Pilotta and go up this lovely bridged street. After passing the Gregorian University you soon turn right at Largo Pietro di Brazza to the Quirinal. (If you keep straight on you quickly reach the Trevi Fountain.)

Occupying the site of a former Roman temple, the Quirinal Palace was comissioned by Pope Gregory XIII as a summer residence, away from the stench and malaria of the Tiber. Begun in 1574 it was not completed until 1730 and many fine architects have had a hand in it, including Borromini and Bernini, and Carlo Maderno, who designed its great Paolina Chapel, the Sala Regia, and the Papal Apartments. Thirty popes have resided here: the first was Sixtus V (1585–90), who as we have seen was responsible for turning round the fortunes of the city and the Church, and the last, Pius IX. The palace was the venue for papal conclaves in 1823, 1829, 1831 and 1846. Since 1871 it has accommodated four kings and twelve presidents. Most of the paintings and furnishings belonged to the Italian Royal Family.

The obelisk in the piazza in front of the palace is one of a pair which originally stood at the entrance to the Mausoleum of Augustus: for its pair see p. 171.

Palazzo Doria-Pamphilj Art Gallery

Via del Corso, near Piazza Venezia (Map p. 24). For Saturday morning concerts and guided tours, see p. 8.

The Palazzo Doria-Pamphilj houses one of the finest private art collections in the world open to the public, in a glorious building dating back to 1435, constructed around a courtyard with lovely colonnades. A visit includes the chapel, designed by Carlo Fontana, and splendidly decorated rooms and galleries, hung with tapestries and paintings, including the Galleria degli Specchi. In  the Velázquez Room you will find Velázquez's superb portrait of *Pope Innocent X*, a Pamphilj himself, who started the collection— Sir Joshua Reynolds considered it the best portrait in Rome. Busts of him by Bernini and Algardi are in the Velvet Room. In the Red Room are works by Jan Brueghel the Elder: *Spring*, *Summer*, and *Winter*, and the *Garden of Eden*.

Many greats are in the Sala Aldobrandini, among them Titian's *Salome with John the Baptist's Head*, José de Ribera's *St Jerome*, Caravaggio's *Penitent Magdalen*, his cheeky young nude *John the Baptist*, and tender *Rest on the Flight into Egypt*, and Raphael's *Double Portrait*. This room also contains a rich array of Roman sculpture including a *Bacchus* in red basalt and a *Centaur* in red and black marble. An exquisite *Annunciation* by Filippo Lippi is found in the Sala dei Primitivi. Pieter Brueghel the Elder's *Battle in the Gulf of Naples*, the first representation of a real seascape in art, is in Galleria Pamphilj. You will also find paintings by Guido Reni, Correggio, Giovanni Bellini, Parmigianino, Carracci, Hans Memling among others, as well as a bookshop and café.

The second floor is home to the **Anglican Centre**, established by Pope St Paul VI and Archbishop Ramsey of Canterbury in 1966, to facilitate study and unity between the Catholic and Anglican Churches. Its entrance is at the back of the palazzo in

Piazza del Collegio Romano through the large doors at No. 2 (ring bell 07).

Palazzo Farnese

Piazza Farnese, 67. For tours see p. 8.

Occupied since 1936 by the French Embassy, this most magnificent of all Rome's Renaissance palaces was designed by Antonio da Sangallo the Younger and completed after his death in 1546 by Michelangelo. Sangallo's courtyard is modelled on the arcades of the Theatre of Marcellus; Michelangelo's contribution is visible in the window frames and the most impressive cornice at the top. The Galleria was brilliantly decorated by Annibale Carracci, and in the Salone d'Ercole are tapestries copied from the Raphael Rooms in the Vatican. The granite basins in the piazza were discovered in the Baths of Caracalla and turned into fountains in 1626.

Stand facing the palace and look to the right; on the corner you will see the curious campanile of the Bridgettine Convent, founded by St Bridget of Sweden in 1344. The nuns' life of prayer is combined with offering hospitality in their guest house (a very good one), and with parish work among children, the sick and the elderly. Just round the corner, in Via di Monserrato, is the **Venerable English College** *(p. 222)*

Vatican Museums (Musei Vaticani)

Viale Vaticano (Map p. 240). Open: 9:00–18:00 (final entry 16:00). For online booking and Friday evening visits, see p. 4.

The only way there, apart from by taxi, is to walk alongside the walls of Vatican City from Piazza del Risorgimento (you will spot the arrow on the Musei Vaticani sign on the corner). Getting back is easier. Turn left from the exit and you come to a stop for the 49 bus which passes through Piazza del Risorgimento, and stops just beyond it in Via Crescenzio. For the 23, turn right from the exit and left into Via Leone IV, where there is a stop. The 23 goes through Piazza del Risorgimento, past Castel Sant'Angelo, and along the Trastevere side of the Tiber. You may be ready to get off at Lgt. Sanzio, the stop after Lgt. Farnesina/Trilussa, and collapse for a meal or drink in Trastevere. Or go to the next stop, Lgt. Alberteschi, beside the Tiber Island.

It is likely that most visitors go to the Vatican Museums in order to see the Sistine Chapel. But in its own right it ranks as one of the world's greatest museums and is generally packed with visitors. Unless you intend to spend the day there (and you can pre-book breakfast and lunch) you need to be selective. The building itself is wonderful: it started off around AD 500 as a guest house for sovereigns and other notables visiting the pope. Neglected and restored over time, it was turned into the Vatican Palace by Donato Bramante at the invitation of Pope Nicholas V. Much has been built on to it over the centuries since. The spectacular double-helix spiral staircase, the finest in the world, was added by Giuseppe Momo in 1932, and you will see it near the exit. Don't confuse it with the modern one. The Vatican contains all you would expect in a great museum: Egyptian, Etruscan, Greek and Roman Collections in the Pio-Clementine rooms; some of the world's most famous sculpture like the *Laocoön*, the *Apollo Belvedere*, the *Belvedere Torso*, the Etruscan bronze of *Mars*, the *Athlete Washing*, another *Discus Thrower* (probably a later copy than the one in the National Museum), and many more. The Picture Gallery (*Pinacoteca*) is full of works by well-known masters: Pinturicchio, Bellini, Guido Reni, Caravaggio, Domenichino, Pietro Lorenzetti, Fra' Angelico, Simone Martini, Stefano di Giovanni, Melozzo da Forlì, Leonardo da Vinci and Van Dyck, to name some at the risk of leaving out your favourites. Nor is Modern Religious art neglected, for a remarkable collection of over eight hundred paintings, drawings, sculptures, mosaics, stained glass, and ceramics by notable artists like Paul Klee, Henry Moore, Edvard Munch, Pablo Picasso and Graham Sutherland, was begun by Pope St Paul VI, in his desire to reinstate the dialogue between the Church and contemporary culture. There is a gallery of fifteenth and seventeenth-century tapestries, and the fascinating map gallery (Galleria delle Carte Geographiche) the walls of which were painted in brilliant colours in the early 1580s with forty large-scale maps of the Italian peninsula. There are some fascinating details, and if you locate Liguria, the region around Genoa, you will spot Christopher Columbus dressed like a Roman Emperor speeding down the coast in a golden chariot, compass in his hand, drawn by horses and led by Neptune waving his trident.

In making your choices of which collections to see, bear in mind that there are galleries in the Vatican Museums you will find nowhere else. There are unique stamp and coin collections. Nowhere else will you find four  rooms decorated by Raphael. The Pio-Christian Museum comprises ancient sculptures and inscriptions, many from the catacombs, including the famous Good Shepherd statue. Not to be missed is the magnificent 'Jonah Sarcophagus', dated *c*.390, with the story of his life. The Hebrew Lapidary contains inscriptions from ancient Hebrew cemeteries in Rome. The Chapel of Pope

Nicholas V was painted by Fra' Angelico. In the Missionary-Ethnological Museum there are thousands of beautiful and curious objects from all over the world given to the pope by private donors, and from the missions, and from four hundred dioceses for the great Exhibition of 1925; they include early ethnic statuary from South America, ceremonial objects from New Guinea, plaster portraits of the American-Indian populations made by the German sculptor Ferdinand Pettrich, and prehistoric objects from the British School of Archaeology in Jerusalem. The Carriage and Automobile Museum contains sedan chairs, carriages and cars used by popes and cardinals down the years, including the 'Gala Berlin' carriage used by Leo XII in the 1820s, and the popemobile in which Pope St John Paul II was shot. There is also the last Volkswagen Beetle made, and a model of a locomotive used on the Vatican Railway.

The Sistine Chapel

While Raphael was hard at work in the Vatican Palace, Michelangelo was only steps away painting the ceiling of the papal chapel, known as the 'Sistine' Chapel after Pope Sixtus (Sisto) IV, who commissioned it in 1475. Its dimensions correspond to Solomon's Temple. Michelangelo began the ceiling in 1508 when he was 33, and from the start he was beset with difficulties. He had to invent the scaffolding; there was insufficient light; his assistants were more a hindrance than help, so in the end he dispensed with them, working alone, trying to guess what his painting looked like from twenty metres below. He was always covered with paint and damp plaster (for it is a fresco) as he stood with his head tilted back for over four years till it was completed. It became the exemplar of the Mannerist style, with its colourful figures in complex poses, and is one of the most famous works of art in the world.

There are nine central panels. Starting at the altar end they depict: (1) the separation of light from darkness; (2) the creation of the sun and moon; (3) the separation of land from water; (4) the dramatic creation of Adam (perhaps the most famous); (5) the creation of Eve; (6) original sin and Adam and Eve's expulsion from Eden; (7) the sacrifice of Noah; (8) the Flood (the first to be painted); and (9) the drunkenness of Noah. In the corners between the panels Michelangelo painted twenty heroic male nudes, known as the 'Ignudi'. In the lunettes and surrounding panels are Sibyls, Prophets, Jonah and other forerunners of Christ.

The *Last Judgement*, which dominates the sanctuary, was commissioned by Pope Clement VII only days before he died. Michelangelo started work on it when he was 61, and it took him from 1536 to 1541. The subject was to have been Christ's Resurrection. But Rome was still shell-shocked after the Sack of 1527, which left up to 12,000 dead, and a very sombre new Pope Paul III changed it to the Last Judgement. Michelangelo too was badly affected by the event, which some say explains the violence he depicts. Personal anguish is revealed in his self-portrait on the flayed skin which the bearded St Bartholomew is holding just beside Christ's left leg. Tragic as it is, it remains the masterpiece of his mature years.

> If before the Last Judgement we are dazzled by splendour and fear, admiring on the one hand the glorified bodies and on the other those subjected to eternal damnation, we also understand that the entire vision is deeply permeated by one light and one artistic logic: the light and logic of the faith that the Church proclaims by confessing: I believe in one God ... creator of heaven and earth, of all things visible and invisible.
> Pope St John Paul II.

To make space for the *Last Judgement* some earlier frescoes on this wall were sacrificed. They had formed part of the two sequences of paintings on the side walls of the chapel executed between 1481 and 1483 by the best painters Sixtus IV could find, who included Botticelli, Ghirlandaio and Perugino. On the right (south) wall, as you stand with your back to the *Last Judgement*, are scenes from the life of Moses, and on the left scenes from the life of Christ, the 'new Moses.' First in the Moses sequence is Moses' journey into Egypt; then more scenes from Moses in Egypt (including the burning bush); the crossing of the Red

Sea; Moses receiving the tablets of the Commandments; the punishment of Korach, Dathan and Abiram; and the testament and death of Moses (in the background the Archangel Michael shows him the promised land he will never reach). The life of Christ begins with his baptism; then the temptations; the calling of St Peter and St Andrew; the Sermon on the Mount; Jesus entrusting the Keys to St Peter; and the Last Supper. The 'lost' scenes on the west wall were Moses in the bulrushes, and the Nativity.

Catacombs and Churches

Catacomb and Basilica of Sant'Agnese fuori le Mura, and the Mausoleum of Santa Costanza

Via Nomentana, 349. Open: see page 7.

Catch the 82 bus from Termini (Bay D). The stop before you alight is Nomentana/XXI Aprile; the bus goes over Via di S. Costanza at the crossroads, and you alight at the next stop, Nomentana/S.Agnese. Just a few yards further on, turn left along Via di S. Agnese and you reach the entrance to the church.

Constantia (*Costanza*), the elder daughter of Constantine, erected a small chapel over the tomb of St Agnes in the catacomb, and nearby she built a huge basilica in AD 325. In the basilica she incorporated a mausoleum for herself and her sister, Helena. The basilica has been destroyed, though traces of its apse still exist in the grounds, but the mausoleum was carefully preserved.

The story of St Agnes was told on p. 143 in connection with the Church of S. Agnese in Piazza Navona. She is buried with S. Emerentiana, the daughter of her nurse, who was martyred after being spotted praying and grieving beside her little friend's grave. About 630 the chapel over their tomb was converted into the present church by Pope Honorius I. Ancient pillars were used in its construction and a gallery admits worshippers from the street level, for the church floor is close to the level of the catacomb. The sumptuously decorated church is much as it was when it was built. The three figures in the apse mosaic are: Pope Honorius I, presenting his church; St Agnes in Byzantine apparel, surrounded by flames which do not touch her; and Pope Symmachus who is thought to have restored the basilica. The exceptional paschal candlestick, by a Graeco-Roman artist, came from the mausoleum.

The catacomb is entered through a door to the right of the altar, but you can pray beside the tomb of St Agnes and St Emerentiana without going into it. No paintings have survived in the catacomb, and its main interest is that many tombs are still sealed and undamaged. Nor need you make a visit to see a great number of inscriptions from it, for if you leave the church by the doors at the back on the right side you can walk up a flight of steps to ground level past walls covered with engraved marble slabs. Among them you will spot St Agnes with her arms outstretched praying, and a eulogy praising her composed by Pope Damasus, exquisitely carved by the distinguished fourth-century calligrapher, Furius  Dionysius Filocalus. There are many Good Shepherds, Chi-Rho, anchors, doves, olive branches and other ancient symbols.

Should you be in Rome on 21 January, the Feast of St Agnes, be sure to get there for Mass when two lambs are blessed. The nuns of S. Cecilia in Trastevere weave the wool into *pallia*, the neck-stoles given by the pope to new archbishops as a sign of their communion with him as pastors. The custom is very ancient, and Pope Gregory gave one to St Augustine when he appointed him Archbishop of Canterbury.

In the garden is the Mausoleum of S. Costanza, circular like Hadrian's and others, and quite exceptional in its grace and beauty: it has been a church since the ninth century. The dome is supported by an arcade formed by twelve pairs of granite columns. The fourth-century mosaics in the vault are stunning, more pagan than Christian, with wonderful scenes of grape harvests and cherubs treading grapes, human figures, animals and exotic birds. The floor mosaics are similarly covered with cherubs, birds, grapevines and the head of Bacchus. A replica of Costanza's porphyry sarcophagus is here (the original being in the Vatican Museums), and in the side niches are slightly later mosaics of Christ presenting St Peter with a scroll of the Gospel with the words, *Dominus legem dat*: 'The Lord gives the Law'. Some sheep remind Peter to be a shepherd. St Paul is there too. In another niche Christ gives the Keys of the Kingdom to St Peter. These are thought to be the oldest surviving pictures of Christ as the Pantocrator, a word used in the Greek Old Testament for 'Almighty God', and by St Paul of Jesus (2 Corinthians 6:18).

Leave the complex by going through the courtyard of the abbey of the Canons Regular of the Lateran, who have been serving these churches since 1489, and on Via Nomentana you will see a bus stop with the 82 and other buses going back into the city centre.

Catacomb of Priscilla

Via Salaria, 430. Open: see page 7.

Get the 310 bus from Termini (Bay E). The stop before you alight is Nemorense/Acilia. Your stop is Priscilla. (If you miss it you reach the terminus, Vescovio.) Go back the way the bus came, then take the right fork, Via di Priscilla. This leads you into Piazza di Priscilla. Cross over to the far corner and the entrance to the catacomb is in the ochre-coloured building on your left. It is about 300 metres.

Priscilla was probably the woman who founded the cemetery or donated the land. An inscription in the catacomb attests that she was related to Acilia, identified as a consul who was martyred by Domitian. Among the martyrs buried here are the brothers Felix and Philip, who were condemned with their mother, St Felicitas (Felicity), by Diocletian. Some early popes are also buried at Priscilla: Marcellinus (d. 304), Marcellus (d. 309), Sylvester (d. 335), Liberius (d. 366), Siricius (d. 399), Celestine (d. 434) and Vigilius (d. 555).

This catacomb is especially rich with paintings dating back to the second half of the third century in a remarkably good state of preservation. The *Cubiculum of the Veiled Woman* shows a young woman in prayer, also the Good Shepherd, peacocks and doves. Also there is Jonah spewed out of the whale; the sacrifice of Isaac; and the three young men in the fiery furnace. The *Greek Chapel* is renowned, richly decorated with stuccoes and paintings reminiscent of Pompeii: over the arch are the Wise Men offering their gifts, as we do at the Offertory in Mass; in the apse is the Eucharistic Banquet with seven people at the table, including a priest consecrating the bread as he stretches out his hands. There are seven baskets, signifying the miraculous multiplication of the loaves and fishes, when Jesus promised the bread of eternal life. Other paintings show Moses making water run from the rock, a prophecy of the saving waters of baptism; Noah on the ark; and three stories of miraculous deliverance from the book of Daniel—Daniel among the lions, the three young men in the fiery furnace, and Susanna saved by Daniel from her accusers. Scenes from the New Testament include the resurrection of Lazarus and the healing of a paralysed man.

Most prized of all, through water-damaged, is the oldest surviving depiction of Our Lady. A prophet stands near her, holding a scroll in his left hand and pointing to a star with his right, probably an allusion to the prophecy of Balaam, *'A star shall rise out of Jacob, and a sceptre shall rise out of Israel'* (Numbers 24:15–17).

Sant'Andrea della Valle

Corso Vittorio Emanuele II (Map p. 149). Open: 7:00–12:30; 16:00–20:00.

Like the Gesù and the Chiesa Nuova, this is one of the great preaching churches established by new Religious Orders in the sixteenth-century renewal of the Church: in this case, the Theatines, who were founded by St Cajetan of Thiene in 1524 to preach the Gospel and give apostolic service. S. Andrea, which they still serve, was built for them. In 1539 Cajetan opened the Monte di Pietà as an alternative to loan sharks—something which resonates with us today: it later became the Bank of Naples. His remains are in the church, under the altar in the left transept.

At S. Andrea you see again the hand of the great Carlo Maderno, who was called upon to complete St Peter's when Michelangelo died. Here, in 1608, he was similarly commissioned to complete the original 1590 designs of Giacomo della Porta and Pier Paolo Olivieri. Maderno was responsible for the magnificent dome, the highest in Rome after St Peter's. The façade was added by Carlo Rainaldi in the 1660s. Maderno also designed the fountain in the piazza opposite.

The painting in the dome of the *Glory of Paradise* is regarded as Giovanni Lanfranco's great masterpiece; the Four Evangelists in the pendentives were painted by his famous contemporary, Domenichino, who also decorated the semi-dome of the apse with scenes from the life of St Andrew. The three large panels on the apse walls of the *Martyrdom, Crucifixion* and *Burial of St Andrew* are by Mattia Preti. To the left of the high altar is an octagonal chapel containing *Our Lady of Purity*. The sepulchres of two popes, Pius II (d. 1464) and Pius III (d. 1503) were moved here from St Peter's, and now face each other across the last bay of the nave. Pius II (on the left) was a prolific writer of history, poetry and novels, as well as on ethics and theology, including a refutation of Islam. Pius III's pontificate, like that of John Paul I, lasted for only a month.

The first Act of Puccini's *Tosca* takes place in this church, but his 'Attavanti Chapel' is an invention. The actual Strozzi Chapel, second on the right, is thought to have been designed by Michelangelo, and the bronze statues on the reredos include a copy of his famous *Pietà* in St Peter's. The first chapel on the right, with its green marble columns, was designed by Carlo Fontana. The first chapel on the left has four statues: one of them, St John the Baptist, sculpted by Pietro Bernini, Gian Lorenzo's father.

Outside, standing against the wall of the church in Piazza Vidoni is another Talking Statue—Abbot Luigi.

Santi Dodici Apostoli (Twelve Apostles)

Piazza SS. Apostoli. Open: 7:00–12:00; 16:00–19:00.

Go to Piazza Venezia (Map p. 149). The second turning on the left after Via del Corso is Piazza SS. Apostoli: the church is on the right, and the Muti Palace, the Stuarts' residence in Rome, at the far end of the piazza (p. 134).

There may have been an earlier church here, but there certainly was one in the mid-sixth century, and you can still see some of its pavement beneath glass in the Chapel of Cardinal Bessarion, the third chapel on the right. The Chapel of the Crucifixion, at the end of the right nave, has eight columns from that church. In 890 the church was restored to receive the remains of many martyrs from the catacombs; Pope Stephen VI, barefoot, helped carry them here, and it is a moving place to pray. During the alterations were found the tombs of the Apostles St James the Less and St Philip, to whom the church was originally dedicated. If you haven't time to visit a catacomb, the crypt, remodelled in the nineteenth century, is a good place to see reproductions of catacomb art. Sadly the church was wrecked by an earthquake in 1348 and abandoned for seventy years before being restored. Carlo Fontana and his son Francesco almost completely rebuilt it to much as you see it now, spacious and richly decorated in white and gold. They finished it in 1714, the year Carlo died. The painting of the *Martyrdom of St Philip and St James* on the high altar by Domenico Muratori, the altarpiece specialist, is said to be the largest in Rome. Pope Clement XIV's monument, over the sacristy door at the end of the left aisle, was Canova's first major work in Rome and won him wide acclaim.

Michelangelo lived in this parish, and after he died, suddenly in 1564, his body was laid here before being taken to rest in S. Croce in Florence. You can see a lovely monument to him on the right wall of the second cloister, reached (when open) through the corridor on the left of the portico (No. 51).

The other famous residents were the Stuarts, and there is a pretty monument by Filippo della Valle on a pillar on the right, with putti frolicking in clouds and drapery over an urn enshrining the heart of Maria Clementina Sobieska.

Carlo Rainaldi designed the balustrade with the statues of Christ and his Apostles in 1665, and inserted the Baroque windows in the formerly open second storey of the portico. The façade above the portico was designed by Giuseppe Valadier as part of a restoration in 1827, making the church look more like a palace. On the right wall of the portico is a second-century AD Roman bas-relief depicting an eagle holding an oak-wreath tied with ribbon. It was found in the nearby Forum of Trajan, and was copied and notoriously used by the Fascists and the Nazis. Below it is a twelfth-century stone lion by Pietro Vassalletto. The pair of red marble lions flanking the doorway are of the same period; one of them is holding his lunch, a lamb. Also in the portico is a memorial by Canova to his teacher, Giovanni Volpato.

Chiesa Nuova

Corso Vittorio Emanuele II (Map p. xxx). Open: 7:30–12:00; 16:30–19:00 (19:30 in summer).

Guided tours of the church and the rooms of St Philip Neri on Saturday mornings (see p. 138)

Next door to this church lived St Philip Neri, the 'apostle of Rome'. Born in 1515, and raised up by God for the renewal of the Church in the sixteenth century, when churches in Rome were crumbling through neglect and Mass attendance was low, St Philip began by enthusing other young men to join him in prayer, and to make pilgrimages to the seven major Basilicas. They cared for those who were sick, mentally ill and destitute, and for impoverished pilgrims to the city. He realised that people unused to the Mass required a simpler Service of Prayer and Preaching, and he recognised the power of good music to touch the soul. The word 'Oratory' came to be used not just for the church itself, but also for the community he founded, the Oratorians (Congregation of the Oratory), living together 'with no rule but love'. The word Oratorio was coined for the musical form he pioneered. Palestrina was one of his admirers, and composed music for the services. St Philip's rooms, containing interesting artefacts of his life, are included in the tour.

The original church on the site, founded by St Gregory the Great in the sixth century, proved too small for the crowds who came, and St Philip had this large new church built in 1575, one of the great preaching churches of the city, and still called Chiesa Nuova, though its dedication is S. Maria in Vallicella. The architects were Matteo Bartolini and Martino Longhi the Elder. Like all the churches of that reforming age it was austere, but in a later century was embellished by the most prestigious artists of the day, among them Pietro da Cortona who painted *St Philip's Vision of Our Lady* (on the ceiling); *Christ Interceding with the Father* (in the dome); *Isaiah, Jeremiah, Ezekiel* and *Daniel* (in the pendentives); and the *Assumption* (in the apse). Just before he left Rome in 1608, Rubens was commissioned to paint the three saints around the altar, *Domitilla, Nereus* and *Achilleus*. The Madonna is painted on slate which can be lowered to reveal a much older image of the Madonna dating from c.400 AD behind: the older image is shown every weekend between 19:00 on Saturday and 19:00 on Sunday. The ten side chapels contain scenes from Our Lady's life: the *Visitation*, fourth chapel on the left, and the *Presentation in the Temple*, chapel in the left transept, are both by Federico Barocci, a highly influential artist. In the eighteenth century the interior of the nave was further enriched with ornamentation and gold stucco. St Philip Neri lies in the splendid chapel to the left of the apse, a Baroque jewel, with scenes from his life by Cristoforo Roncalli from Tuscany. Above the altar is a copy in mosaic of Guido Reni's famous painting of the saint now in the Vatican Museums.

Santi Giovanni e Paolo (Saints John and Paul)

Open: 08:30–12:00; 15:30–18:00.

Visit this church and the Roman houses on the Caelian Hill when you are in the region of the Colosseum. It is very close to S. Gregorio Magno (Map p. 104).

Outside the church stand the remains of the massive Temple of Claudius on which the superb twelfth-century campanile rests. There was a church here at the beginning of the fifth century, the *Titulus Pammachi*, a house where early Christians may have worshipped. The façade, with its five arches that go back to the fifth century, was restored by Cardinal Francis Joseph Spellman, Archbishop of New York (1939–67) and the titular Cardinal Priest of this church, with generous support from Joseph Kennedy, President Kennedy's father. The twelfth-century portico was built by the English Pope, Adrian IV.

The two saints of the dedication, John and Paul, were court officials of Constantine martyred on 27 January 361, when the Emperor Julian turned back the clock during his two-year reign, making paganism the state religion and harassing Christians. Their remains are contained in a porphyry urn incorporated in the marble high altar (by Francesco Ferrari). However, this story has been questioned because it is not certain that Julian did martyr any Christians.

Invasions and changing fashions inevitably necessitated restorations over the years. In the thirteenth century much new work was done, including the Cosmati floor, and in a room to the left of the high altar is a great Byzantine-style fresco of *Christ with his Apostles*, dated to 1255. The ceiling was installed in 1598. Otherwise you are in a splendid eighteenth-century interior, lit by 30 crystal chandeliers, which nonetheless retains its fifth-century form. The second altar on the right is dedicated to St Pammachius, the Roman senator who gave the first titular church. The altarpiece showing the saint with a plan of the earlier basilica is by Aureliano Milani, a prolific painter in Rome in the first half of the eighteenth century.

The church became a shrine to St Paul of the Cross, who founded the Passionist Congregation in 1725, to 'teach people to pray', and always to have in mind the Passion. Their work is mainly missions and retreats, and they serve this church. In 1850 a Passionist priest, Fr Rossi, founded the Congregation of Sisters, who share the work. Blessed Dominic Barberi, who established the Passionist Order in England and received Newman into the Catholic Church, lived in the monastery. The English Passionist, Fr Ignatius Spencer, son of the second Earl Spencer, stayed here for several months when he came to Rome in 1851 to raise funds for his missionary work in England and to seek approval for his proposals to encourage Catholics across the world to work and pray for the conversion of England.

> It is an excellent and holy practice to call to mind and meditate on our Lord's Passion, since it is by this path that we shall arrive at union with God. In this, the holiest of all schools, true wisdom is learned, for it was there that all the saints became wise.
> St Paul of the Cross.

*If you didn't walk up from S. Gregorio, do walk back that way (turn right from the church). You are walking down the Clivo di Scauro, a street dating back to 109 BC which has retained its original name—in Latin Clivus Scauri (clivus means a 'rise' and scauri 'swollen ankles', which you may have by now). Arches were added in the twelfth century, though the furthest one may be third century. The entrance to the **Case Romane** (Roman Houses) beneath the church is on the right. The side wall of the church is ancient, and used to be the street frontage of houses and shops dating from the first to the fifth centuries, a remarkable survival. You can see blocked windows above.*

Sant'Ignazio

Open: 07:30–19:00. Next to the Collegio Romano (Map p. 149). The entrance is in the charming eighteenth-century Piazza S. Ignazio.

The Church of St Ignatius of Loyola was consecrated in 1650 as a chapel for the Collegio Romano (pp. 154 and 156), when the original chapel became too small for its two thousand students. The project was overseen by a Jesuit mathematician, Father Orazio Grassi; several leading architects were involved, including Carlo Maderno. Most of the decoration, and the high façade, was the work of Brother Andrea Pozzo, whom you met in the Gesù.

On entering the church you are struck by Pozzo's grandiose fresco in the vault of the nave. It celebrates the work of St Ignatius and the Society of Jesus all over the world by allegorical representations of the four (as it was then thought) continents. The saint is welcomed into paradise by Christ and Our Lady. A marble disc in the centre of the nave indicates the position from which you see it best, though it is less of a strain on the neck to use the modern mirror. Pozzo was a master of perspective (he wrote a treatise on the subject) and he created the illusion of a dome, because the money ran out before a real dome could be built. Another marker on the floor gives you the full effect of this flat 'dome' painted on canvas. The original painting was actually destroyed by fire, but in 1823 was faithfully copied by Francesco Manno from Pozzo's original drawings.

The conversion of Ignatius, a soldier, occurred when he was convalescing after being badly wounded in the Battle of Pamplona, and Pozzo depicts this in the soffit of the sanctuary arch. He painted more scenes from the life of Ignatius in the apse. The central panel over the altar celebrates the saint's vision at La Storta, where he received his calling; on the left he sends St Francis Xavier on his mission to India, Japan and China; on the right he receives St Francis Borgia into the Society of Jesus; and in the semi-dome he is administering to the poor and victims of the plague.

> I wish not merely to be called Christian, but also to be Christian.
> St Ignatius of Loyola.

In the right transept you should note the chapel dedicated to St Aloysius (Luigi) Gonzaga, with a large marble high-relief by the French sculptor Pierre Legros, depicting him in Glory. Aloysius was a student at the Collegio Romano, when he died at the age of 23 caring for plague victims. He is buried under the altar in a sarcophagus of lapis lazuli. Opening off this transept on the left, the Ludovisi Chapel contains the very elaborate funerary monument of Pope Gregory XV and his nephew Cardinal Ludovico Ludovisi, made by Legros and another French sculptor Pierre-Étienne Monnot some sixty years after the pope's death in 1623: the female figures flanking the sarcophagus represent *Magnificence* and *Religion*. Gregory XV canonised both Ignatius and Francis Xavier.

Art lovers should not miss the chapel in the left transept, which has a marble altarpiece of the *Annunciation* by Filippo della Valle, with allegorical figures and angels by Pietro Bracci, and a frescoed ceiling of the *Assumption* by Ludovico Mazzanti. Buried under the altar here, in a later copy of Gonzaga's lapis lazuli sarcophagus, is the Jesuit Cardinal St Robert Bellarmine, one of the great leaders and theologians of the renewal of the Church after the Reformation. He lived an austere life, giving the tapestries from his rooms to the poor, saying that walls couldn't catch cold. The second chapel on the right, expensively decorated with rare marbles, has an altarpiece of the *Death of St Joseph* by Francesco Trevisani, a Rococo artist from Venice. A curiosity in the first chapel on the right is the wooden model of the Temple of Christ the King, by the Neapolitan cabinet-maker Vincenzo Pandolfi (1905–2005). Its central domed 'temple' is ringed by little models of some of the most famous churches and places of worship around the world

At Christmas time all Roman churches create wonderful cribs, and this church has one of the best. It is a modern copy of an eighteenth-century Neapolitan original and is on permanent display in the first chapel on the left.

Basilica of San Lorenzo fuori le Mura

Open: 7:00–12:00; 16:00–19:00.

Experience a 50-minute journey on the No. 19 tram from Piazza del Risorgimento to Verano. The previous stop is Università la Sapienza. You will see a column outside the basilica to your left. Or else, take the 492 bus from Piazza del Risorgimento (the stop is in Via Crescenzio just before it reaches the piazza). This route takes you to Piazza Aracoeli, near Piazza Venezia, and on to Termini. If you catch it at Termini the stop is just round the corner in Via Volturno (Map p. 180). You get off at Verano, where you will see the basilica. The column in front, erected in 1865, replaces a smaller one: it is 21 metres high and on the top is a bronze statue of St Lawrence by Stefano Galletti.

One of the Seven Pilgrimage Churches of Rome, S. Lorenzo is well worth the journey to get there, and of course essential visiting if you are making the pilgrimage. The basilica enshrines the tomb of St Lawrence, a deacon of Pope Sixtus II, who was martyred in 258 under Emperor Valerian, a few days after the pope himself and other clergy. Many other saints are buried here, as is Blessed Pope Pius IX. Pius had originally planned to be buried in St Mary Major's, but changed his mind and chose instead to be buried 'among the poor', for this is a poor part of the city. Popularly acclaimed as a great liberal, he was a very influential pope and innovator: religious vocations, new foundations and structures flourished under him, and he convened the First Vatican Council. He built railways in Italy and installed gas street-lighting in Rome. But in his reign of 31 years (from 1846 to 1878), the longest of any pope, he lived through a time of huge upheaval in Europe; and the unification of Italy in 1871, with Rome as its capital, entailed the loss of the Papal States and of the Pope's dominion in Rome. Pius IX never accepted this, and the problem remained unresolved until the signing of the Lateran Treaty in 1929, which gave the Vatican substantial compensation and recognition as a separate state, with the benefit of ensuring the Pope's political independence and freedom.

The basilica looks slightly odd because it is really two churches turned into one and not quite in alignment. The first church was originally a small chapel built by Constantine over St Lawrence, who is buried in the catacomb beneath. In 580 it was reconstructed by Pope Pelagius II and remains today beyond the altar. In 1216 Pope Honorius III reversed its orientation, demolished its apse, and built a second church in front, turning Pelagius's church into the choir and sanctuary. Hence the restored sixth-century mosaic on the triumphal arch now faces away from the congregation: it shows Pelagius offering his church to Christ in the company of Saints Peter, Paul, Lawrence, Stephen and Hippolytus.

You enter the church of Pope Honorius through an impressive portico with six different antique columns unified by ionic capitals. The church was badly damaged in 1943, hit by an allied bomb aimed at the nearby railway yard when Rome was occupied, but you would never know it, so perfect is the restoration. The nave ceiling is an exact replica of the war-damaged nineteenth-century ceiling made by Virginio Vespignani. Towards the altar is a fine Cosmatesque choir enclosure with a great paschal candlestick and two early thirteenth-century ambos in Cosmati work: the one on the right, said to be the finest in Rome, for the Gospel. Behind this fine ambo is an antique ionic column, and carved in the volutes of the capital is a rather sweet lizard with a frog for company. It may have come from the Portico of Octavia. The tomb of St Lawrence and relics of the Deacon St Stephen are under the high altar in a crypt chapel entered from the nave.

Steps on both sides of the entrance to the crypt chapel lead up to the chancel, a space of great beauty within the sixth-century church. A raised floor was inserted here so that you only see the tops of the fluted antique marble columns with their richly carved capitals which separated the nave of Pelagius's church from its two aisles; the bases rest on the original floor below. The two columns nearest the altar are decorated with Roman armour. Above the aisles are arcaded galleries for the women. The baldacchino over the high altar, introduced in 1148, is signed by stonemasons Johannes, Petrus, Angelus, and Sasso, the sons of master mason Paolo Romano. The bishop's throne, from 1254, is richly decorated with little mosaic columns, pieces of porphyry and serpentine.

In the nineteenth century the original floor level and narthex of the sixth-century church were uncovered and can be reached by steps on both side of the chancel. Here, in the narthex, now decorated with modern mosaics of the Venetian School, you will find the tomb of Blessed Pope Pius IX. The campanile and the cloister date from 1190. In the cloister, which can be entered from the sacristy, is a collection of inscriptions from the catacomb: the catacomb itself is devoid of paintings.

As you leave the church prepare to be amused by the tomb on your left of Cardinal Guglielmo Fieschi (d. 1256). It is a magnificent Roman sarcophagus, very beautiful, but a rather curious choice for a cardinal, since it depicts a pagan wedding festival and protective deities.

There is a lovely story told about St Lawrence. As deacon he was entrusted not only with supporting the sick and poor, but also with keeping safe the gold chalices and other valuables. Aware of this, the magistrate ordered him to surrender the treasures of the church. Lawrence returned with a crowd of sick, poor and disabled people, and with his arm over them told the furious magistrate, 'These are the treasures of the Church'.

As you leave the basilica you can see on your left the Cemetery of Rome and all the flower stalls outside the entrance. To get back on the 492 bus cross the wide Via Tiburtina with its tram lines and head left on Via Cesare de Lollis. You will find the stop a short way along there to your right.

San Pantaleo

Corso Vittorio Emanuele II (Map p. 138)

Open: 7:00–12:00; 16:00–19:30.

The simple white façade conceals an elegant thirteenth-century church dedicated to St Pantaleon, a martyr in the persecution of

Diocletian whose Greek name means *compassionate one*. Restored several times, the interior is much as it was when Giovanni Antonio de Rossi designed it in the seventeenth century. The façade was added in 1806 by Giuseppe Valadier. It is worthy of a visit and a prayer to St Joseph Calasanz, who lies beneath the altar. A pioneer in education, this Spanish priest opened the first free school in Europe in 1597, and founded the Piarists, who still provide free education all over the world. Radical in his day, he admitted Jewish and Protestant children into his schools, and was even asked by the Turks to educate Moslems; only a lack of teachers prevented him from doing so. He placed emphasis on mathematics and science, and became a friend to Galileo in his troubles. Anticipating the nineteenth-century philosophy of St John Bosco, and late twentieth-century educational theory, he strongly opposed punishment, preferring encouragement. For all these reasons he faced much criticism.

In thanksgiving for their dedication, we ask your grace, Lord, for all those who teach and guide the minds of the young. Give them encouragement when they feel unappreciated, so they may rise to every challenge. Grant them wisdom, so that they may find fulfilment and joy in their vocation to educate, care and love each child and develop their potential for life, through Jesus Christ our Lord.

Amen.

The statue in the piazza outside is of Marco Minghetti, Prime Minister in 1863 and again in 1873, and a strong supporter of both Italian unification and the Pope.

Santa Prisca

Open: 8:30–12:00; 16:30–18:30. This church is on the Aventine (Map p. 104). From Circo Massimo station walk up the left side of the Circus Maximus, and take the first left into Via della Fonte di Fauno. Keep on it and soon after it bends right, at the

T-junction turn right into Via di S. Prisca. The church is on your right.

There is some confusion about its origins. One tradition is that Prisca was a young martyr: the other, more intriguing, is that she was Priscilla, wife of Aquila who, according to the Acts of the Apostles (18:2–3), was expelled from Rome together with his wife by Emperor Claudius in AD 49. The historian Suetonius explained: *'Since the Jews constantly made disturbances at the instigation of Chrestus, [Claudius] expelled them from Rome'.* It is assumed that 'Chrestus' is a reference to Christ, and that, as in other cities, there was conflict between those Jews who became Christians and those who did not. So Claudius banished them all. St Paul stayed with Priscilla and Aquila in Corinth, where they had found refuge, and took them with him to Syria (v. 18). Like Paul, Aquila was a tentmaker, and he and his wife were missionaries. By 56 they had returned to Rome, for in his Letter to the Church in Rome Paul greets them (Romans 16:3–4), mentioning that they risked death to save his life, so they must have been delighted when he came to live in Rome.

Archaeologists investigated the tradition that Prisca's house, *Titulus Priscae*, was beneath the present church, and in 1934 they did discover a house and chapel close by and some terracotta lamps with the Chi-Rho monogram. By the fifth century it had been converted into a church and there is documentary evidence of restorations in the eighth century. Damaged by the Normans in 1084, it was rebuilt by Pope Paschal II, and again after a major fire in 1414. Benedictine monks served it from 1062, but soon after the fire they were replaced by Dominicans. In 1660 Augustinians took over. More restoration followed in 1728, when the ancient columns were embedded in pilasters to strengthen them. For many years after Napoleon's occupation of Rome in 1798 the church was in ruins, and there is not a lot to see. The body of S. Prisca lies under the high altar. The surviving frescoes in the nave, by the Florentine artist Anastasio Fontebuoni, and the picture above the altar of *St Peter baptising Prisca* by Domenico Passignano, date from about 1600.

Santi Quattro Coronati

Open: 10:00–11:45; 16:00–17:45. Near S. Clemente (Map p. 9).

Popular for weddings, like many churches in the historic centre, Santi Quattro Coronati is cared for by a community of contemplative Augustinian nuns. As you approach it, the outside of the building has the appearance of a fortress. It is one of the oldest churches in Rome, originally *Titulus Aemilianae*, whose villa is beneath the church. In the sixth century a church was built over it, which Pope Leo IV greatly enlarged in the ninth century. During the Norman Sack of Rome it was burned to the ground and rebuilt by Pope Pascal II in more modest style, with a second courtyard replacing part of the nave. He saved the squat campanile, the oldest in Rome, though it was rebuilt in 1914, and retained the dimensions of the earlier apse, which is why it looks so big for a small church. Little has been changed since, apart from the additions of a fine sixteenth-century wooden ceiling and some good paintings and, in the right aisle, some fourteenth-century frescoes. On the left side there is a bell, and a sister will admit you to the lovely thirteenth-century two-storied cloister (built by a famous stonecutter, Pietro de Maria), with delicate arcades, architectural fragments, flowers and a very fine fountain made a century earlier. St Barbara's Chapel, off the cloister, belonged to Leo IV's church and has faded frescoes of the ninth to twelfth centuries.

On the left of the courtyard as you leave, is another chapel from Leo IV's church. If you go to the barred window, ring the bell, and say 'San Silvestro' to the sister, she will admit you to this chapel dedicated to St Sylvester, whom Constantine persuaded to leave his hermitage to become pope, and who it was said cured the emperor of leprosy. Offer a euro for the sister to turn on the lights and you will see the famous thirteenth-century frescoes of the legend of Constantine and Sylvester. They include the emperor lying in bed with leprosy, his face covered with sores; his dream of St Peter and St Paul urging him to see Pope Sylvester; the emperor kneeling before the pope, the so-called 'Donation of Constantine'; and Constantine's baptism by the pope. In 2002 important (but inaccessible) frescoes were discovered in the monastery.

Pope Honorius III is said to have greeted St Francis at this church. The four crowned saints (*Quattro Coronati*) of the dedication are thought to have been Roman stonemasons, martyred for refusing to carve a statue of Aesculapius.

Continue along Via dei SS. Quattro Coronati or along Via di S. Giovanni in Laterano, and you will reach St John Lateran.

Santuario del Divino Amore

Open: 8:00–12:00; 15:00–18:00 (19:00 in summer).

Take bus 218 from St John Lateran to the catacombs (Maps pp. 89 and 83) and stay on until you reach Santuario del Divino Amore. The previous stop is Castel di Leva/Ardeatina.

Pope St John Paul II made this an alternative to the Basilica of S. Sebastiano on the Seven Churches Pilgrimage for the Holy Year 2000, and it is indeed loved by the people of Rome. Every Saturday night, from Easter until the end of October, a walking pilgrimage sets out at midnight from Piazza di Porta Capena, just across the road from FAO, near S. Gregorio (p. 104), reaching the sanctuary for the first Sunday Mass at 5:00.

The sanctuary houses a medieval fresco of Our Lady which formerly decorated the gatehouse of the Castel di Leva. In 1740 a traveller was being attacked by a pack of dogs, when in a vision he saw this image and cried out to Our Lady for help. The dogs quietened down and he was saved. So popular did the image become that the Shrine of Divine Love was made for it in 1745. During the Second World War it was kept in S. Ignazio and taken around the churches of Rome, where people came to pray for peace and protection. In 1999 a sensational new church, nicknamed the 'Blue Grotto' on account of its sparkling glass, was consecrated by Pope St John Paul II. Retreats and charitable activities are undertaken by the Oblate Sons of Our Lady of Divine Love, who serve the parish and the shrine.

O beautiful Immaculate Virgin Mary, Mother of God and our Mother, O Lady of Divine Love, we turn to you in confidence that you will obtain for us the grace we sorely need. We know that you will never turn us away, you who have been worthily greeted by an angel with the words 'Hail, full of grace!'

Grant peace and prosperity to Italy and to the whole world; protect our Holy Father; bring into perfect unity all Christians according to the desire of your divine Son; illumine with the light of the Gospel all who have not yet come to the true faith; convert poor sinners; give us too a sincere contrition for our sins; render us always strong enough to say 'no' when temptations assail us; lead us along the path of fraternal love and charity; and, finally, when God would beckon us, open to us the portals of heaven. You who see us mourning and weeping in this vale of tears, come to our aid when we are weighed down by the load of our miseries; give us strength to accept the inevitable difficulties and trials of life; grant, O Mother of Grace, health in mind and body to all who turn to you.

San Silvestro in Capite

Open: 7:00–18:30. Mass in English: Sunday 10:00 and 17:30.

*A pleasant way is to walk on the left side of Via del Corso from Piazza Venezia to Piazza Colonna where you will see the **Column of Marcus Aurelius**, erected after the emperor's death in AD 180, probably by his son, Commodus. It celebrates his father's victories over the Germanic tribes and Sarmatians. The bronze statue of St Paul on the top was placed there by Pope Sixtus V, probably replacing one of the emperor. Then cross the Corso, turn right into Largo Chigi, and the second turning left will bring you into Piazza di S. Silvestro; the church is on the far side next to the large central Post Office.*

The original church was erected in the eighth century on the site of an ancient building, probably Aurelian's Temple of the Sun. It was built to house remains from the catacombs, and the names of various martyrs are recorded on two tablets in the portico on either side of the central door—men to the left, women to the right (their tablet is incomplete). The men include St Tarcisius (on line 18), a layman, who was carrying the Blessed Sacrament to Christians in prison when he was set upon and killed for refusing to surrender the Most Holy.

Pope Sylvester is credited with baptising Constantine, but he was not adopted as the patron saint of this church until the twelfth century. Like S. Maria in Aracoeli, S. Maria in Cosmedin, and other churches, it was served by Byzantine monks. When they returned home in the tenth century Benedictines replaced them. The campanile, an attractive landmark with its Romanesque arches and embellishments of purple porphyry and green serpentine, was built in 1216. Its tiled pyramidal cap used to support a bronze cockerel, recalling the cock that crowed at Peter's third denial of Christ.

In 1286 the convent was given to a new movement, the Poor Clares, who remained for six hundred years. In 1588 they began rebuilding the church. Carlo Maderno was their principal architect, and Carlo Rainaldi was responsible for the sanctuary and high altar (though it is thought Michelangelo influenced its design). Rainaldi also provided the organ with its intricately-carved case. Other architects worked here until the rebuilding was finished in 1697. The nuns got hold of the rather doubtful relic of St John the Baptist's head (now shown, in a golden reliquary, in a room to the left by the entrance), and added 'in capite' to the church's name. In 1849 the poor sisters were brutally ejected by Garibaldi and their convent turned into a barracks. After the French occupied the city later in the same year the sisters returned, but only until 1876, when their convent was turned into the central Post Office.

The street door opens into an atrium with a drinking fountain on the left; around and on the walls are the usual architectural fragments, inscriptions and sarcophagi, which you may be so used to seeing that you have forgotten how wonderful they are. The interior is richly decorated with fresco and stucco work, much of the latter gilded. Two recurring themes are the head of St John the Baptist on a platter, and the face of Christ on a veil. The face of Christ was painted on wood, which the nuns certainly had in 1517 but since 1870 it has been kept in the Matilda Chapel in the Vatican Palace. A good example of the head and the face can be seen on the pulpit. The ceiling fresco, by Giacinto Brandi, depicts the *Assumption of Our Lady*. You may notice that the dome is false and oval-shaped; the *Glory of the God the Father*, was painted by Cristoforo Roncalli, who like Brandi worked extensively in seventeenth-century Rome. In the apse the paintings on either side of the altar are of the *Martyrdom of St Stephen* (right) and Pope Sylvester being summoned by Constantine's messengers (left), while in the semi-dome is a painting by Ludovico Gimignani of Sylvester baptising Constantine.

The *confessio* (not always accessible) is a late addition, excavated in 1906: it holds remains from the catacombs. Note on the wall a Roman mosaic of birds at a bath. The relics of three popes, Saints Sylvester, Stephen I and Dionysius, are enshrined in the high altar. There are some lovely devotional paintings in the side chapels, among them the *Virgin and Child with Saints* by Baccio Ciarpi in the right transept (Colonna Chapel). The second chapel on the right has an altarpiece of *St Francis receiving the Stigmata*, painted *c.*1616 by an admirer and imitator of Caravaggio, Orazio Gentileschi, who spent the last thirteen years of his life working in England. In the first chapel on the left are late-seventeenth-century paintings of the *Passion* by Francesco Trevisani.

S. Silvestro has been served by Pallottine Fathers since 1890 for the benefit of the English-speaking community in Rome, and visitors. It was the titular church of the popular and revered Cardinal Hume of England. It was the first in Rome to get electric light.

Santa Susanna

Maybe closed for restoration—check before visiting.

Red Linea A to Repubblica, or walk from Termini (Map p. 180).
Leave Piazza della Repubblica by Via Vittorio Emanuele Orlando,
and turn left into Piazza di S. Bernardo. The church is in front of
you. Buses 60, 61, 62, 175 and 492 stop in Largo S. Susanna near
to the church.

This late Renaissance gem was entrusted to the Paulist Fathers
for American Catholics in 1922, but in 2017 they moved to St
Patrick's in Via Boncompagni. There was a *titulus* here in 280,
perhaps owned by Pope Caius, which was replaced by a church
around 330. Pope Gregory the Great later dedicated it in honour
of the young Susanna, martyred with her brother, Gabinus, under
Diocletian. Remains of what may have been the early house-
church have been found beneath the present building.

The church was entirely rebuilt under Pope Leo III (795–
816), again by Sixtus IV (1471–84) and yet again between 1593
and 1603, to much as you see it now, bright and spacious. All
the walls are frescoed: those in the nave by Baldassare Croce,
later framed to look like tapestries, tell the story of the saint's
Old Testament namesake, whom the youthful Daniel saved from
the condemnation of the lecherous elders. In the apse, paintings by Cesare Nebbia show scenes from the life of the martyr
Susanna: on the left she is being accosted by Diocletian's son,
Maximian (or perhaps by General Galerius), with an angel in-
tervening, and on the right she refuses to burn incense to Jupiter.
In the semi-dome above you see her being crowned as a martyr
by Christ, flanked by angels playing sixteenth-century instruments. Above the high altar is the *Martyrdom of S. Susanna* by
Tommas Laurenti of Palermo, dated 1592. Caravaggio is said to
have studied it before completing his great *St Matthew* paintings
in S. Luigi dei Francesi.

The façade was designed by Carlo Maderno. Completed in
1603, it was his first major project, and led to his appointment at

St Peter's. On the façade are statues of Saints Caius, Gabinius, Felicitas and Susanna.

*The church on the opposite corner just across the road from S. Susanna, S. **Maria della Vittoria**, contains, in the third chapel on the left, one of the most celebrated of all Bernini's religious sculptures, St Teresa in Ecstasy. On both sides of the chapel members of the Cornaro family, who commissioned the work, look on from their boxes, like spectators at a theatre.*

*Diagonally across Via XX Settembre from S. Susanna, is the monumental **Fountain of Moses** (1585–8) designed by Domenico Fontana to celebrate the aqueduct built by Pope Sixtus V, restoring water supplies to Rome. The design of the mostra or public terminus of the aqueduct was inspired by a Roman triumphal arch. In the central opening is a large statue of Moses, who having made water spring from the rock quenched the thirst of his people (just as Sixtus had done with this new fountain; the parallel would not be lost). In the arches to right and left are reliefs depicting other episodes related to the Exodus of the Jews from Egypt. That on the left shows Aaron gathering Manna to feed the people, while on the right Joshua prepares them for battle. The figure of Moses, carved by Prospero Bresciani, drew immediate criticism for its ungainly proportions. The four amiable lions spouting water are nineteenth-century replacements.*

Tre Fontane

Via Acque Salvie, 1.

Open: 9:00–12:00; 16:00–18:00.

*Metro Blue Linea B to Laurentina. Turn left from the metro station, passing the clothing kiosk and along the island with its clothes stores and trees on Via Laurentina. At the T-junction you will see the 761 bus stop, Laurentina, direction of Arco di Travertino. It is only 3 stops to Laurentina-Tre Fontane (the previous one being Laurentina-Mendoza). Get off and continue walking in the same direction about 100 metres to a sharp right turn marked by a notice **Abbazia delle Tre Fontane**. To come back to the metro get the 761 across the road from where you got off.*

You will pass St Benedict with his finger to his lips to invite silence, a statue inscribed with his words, *Ora et Labora,* 'Pray and Work'. This is a beautiful oasis of pilgrimage and retreat, the place where St Paul is thought to have been executed. There are three churches: the **Monastery of SS. Vincenzo e Anastasio,** the **Church of S. Maria Scala Coeli,** and **St Paul's,** which marks the place of his martyrdom. The monastery was built by Pope Honorius I in 626 and given to Byzantine monks. In 1140 Pope Innocent II entrusted it to St Bernard, and it has remained Cistercian to this day. Restored by Pope Honorius III, who consecrated it in 1221, it is typically austere.

S. Maria Scala Coeli, dedicated to Our Lady of Martyrs, was built in 1582 by Giacomo della Porta, and restored in 1925: the crypt (which you can visit) is part of the earlier church it replaced. The martyrs were St Zeno and the thousands of slaves who worked on Diocletian's Baths in the city, who were allegedly killed when it was finished. There is uncertainty about this, and also whether St Zeno is to be identified with the St Zeno buried in S. Prassede, but certainly part of a large Christian burial area was unearthed here in the nineteenth century. The name Scala Coeli, 'Ladder to Heaven', recalls a vision of souls entering Heaven (attractively depicted in a mosaic in the chapel on the left) which St Bernard had while celebrating Mass here.

S. Paolo alle Tre Fontane (St Paul at the Three Fountains) was built on the site of a Roman garrison where it is thought the apostle was executed. An early Greek life of St Paul says he was beheaded beside three springs near a stone pine tree (*pinus pinea*): these springs are still to be seen. Somehow a legend grew up that his head bounced three times, causing the three springs to spout from the earth. It is not known when the first church was built, but one existed in the seventh century. The present one, like S. Maria, was built by della Porta.

Tre Fontane is also home to the Little Sisters of Jesus, part of the Spiritual Family of Charles de Foucauld, who witnessed to Christ among the Tuareg people of Southern Algeria until he was killed in 1916. The Sisters' lives are spent in the most dangerous and poverty-stricken countries of the world, including the Middle East; they welcome visitors and are given to hospitality.

> As for me, my life is already being poured away as a libation, and the time has come for me to be gone. I have fought the good fight to the end; I have run the race to the finish; I have kept the faith; all there is to come for me now is the crown of righteousness which the Lord, the faithful judge, will give to me on that Day; and not only to me but to all those who have longed for his appearing.
>
> St Paul (2 Timothy 4:6-8).

*While in this part of Rome, for something entirely different, you could go on the metro to the next stop, EUR Fermi, and look round **EUR** (p. 230).*

Trinità dei Monti

At the top of the Spanish Steps. Open 6:30–20:00. Thursdays to 23:59. Closed Monday.

As already mentioned, this church at the top of the Spanish Steps was built by the French, and it remains the responsibility of the French State. Originally proposed by Charles VIII of France in 1494, it was begun in 1502 by his successor Louis XII, and building work continued throughout much of the sixteenth century. During the Napoleonic invasion of Rome in 1798 it was severely damaged, like many other churches, but in 1816 was restored by François Mazois and students from the nearby Académie de France, at the expense of Louis XVIII.

The distinctive façade with its two campanili, now bright and white after a major restoration in 2013, was designed in 1584 by Giacomo della Porta. The elegant double staircase by Domenico Fontana was built in 1587 at the expense of Pope Sixtus V, who found the previous staircase too steep. One curiosity is that the campanili had two different clock faces. That on the right showed the Italian (originally ancient Roman) method of telling the time, which is now completely unfamiliar. Daylight was divided into twelve 'hours': zero hour was sunrise, and the end of the twelfth hour was at sunset. This meant the hour had no fixed duration. Incredibly, Rome persisted with this method of telling the time until 1842, when it began to conform to the rest of the world, and the clock was replaced by a sundial. The clock on the left showed *Tempo Ultramontano*, 'the way they tell the time on the other side of the Alps'. Pairs of clocks like these also operated at St Peter's and Sant'Agnese in Agone.

At first glance the interior looks like a fairly typical example of a Roman church of the sixteenth and seventeenth centuries, but its original style was gothic and traces of this survive, particularly the tracery of the vault immediately before sanctuary. The two free-standing barley-sugar columns in the sanctuary are thirteenth-century copies of the serpentine columns that embellished the old St Peter's. Daniele da Volterra, a Tuscan artist and friend of Michelangelo, painted the third chapel on the right with a *Presentation of the Virgin* on the right wall, and an *Assumption* over the altar, in which he included Michelangelo (the last figure on the right). He also painted the second chapel on the left with a fine *Descent from the Cross*.

Nowadays the church is noted for the vigour of its spiritual life, for it is served by the Fraternités Monastiques de Jérusalem, a new Catholic Order founded to live the monastic life in the heart of modern cities.

The 'Egyptian' obelisk in front of the church is in fact a Roman imitation from the Gardens of Sallust: it was erected here in 1789.

*From the church you can turn right to the entrance of the metro or go on and make your way into the **Borghese Gardens** from where the views over the city are worth seeing. You will pass the **Villa Medici**, home since 1803 of the Académie de France à Rome which offers courses in classical art, as it has since the seventeenth century. There are guided tours of the gardens and the rooms of Cardinal Ferdinando de' Medici, Tuesday to Sunday, 10.00 am to 7.00 pm. It is a long walk from here to the Villa Borghese.*

Venerable English College

Via di Monserrato, 45 (Map p. 138).

This is the oldest existing English Institution outside England. Its beginnings go back to 1362 when John Shepherd, a Rosary merchant and his wife, established a pilgrim hospice here for the convenience of 'poor, sick, needy and distressed people coming from England to the City'. In 1579 it became the English College for the training of priests, which it still is: 'Venerable' because during the Reformation period young men from England studied here before returning home to face certain martyrdom. St Philip Neri, who lodged opposite the college, would greet and bless them, and it is said he kissed their footprints. In the tribune of the College chapel there are frescoes of English martyrs, from St Alban in 209 to those who died in the sixteenth and seventeenth centuries, which you may see if you ask. Behind the altar hangs a large painting of the *Blessed Trinity* by Durante Alberti (1581) which includes images of two English martyrs, St Thomas of Canterbury and St Edmund: according to tradition the students gathered in front of this painting to sing the *Te Deum* each time news reached Rome of the martyrdom of one of their brothers. The custom continues today when present students gather in front of the painting on 1 December, 'Martyrs' Day', to remember those young men who were mercilessly hung, drawn and quartered for celebrating Mass and keeping the Catholic Faith alive in England.

> God of patient love, who gave to our martyrs courage to endure death and the vision of a nation renewed in faith, grant that the prayers of those who suffered with Christ may lead all Christians of our land into one communion with Christ's risen body and encourage them to await in hope the fullness of your promised kingdom. We ask this through our Lord Jesus Christ, your Son, who lives and reigns with you in the unity of the Holy Spirit, God for ever and ever. Amen.

Other Places of Interest

Campo de' Fiori

Market every morning except Sunday.

Just beyond the Church of S. Andrea della Valle, turn left down Via dei Baullari. It leads into Campo de' Fiori (Map p. 138)

Literally 'Field of Flowers', this is Rome's oldest and liveliest market for flowers, fruit and vegetables, spices, food, clothes and kitchenware. In the centre, not much to the credit of the Church is a late-nineteenth-century statue of Giordano Bruno, the Dominican friar, philosopher, mathematician, poet and astrologer, who was burned at the stake here in 1600 for his heresies; accused, among other things, of denying several Catholic doctrines, including the Trinity, the divinity of Christ, the virginity of Mary, and transubstantiation. In 2000 Pope St John Paul II made a general apology for the deaths of thinkers in the Middle Ages. In medieval days the square was full of inns, one of the best known being the Hosteria della Vacca, 'Cow's Inn', at the southwest corner, on the angle between Via dei Cappellari and Vicolo del Gallo. It was the home of Vannozza dei Cattanei, the lover of the notorious Borgia Pope Alexander VI, and mother of his daughter, Lucrezia. Her coat of arms quartered with that of her third husband and the Borgia pope is still on the house façade at No. 13 Vicolo del Gallo. Alexander VI has gone down as the worst pope in history, and Julius II, his successor (after the very brief reign of Pius III), was so appalled by him that he declared:

> *I will not live in the same rooms as the Borgias lived. He desecrated the Holy Church as none before. He usurped the papal power by the devil's aid, and I forbid under the pain of excommunication anyone to speak or think of Borgia again. His name and memory must be forgotten. It must be crossed out of every document and memorial. His reign must be obliterated. All paintings made of the Borgias or for them must be covered over with black crepe.*

If you continue down Via dei Baullari from Campo de' Fiori, you will come into Piazza Farnese, where you will see the Farnese Palace and be very close to the English College (Map p. 138.)

Case Romane del Celio (Roman Houses)

Clivo di Scauro. Near SS. Giovanni e Paolo and S. Gregorio. (Map p. 104)

Excavations begun in 1887 found not only the *Titulus Pammachi* they were looking for beneath the Church of SS. Giovanni e Paolo (see p. 202), but also a labyrinth of twenty rooms belonging to Roman houses dating from the first to the fourth centuries, many of them beautifully frescoed. One is a chapel: on the right-hand wall the upper scene shows two men and a woman blindfolded and awaiting execution. Three bodies were buried here in the fourth century, and are presumed to be Saints Crispin, Crispianus and Benedicta who, it is said, were martyred during the reign of the apostate Emperor Julian in 361, not long after the two saints commemorated in the church above. There is a youthful Christ in a long tunic with two figures prostrating before him, and a praying figure with arms outstretched; and sheep. One room was originally a courtyard with a nymphaeum, an installation of fountains, with a mosaic floor. It contains an elegant second or third-century fresco thought to show Proserpine, with other divinities and cherubs, in a boat. Another room is a private bathroom. Everywhere you will see wonderful cupids and flowers, sea-monsters, peacocks and birds, garlands and people, and much more besides. It is a uniquely preserved row of Roman houses.

Castel Sant'Angelo

Lungotevere Castello

This massive structure, a prominent landmark on the banks of the Tiber at the opposite end of Via della Conciliazione to St Peter's, started off as the grand marble-covered mausoleum which the Emperor Hadrian commissioned for himself in AD 128. The remains of this man, who also built Hadrian's Wall to secure the northern border of Britain, were buried deep within, as were his six successors. It was fortified and incorporated into the Aurelian Wall in 271. You may have noticed a long wall linking it to the Vatican: this was built in 850, and a corridor was later constructed on top, the Passetto di Borgo, to provide an escape route for the pope, which Pope Clement VII was glad to make use of during the Sack of Rome in 1527. His successor, Paul III, built an apartment in the castle to ensure more comfort in the future. It makes a very interesting visit, combining the mausoleum, the fortifications, a military museum of medieval firearms and memorabilia, sculpture and paintings, as well as the papal apartments, a coffee shop and great views over the city. One canvas of special English interest in the Sala Festoni is *The Entry of James III of England into Bologna*. James is wearing a bell-bottomed wig and a pale blue silk coat with the Garter Riband and Star. Among his entourage is the young Bonnie Prince Charlie. A welcoming cardinal doffs his red biretta while a woman points out the king to her children. Sometimes this room is closed and you may have to ask an attendant if you wish to see it.

Hadrian's mausoleum was renamed Castel Sant'Angelo because Pope Gregory the Great mobilised the clergy and people of Rome into a Penitential Procession in 590 to beseech God to end a terrible plague. As they passed the mausoleum they saw, on the top, a vision of St Michael the Archangel sheathing a flaming sword as a sign that the plague had ended. Immortalised in  bronze by the Flemish sculptor Peter Anton von Verschaffelt in 1753, the figure of St Michael on the roof of the castle replaced an earlier marble statue by Raffaello da Montelupo, which is now in the museum.

Domus Aurea

Entrance is four minutes' walk from Colosseo metro station. Turn left out of the station, walk along the footpath into the park, and on the left you come to the entrance in Via della Domus Aurea. Tickets must be purchased in advance (p. 7).

After the great fire in AD 64, which it was suspected that he started, Emperor Nero built an unimaginably vast complex called the Domus Aurea, 'Golden House', covering perhaps 300 acres, where the Colosseum now stands, and spreading to the Palatine, Caelian and Esquiline Hills. Nero never lived there: the whole place, including three hundred richly decorated rooms, was for entertainment. Nero's extravagance ended in his suicide, and his successors tried to bury every trace of the house. Where there had been a lake Vespasian built the Colosseum to pacify the people. The Golden House was lost until the end of the fifteenth century when a young man fell down a shaft and discovered it. So fabulous are the frescoes that famous Renaissance artists including Michelangelo, Raphael and Pinturicchio crawled around to study them, even signing their names down there, a breathtaking window for them into the classical world they were re-inventing. After decades of restoration it was eventually opened to the public, but closed in 2005 for restoration work, and yet again in 2008 for safety concerns. Part of it is now open for guided tours which must be booked in advance, but you do not see many frescoes at present.

Mausoleum of Augustus and the Altar of Peace (Ara Pacis)

With the Spanish Steps behind you, turn right down Via del Babuino, then left along Via Vittoria. Cross the Corso and continue along Via dei Pontifici, which brings you to the Mausoleum of Augustus and the Altar of Peace (Ara Pacis).

*From Castel Sant'Angelo, turn left alongside the river past two prominent landmarks: first Calderini's impressive **Palace of Justice**, then the extraordinary, white, neo-gothic reinforced concrete façade of*

Sacro Cuore di Gesù in Prati (also called Sacro Cuore del Suffragio).
Built in 1917 for the French Missionaries of the Sacred Heart, who
still serve there, it is the local parish church and worth popping in as
you pass. The floor is very attractive; the nave, punctuated by good
stained-glass windows, is long, narrow and high. A little further on
you reach Ponte Cavour; cross it and turn left; the Ara Pacis is beside
the river, and the mausoleum behind it.

Compared with the great circular Tomb of Hadrian, the
Mausoleum of Augustus presents a sad sight of ruins and veg-
etation, and is not open to the public. But there are plans for
its restoration which include a multi-media presentation of the
emperor's achievements. Augustus had it built for himself and his
family in 27 BC. He was buried there, as were Emperors Tiberius,
Claudius and Nerva and other members of the imperial family.
Across the road is the *Ara Pacis*, the Altar of Peace, commissioned
by the Senate and dedicated in 17 BC for an annual sacrifice to
the goddess Pax. It commemorates the *Pax Romana*, the great
peace from 27 BC for which Augustus was credited, and which
lasted for more than 200 years. Originally the altar stood beside
the Flaminian Way (now the Corso), on a site which in modern
terms was behind the Church of S. Lorenzo in Lucina. Later
inundations of the Tiber covered it with silt and it was lost, even
to memory, until the sixteenth century, when large fragments
were re-discovered: other fragments turned up in the nineteenth
century, but it was not until 1903 that excavations identified its
precise site. In 1937 the Italian government sponsored further excavations and the altar was reconstructed on its present site beside
the Tiber to commemorate the two thousandth anniversary of
the birth of Augustus. Now protected and displayed within an
uncompromisingly modern building of glass, steel, concrete and
travertine (2006), it is spectacularly illuminated at night.

Perhaps you will not visit it unless you are fond of Roman
sculpture, which indeed is so fine that some experts consider only
Greeks could have made it. The altar is sculpted with sacrificial
processions of Vestal Virgins and priests, and animals being led
to sacrifice. The walls around it are decorated with ox heads (*bu-
crania*) and garlands and fruit. On the outside walls the friezes

include the emperor and his family, priests and others in the act of processing or performing a sacrifice. Some show figures from Rome's mythical past, like the seated figures of Roma and Pax, Romulus and Remus (with the she-wolf), and Aeneas, portrayed as prototypes of Augustus himself, along with vines and wildlife, allegorical depictions of peace, prosperity and piety. Processional friezes along the outer walls are thought to represent the annual sacrificial procession or the altar's dedication ceremony. The movement of visitors as they walk around the monument echoes that of devotees.

Temple of Hadrian

Piazza di Pietra, near the Pantheon (Map p. 149).

The Temple of Hadrian was probably built in AD 145 by Emperor Antoninus Pius, to honour his predecessor, Hadrian. All that remains are eleven impressive Corinthian columns, some of the cella wall and the lower part of the entablature, now incorporated into the façade of a nineteenth-century palace which served as Rome's Stock Exchange and Chamber of Commerce. It is not worth a special visit unless you are in the vicinity of the Pantheon.

8

VISITS OUTSIDE ROME

Those who want a respite from the heat of Rome may enjoy a trip outside the city into the Alban Hills.

Castel Gandolfo

You can travel by train from the Vatican Railway Station (p. 5); otherwise by train from Termini. Follow signs to the town centre (15 minutes' walk). Alternatively, go by metro Red Linea A to Anagnina, where you get the Cotral bus to Castel Gandolfo. Follow signs to town centre. Tours of the garden and part of the palace may be booked in advance (p. 4). Free admission on the first Sunday of the month.

Castel Gandolfo is a picturesque village beside Lake Albano, dominated by the Pope's summer residence, which Carlo Maderno designed for Urban VIII. Many of his successors have enjoyed escaping from the heat of August here. Pope Pius XII chose to die here, as did Pope St Paul VI. The sporty pope, St John Paul II, added a swimming pool, and when officials questioned the cost he responded, 'which would be cheaper, a swimming pool or another papal funeral and installation?' (His predecessor, John Paul I, had died within a month of his installation). Pope Benedict XVI spent time here after his resignation. Pope Francis does not use it, and opened the castle to the public in 2016.

The gardens occupy the site of a residence of Emperor Domitian, and Pope Francis opened them for 90-minute guided tours most mornings other than Sundays and festivals. Providing a backdrop to the upper level of the formal garden is the long cavernous portico of Domitian's villa and the ruins of his theatre. Shady walks lead to the Garden of the Madonna, and paths of roses, aromatic herbs and lilies stretch to the Belvedere Garden, with its series of geometrical parterres edged by towering cypresses, stone pines, and old cedars, with a panoramic view across Latium to the sea. In spring you will see masses of begonias, ageratum and pansies.

With the purchase of a new telescope in 1935, the Vatican Observatory was transferred here from the Vatican gardens to escape light pollution. Along with it came the Vatican's meteorite collection, one of the most significant collections of cosmic rocks in the world. In 1993 the work of the observatory was enhanced by a new advanced technology telescope in Arizona, and in 2008 the Castel Gandolfo telescope was moved a mile from the castle to avoid light pollution again.

Pope Pius XII filled the castle with thousands of Jews during the war, just as he sheltered them in the Vatican and in convents and monasteries all over Italy, and forty babies were born there. Tragically, on 10 February 1944, a bomb from an allied plane fell on the castle where a crowd was gathering for the distribution of the daily milk ration, and five hundred people were killed.

EUR

Metro Blue Linea B to EUR Fermi (direction Laurentina).

EUR (Esposizione Universale di Roma) is now a commercial and residential district south of the city centre, but was originally chosen in the 1930s as the site for the 1942 World Fair which never took place due to the Second World War. It was planned by architect Marcello Piacentini for Mussolini, who envisaged a whole new city of Rome that would stretch all the way to Ostia, rivalling the old city built by the Roman emperors and popes. You could say he had a more megalomaniac vision than Nero. Still, it is worth seeing, but will give you a strange empty feeling; a soulless place, built to the glory of man rather than God, with hardly anyone walking about and few restaurants or shops. Severe buildings complete with colonnades and statues loom above its tree-lined streets: the long-gone aesthetics of a Fascist regime. Mussolini loved blank white. One highlight is the **Palazzo della Civiltà Italiana**, known as the 'Colosseo Quadrato' (Square Colosseum). Some people go to EUR simply to visit the **Museo**

della Civiltà Romana, which has a scale model of Imperial Rome as it was in the reign of Constantine. Yet it contains no original objects, only plaster copies and replicas of mosaics, reliefs and utensils that give some insight into daily life in ancient Rome, and a model of the library at Hadrian's Villa at Tivoli. The **Museo delle Arti** gives a picture of Italian life before the Second World War. God is not entirely forgotten; on the highest point at one end of Viale Europa stands the spectacular domed **Church of St Peter and St Paul** built in 1937–41 to designs by Arnaldo Foschini.

Villa d'Este Water Gardens

Open throughout the year, except on Mondays and certain holidays. Tickets may be booked online in advance, and it is wise to check dates and times of opening on the website (p. 8).

Take metro Blue Linea B to Ponte Mammolo, (direction Rebibbia). Follow signs to Cotral and buy 2 blue Cotral bus tickets to Tivoli (one for the return) at the Cotral window (not the ATAC window). The Tivoli bus is 7, usually at platform 2, and leaves every 15 minutes. Get off in Tivoli village square, Piazza G. Garibaldi, (about 50 minutes). You get the bus back across the road. Go straight ahead and then follow the sign Villa d'Este towards the left. There is a Tourist Information Office in Piazza G. Garibaldi.

This sensational water garden makes a refreshing half-day out, or a whole day if you want to take in Hadrian's Villa as well, with time for a good lunch. Cardinal Ippolito d'Este commissioned Pirro Ligorio to turn an old Benedictine monastery into this extravaganza of villa and water garden in the sixteenth century. Out of order for decades, there are now rushing torrents, spouts of water from figures and features, plumes of water above the cypresses, a water staircase, the terrace of a hundred fountains, cascades, and quietly bubbling fountains. A hydraulic organ fountain plays every two hours from 10:30. You can imagine Liszt, who had an apartment here, composing his *Fountains of the Villa d'Este*, with the musical sounds of water all around him.

The villa, with its great views of the garden, was restored by the Government in 2000, after years of decay. Among its decorated rooms is the Cardinal's private chapel, with elaborate murals celebrating the Sibyl, who was believed to have prophesied the birth of Christ to the classical world. The villa often hosts interesting exhibitions.

In Tivoli you will see signs to the **Villa Gregoriana**. There is no such villa, only thick woodlands on a steep gradient, with gorges and the Great Waterfall, and paths to the caves of Neptune and the Sirens. Should you go there you will not have time for Hadrian's Villa on the same day.

Hadrian's Villa

To reach Hadrian's Villa from Tivoli, catch orange CAT bus 4 or 4X in Piazza G. Garibaldi. Buy your ticket, and another for your return, at the CAT office, or from the bar opposite the bus stop. Say 'Villa Adriana' to the driver and he and half the passengers will show you where to get off, from where you walk about 100 metres. To return, leave the villa, walk past the little park and continue straight along the road for a few yards till you find the bus stop. If you are feeling brave you can get off on Via Tiburtina before reaching Tivoli, cross the road and get the Cotral bus back to Rome.

The Emperor Hadrian who built this villa spent the last ten years of his life here, preferring it to his palace on the Palatine. He filled it with replicas of the marvellous buildings he had seen in his expeditions around the world. Covering more than a square kilometre, it was the largest and richest imperial villa in the Empire, and although the decline of the Empire meant its great treasures were carted away, the ruins still make a marvellous sight today. Get an overview by looking at the model near the entrance. Highlights include the Greek-style Maritime Theatre, probably Hadrian's personal retreat, with an atrium, a library, a *triclinium* and small baths, set on an island surrounded by columns. His most impressive project, partially restored, was the *Canopus*, the Sanctuary of Serapis; a long lake adorned with statues and arcades, an elegant hall, a theatre and a network of tunnels. Fine mosaics are preserved in a row of bed chambers, while some of the more recent finds and statues from the site are displayed in the museum.

Ostia Antica

Open: 8:30–16:00. Closed Monday.

*Getting there is easy. Take Blue Linea B metro (direction Laurentina) to Piramide. Following the conquest of Egypt in 31 BC, the Romans developed a taste for Egyptian art and architecture, and the **Pyramid of Caius Cestius** is one of the best examples of this. Dating from c.18–12 BC, it was built by Cestius, a wealthy magistrate, so he could be buried like a pharaoh, and it survived by being incorporated into the Aurelian Wall in the third century AD: but the frescoes which once decorated the burial chamber inside are badly damaged. Visits must be pre-booked (p. 8). Beside the Pyramid, in the shadow of the wall, is the **Testaccio Cemetery** where Keats and Shelley are more modestly buried. (The entrance is in Via Caius Cestius.)*

In the square you will see the Roma Ostia Lido Station from where trains run frequently. The journey takes 30 minutes, and you can use your 100-minute bus/metro ticket. Get off at Ostia Antica, unless you are tempted to go on to Ostia Lido Centro, Rome's nearest beach. There is a free beach as well as paying ones.

Ostia was on the coast before the sea receded and the Tiber estuary silted up. Rome's busiest port, serving the far reaches of the Empire, its magnificent and extensive ruins testify to its economic and military importance on the Mediterranean Sea. Tradition has it founded in 620 BC, but the ruins suggest around 335. Vast as it became, Claudius had to build a second huge port,

Portus, for Rome's increasing trade, but by the fifth century both were abandoned and fell into ruin.

The pilgrim might like to start by recalling the moving account of St Augustine's farewell to his mother, Monica, whose prayers and tears over many years led to his conversion and baptism in 387. She was waiting for a ship to her home town of Tagaste in North Africa.

She and I stood alone, leaning out of a certain window overlooking the garden of the house we occupied at Ostia [conversing about] the nature of the eternal life of the saints: which eye has not seen, nor ear heard, neither has entered into the heart of man … Then my mother said: 'Son, now that my hopes in this world are satisfied, I do not know what more I want here or why I am here. There was indeed one thing for which I wished to tarry a little in this life, and that was that I might see you a Catholic Christian before I died. My God hath answered this more than abundantly, so that I see you now made his servant and spurning all earthly happiness. What more am I to do here?' [Five days later she was suddenly taken ill, probably with malaria, and at death's door, in and out of consciousness. Coming round] she asked, 'Where was I?' 'Then looking intently at us, dumb in our grief, she said, 'Here in this place shall you bury your mother'. I was silent and held back my tears; but my brother said something about wishing her the happier lot of dying in her own country and not in Italy. When she heard this, she fixed him with her eye and an anxious countenance, because he savoured of such earthly concerns, and then gazing at me she said, 'See how he speaks'. Soon after, she said to us both: 'Lay this body anywhere, and do not let the care of it be a trouble to you at all. Only this I ask: that you will remember me at the Lord's altar, wherever you are'. And when she had expressed her wish in such words as she could, she fell silent, in heavy pain with her increasing sickness. After she died, I closed her eyes; and there flowed a great sadness on my heart, passing into tears … and sorrow was in me like a convulsion'.

St Augustine.

Slowly they became composed and sang the Psalm, 'I will sing of mercy and judgement unto thee, O Lord', and other faithful came to join them. She was 56 and died but a few weeks after her son's baptism.

Monica was buried in the local cemetery, but her body was transferred to S. Aurea in the sixth-century, before being moved to the Church of S. Trifone in Posterula, and finally to S. Agostino in central Rome.

The excavation of Ostia began in 1801 at the instigation of Pope Pius VII, and although only a third of the huge city has been unearthed, its well-preserved buildings, magnificent frescoes, and beautiful mosaics enable you to see exactly what a Roman city was like. An audio-guide is a helpful investment. From the ticket office you come to the cemetery, where Monica was first buried, then enter the city through the *Porta Romana* into Piazzale della Vittoria, with its colossal statue of *Minerva*. Very helpfully you are given five suggested routes to follow according to your inclination and available time. There are some things you must see, like the *Baths of the Charioteers* with black and white mosaics of chariots, on Decumanus Maximus, the main street. Further down are the *Baths of Neptune*, where you can go up on a platform to see great mosaics of Neptune and tritons, dolphins and mythical creatures. Ostia's *Theatre* (still used) was built by Agrippa, the great building collaborator of Augustus, and was enlarged by Septimius Severus to hold 2,700 spectators. Past the Theatre and *Porta Orientale*, Via di Diana is worth exploring for its houses, like the fine *Casa di Diana* and the *Thermopolium*, a fast-food outlet with wall paintings of fruit and vegetables, and the four-storeyed *Casa dei Dipinti*. You may want to stop at the excellent museum where you can have a coffee or lunch. Back on the Decumanus Maximus you enter the Forum area with the remains of several temples, including the *Capitolium*, dedicated, like Rome's, to Jupiter, Juno and Minerva. From the Forum take a left turn along Cardo Maximus and on the right see the *Nymphaeum*, with its colourful mosaics of a goose and a duck, the sea with fishes, and a boat with one man rowing, another catching an octopus, and a fisherman with a blue hat. Close by is the *Domus delle Colonne* with its white columns and office (*tablinum*). Near it is the Christian *House of the Fish*, so-called because a mosaic depicts a chalice and fish. Back on Decumanus Maximus you come to *Porta Occidentale* and the fish shops, from where follow the Decumanus as it veers to the left. On the right is the *Christian Basilica*, adapted from a bath house in Constantine's time, or just after. Here you can be certain Monica went to Mass for the last time, accompanied by Augustine.

> O sacrament of love, sign of our unity, bond of our fidelity, we who long for life have here its very source. Let us come here and believe, unite with you and live.
>
> Let us pray:
>
> Lord, we give you praise in the Eucharist, the memorial of our salvation in Christ. Let it be for us a sign of our unity in Him, binding us together in communion of love. We ask this through Christ our Lord. Amen.
>
> St Augustine.

*If you would like to visit **Sant'Aurea**, where St Monica was reburied, head back towards the station, but instead of turning to it, stay on the main road to the village, following it around the castle to Piazza della Rocca, a pretty medieval square with a restaurant, some cottages, and the church.*

The small village Church of S. Aurea was built at the end of the fifteenth century, but there was a church here long before that, for the patron saint of Ostia, the martyr St Aurea, was buried here, and later St Monica. The apse is decorated with sixteenth-century frescoes, and St Monica's Chapel has a painting of her in ecstasy by the famed seventeenth-century artist Pietro da Cortona. It also contains a piece of her tombstone, found in 1945 by two boys who were digging a hole for a football goal-post in the courtyard beside the church. Her body was transferred to S. Agostino (p. 139) in 1430.

USING THE BUSES AND METRO

Visitors are often anxious about using buses in cities they don't know well, but in Rome it is really easy. *Remember to buy your ticket before you get on.* These are sold at tobacconist shops (*Tabacchi*) displaying a T, at newsagent kiosks and at metro stations. They are not expensive. The same ticket is used for both buses and the metro. A ticket allows 100-minutes travel on any number of buses, including one metro trip. A 1-day ticket (expiring at midnight) is worth it only if you expect
to use it 5 times or more; a 2-day ticket, 8 times; a 3-day, 12; and a 7-day for 16 or more. These tickets permit any number of metro trips, which may be an advantage. *Inside buses there are yellow machines where you must validate your ticket the first time you use it.*

Bus stops (*Fermata*) and Terminus stops (*Capolinea*) display a list of places on the route. The stop where you are standing is marked at the top. Find it on the list, and the bus will stop at the places below it; so you can be sure you are going in the right direction. Out of town you may need to ring the bell. Buses are often crowded, so you may have to stand, but they are part of Roman life and are generally fun to experience. There is a most useful bus website: http://atac.roma.it/ Touch Italian and click English. Go to Route Planner and you can put in a bus number and get a list of its stops and the route. It will also plan you a route, including walking to the stop, providing you accurately put in your starting-point and destination. It will help locate the nearest bus stop to your hotel. You may buy a street-map called *Roma Metro-Bus* from *Tabacchi* and kiosks.

Bus stops at Stazione Termini

(**A** to **M** denotes the Bay. The most useful numbers are in **bold**)

A – 50

B – **714** to St Mary Major (S. Maria Maggiore) and St John Lateran (S. Giovanni Laterano).

C – 90

D – **82** to Catacomb S. Agnese.

E – **310** to Catacomb Priscilla. **223** to Villa Borghese.

F – 38, **92** to Villa Borghese.

G – **40** to Piazza Venezia and St Peter's.

H – **64** to Piazza Venezia and St Peter's.

I – **170** to Piazza Venezia; **85** to Via Veneto, Piazza Barberini, Trevi Fountain, Piazza Venezia, Circo Massimo, Colosseum and St John Lateran.

L – **910** to Villa Borghese.

M – M.

On the right of the Bays, near **B** is a stop for **360** and **590** to St Mary Major and St John Lateran. Near **H** is the **649** stop to St Mary Major and S. Croce in Gerusalemme. Near **L** is the **360** stop for Villa Borghese. On Via Giovanni Giolitti, just past Via Cavour, is the **590** stop for Piazza Barberini, Lepanto, Ottoviano and Piazza del Risorgimento.

Buses near St Peter's Square 1 (Piazza Pia area)

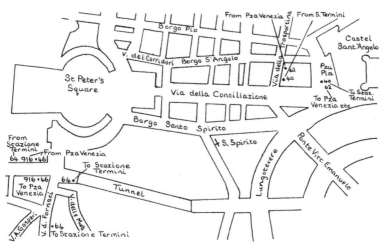

40 – an express bus from its terminus in Piazza Pia to Termini, via Corso Vittorio Emanuele II, Torre Argentina and Piazza Venezia. It returns the same way.

23 – from Piazza Pia to St Paul's Basilica and beyond, alongside the Tiber (Trastevere on your right; Tiber on your left). Returns the same way from the back of St Paul's.

62 – from its terminus in Piazza Pia, via Corso Vittorio Emanuele II, Torre Argentina, Piazza Venezia, Via del Corso, Via del Tritone, Piazza Barberini to Largo S. Susanna and beyond. To return, catch it in Via del Tritone at the bottom of Piazza Barberini, Via del Plebiscito, Piazza Venezia, along Corso Vittorio Emanuele II, including Torre Argentina.

64 – usually packed, from St Peter's to Termini, via Corso Vittorio Emanuele II, Torre Argentina, Piazza Venezia. It returns almost the same way.

46 and **916** – to and from Piazza Venezia.

Buses near St Peter's Square 2 (Piazza del Risorgimento area)

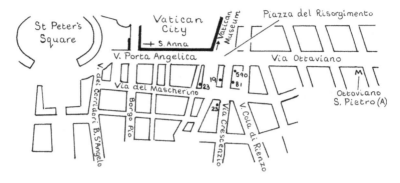

23 – from the side of Piazza del Risorgimento via Piazza Pia to St Paul's Basilica and beyond, alongside the Tiber (Trastevere on your right; Tiber on your left). Returns the same way from the back of St Paul's.

81 – from its terminus in Piazza del Risorgimento to St John Lateran and beyond, via Corso del Rinascimento (near Piazza Navona), Piazza Venezia, passing the Theatre of Marcellus (on your right), S. Maria in Cosmedin (on your left), Circo Massimo, almost reaching the Colosseum before veering right. To return catch it at St John Lateran, Via Claudia (near the Colosseum), Circo Massimo, at the foot of Aracoeli, Via del Plebiscito and Torre Argentina.

590 – from Piazza del Risorgimento to St John Lateran and beyond, via (near) Piazza del Popolo, Piazza Barberini, and Termini. Returns the same way.

19 – a tram to Flaminio (near Piazza del Popolo), to Museo Etrusco, Galleria d'Arte Moderna and Villa Borghese.

Bus stops in Piazza Venezia

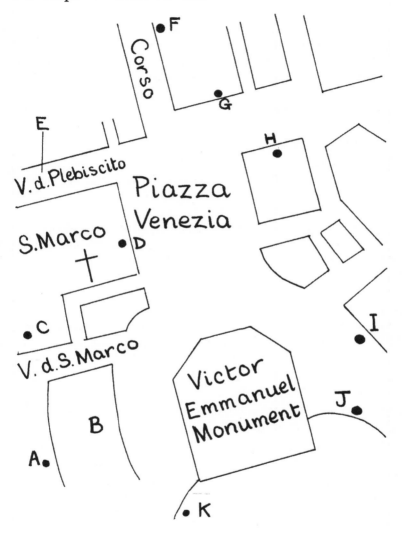

This is a most useful hub with many bus stops, very close to the historic centre. Bus stops marked **A** to **K**.

A – **40**, **H** and **64** to Termini; **62** and **492** to P. Barberini and Largo S. Susanna; **63** to P. Barberini, Via Veneto, Museo Borghese; **70** to St Mary Major's; **81** to St John Lateran; **87** to Colosseum and St John Lateran; **118** to Catacombs; **628** to Circo Massimo. Also 30, 44, 44F, 130, 186, 781, 810.

B – **46**, **916** and **916F** to Chiesa Nuova and St Peter's. Also 60, 80B, 190F, 780.

C – **8** Tram to Trastevere.

D – **51**, **85** and **117** to Colosseum, S. Clemente, St John Lateran; **63** to Monte Savello (for Tiber Island); **80** to P. Barberini and Via Vittorio Veneto; **81** to Circo Massimo and St John Lateran; **160** and **628** to Circo Massimo. Also 60, 170, 810, H.

E – **46**, **62**, and **916** to Chiesa Nuova, Castel Sant'Angelo and St Peter's; **64** to Chiesa Nuova and St Peter's; **70**, **87** and **628** to Rinascimento (near Piazza Navona); **81** and **492** to Rinascimento, (near Piazza Navona), Via Crescenzio and Piazza del Risorgimento. Also 30, 130F, 186.

F – **51** to Colosseum, S. Clemente, St John Lateran; **62** and **492** to Piazza Barberini, Largo S. Susanna; **63** and **160** to Piazza Barberini, Via Veneto and Villa Borghese; **83** to Piazza Barberini and Via Veneto; **85** to Piazza Barberini and Termini. Also 80.

G – **40** and **64** to Torre Argentina, Chiesa Nuova and St Peter's; **70** to Rinascimento (for Piazza Navona).

H – **40**, **64**, and **170** to Termini; **70** to St Mary Major; **117** to Colosseum, S. Clemente and St John Lateran. Also **60**.

I – **85** to Piazza Barberini, Largo Susanna and Termini; **87** to Torre Argentina and Rinascimento (for Piazza Navona). Also **51**.

J – **51**, **85** and **87** to Colosseum, S. Clemente and St John Lateran; **118** for Colosseum, Circo Massimo, and Catacombs S. Callisto and S. Sebastiano.

K – 30 and **130F** to Torre Argentina; **81** to Torre Argentina, Rinascimento (for Piazza Navona) and Piazza del Risorgimento; **83** to Piazza Barberini and Via Veneto; **85** to Piazza Barberini, Largo Susanna and Termini; **87** and **628** to Torre Argentina and Rinascimento (for Piazza Navona); **118** for Colosseum, Circo Massimo, and Catacombs S. Callisto and S. Sebastiano; **160** to Piazza Barberini, Via Veneto and Villa Borghese; **170** to Termini.

Metro

This is very easy to use because there are only 3 lines. Red Linea A and Blue Linea B intersect at Stazione Termini, and these are very useful. A third line, the driverless Green Linea C is not yet finished.

Metro Stations are indicated with a large red M.

Useful Metro Stops:

Linea A:

- Ottaviano-S. Pietro—St Peter's and the Vatican Museums.

- Flaminio—Piazza del Popolo and Borghese Gardens.

- Spagna—Piazza di Spagna (and the Spanish Steps).

- Termini—Stazione Termini (the main Railway and Bus Stations) where Lines A and B intersect.

- S. Giovanni—St John Lateran.

Linea B:

- Colosseo—Colosseum.

- Circo Massimo—Circus Maximus, San Gregorio, and the Caelian Hill.

- Piramide—Testaccio Cemetery, Porta San Paolo and the Station for Ostia and the Lido.

- Basilica S. Paolo—St Paul's Basilica.

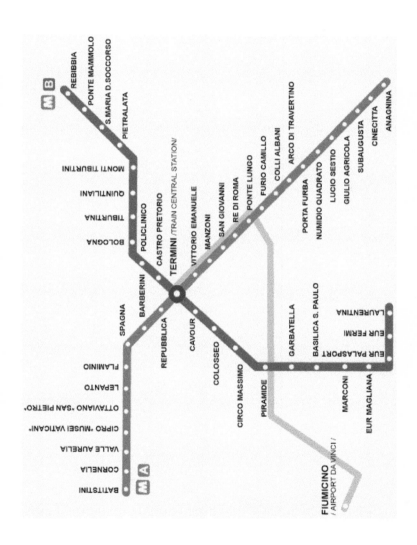

SOME USEFUL INFORMATION

(see also pp. 2–8)

Transfers between Fiumicino and Ciampino Airports and Rome Station

Inexpensive buses from several companies run frequently between both airports and Stazione Termini. You can buy tickets at the bus stop (or online and save a couple of euros, but you may miss the next available bus of a different company). At Ciampino the bus stops are outside Arrivals towards the left. At Fiumicino they are towards the right outside Terminal 3. From Fumicino the 26-km journey takes about 55 minutes; from Ciampino the 15-km journey takes 40 minutes. Some buses terminate in (and leave from) Via Giovanni Giolitti, beside a wonderful market, on the right side of Termini as you face the main entrance; others use Via Marsala on the left. There are taxis in front of the station (Map p. 180). It is a good idea to buy return tickets and leave plenty of time for the return journey.

The Leonardo Rail Express leaves Fiumicino every 30 minutes for Termini and takes 30 minutes. Tickets are available from vending machines inside Fiumicino Arrivals Hall and on the train's departure platform, and from the *Stazione FS* counter (up 2 floors). Cross the road in front of the Arrivals doors to reach the station. *N.B. You must validate your ticket in a **yellow validation machine** on the platform just before using it. Tickets expire 90 minutes after validation.* Trains come into platform (*binario*) 24 at Termini.

Taxis: A fixed price operates from the Airports to anywhere within the 'Aurelian Walls' of the City of Rome—therefore anywhere in the city centre. If you want dropping at a hotel outside the city ask the price, with traffic congestion it may be expensive. The white, official taxis are a good way of getting around the city, and they are not expensive for 3 or 4 persons unless caught in traffic.

Disabled Access: An ancient city with hills and steps everywhere is not easy, but Rome is increasingly assisted-wheelchair-friendly, and most monuments, museums and churches have ramps. Chairs can be borrowed in some places e.g. the Vatican Gardens. www.sagetraveling.com is helpful.

Modest Dress: To enter churches, including St Peter's, the *Scavi* and catacombs, modest dress code is required. This means no bare shoulders and arms, no shorts above knees or mini-skirts. After queuing for a long time to get through security at St Peter's don't be refused entry.

Tipping: A service charge is included in restaurants, hotels, bars and taxis. Nonetheless, waiters gratefully accept a modest tip for good service; porters, maybe €2; taxi drivers, €1.

Passport: Keep your passport in the hotel safe and carry around a photocopy. This may get you concessions.

Free Health Care: Health insurance is strongly advisable.

Theft: As in all cities be vigilant for pickpockets who target tourists, especially on the metro and buses (64 can be bad). Hold handbags tightly on your knees or stomach. Never have a wallet in a back pocket. Use a money belt under your clothes with your cards, and spread cash around different pockets. Carry around no more than you need. Most hotels have secure safes. To report a theft call 06 4686 2102. English is spoken. The best way of carrying things around is to have an ordinary shopping bag, because no one is likely to think it contains anything other than groceries.

Currency: It is useful to bring some euros with you, because although there are many ATMs they are rare in tourist spots.

Climate: July and August are very hot. The most comfortable months are May, June, September, and October. Winters are usually moderate and less crowded.

Where to eat: There are bars and restaurants everywhere. Most display menus in English, particularly around St Peter's and the tourist sites. Many offer a *Menu Turistico*, which are reasonably priced and include drinks. One restaurant should be mentioned to pilgrims and that is *L'Eau Vive*, a French restaurant run by Sisters. It is marked on the Map on p. 149. There are restaurants to suit every pocket, and there are drinks and sandwich vans in tourist areas. However, it is an offence to walk around eating. In most bars you are charged more to sit than stand. Generally you have to pay for what you want before you get it at the bar. Tricky if you cannot speak Italian, but staff are understanding if you point to what you want. You can save money by buying a bread roll and slice of ham etc. from a shop or market. There are drinking fountains all around Rome dispensing fresh pure water, and if you carry a bottle you can refill it.

Crossing the road: Major intersections have coloured signs, green and red, and you should always observe them. Traffic is allowed to turn left when the light is red so be careful not to step into the path of an oncoming scooter or car, even if you have a green light. There are zebra crossings, but unlike in England drivers don't usually stop unless you step just into the road. Watch the Romans and they cross even busy roads by walking straight across, while the cars stop or go round them.

Toilets: There are few public toilets in Italy (St Peter's Square is an exception), but all bars have them and allow you to use them.

Embassies:

- Australia—Via Antonio Bosio, 5. Tel: +39 06 852721.

- Canada—Via Zara 30. Tel: +39 06 854441.

- Great Britain—Via XX Settembre 80/a. Tel: +39 06 4220 0001.

- Ireland—Villa Spada, Via Giacomo Medici, 1. Tel: +39 06 585 2381.

- New Zealand—Via Clitunno, 44. Tel: +39 06 853 7501.

- South Africa—Via Tanaro, 14. Tel: +39 06 852541.

- United States of America—Via Vittorio Veneto 121. Tel: +39 06 46741.

Church Services in English

It is advisable to check that times have not altered.

Catholic, S. Giorgio in Velabro
Via del Velabro, 19 (p. 116).
Sunday Mass: 8.30.

Catholic, S. Silvestro in Capite
Piazza di S. Silvestro, 17A (p. 224).
Sunday Mass: 10:00 and 17:30.

Catholic, S. Spirito in Sassia
Via dei Penitenzieri, 12 (p. 69).
Sunday Mass: 10:00.

Catholic, St Patrick's
Via Boncompagni, 31 (near Via Veneto).
Sunday Mass: Saturday: Vigil 18:00; Sunday: 9:00 and 10:30.

Church of England, All Saints'
Via del Babuino, 153 (near Spanish Steps, p. 162).
Sunday Eucharist: 8:30 and 10:30.

American Episcopalian, St Paul's within the Walls
Via Napoli, 58 (on the left of Via Nazionale, close to Piazza della Repubblica).
Sunday Eucharist: 10:30.

Methodist Church
Piazza di Ponte Sant'Angelo, 68 (coming from Castel Sant'Angelo, just across Ponte Sant'Angelo, Map p. 138).
Sunday Morning Service: 10:30.

Church of Scotland, St Andrew's
Via XX Settembre, 7 (go past S. Susanna towards the Quirinale, and you will reach it on the same side, p. 217)
Sunday Morning Service: 11:00.

Baptist Church
Piazza S. Lorenzo in Lucina, 35 (Just off Via del Corso)
Sunday Morning Service: 10:30.

Other Churches (Liturgies not in English)

Greek Orthodox, S. Teodoro
Via de S. Teodoro, 7 (just passed Hotel Kolbe, and across the road (p. 134).
Sunday: 9:00: Orthros (Lauds); 10:30: Eucharistic Liturgy.

Russian Orthodox, St Catherine's
Via Lago Terrione, 77/79 (64 bus to Piazza della Stazione S. Pietro, take the pedestrian tunnel stairs and turn left onto Via del Lago Terrione).
Sunday Divine Liturgy: 10:00.

Hotels and Places to Stay

This is a very small selection of Hotels and Religious Guest Houses around St Peter's and the Railway Station, convenient for public transport. Religious Houses usually offer excellent value and comfort, and welcome all guests irrespective of Faith.

Near St Peter's

4 Star Hotels:

Palazzo Cardinal Cesi
Via della Conciliazione, 51.
Tel: +39 06 68 40 39. Fax +39 06 68 193 333
www.palazzocesi.it

Hotel Columbus
Via della Conciliazione, 33.
Tel: +39 06 69 345 123
www.hotelcolumbusrome.it

Hotel della Conciliazione,
Borgo Pio, 163/166.
Tel: +39 06 68 75400. Fax: +39 06 68 801 164
www.hotelconciliazione.it

Relais Vatican View
Via del Mascherino, 34.
Tel: +39 06 68 308 456. Fax: +39 06 68 212 899
www.vaticanview.com

3 Star Hotels:

Hotel Sant'Anna
Borgo Pio, 134.
Tel: +39 06 68 801 602
www.santannahotel.net

Hotel Bramante
Vicolo delle Palline, 24.
Tel: +39 06 68 806 426 and 06.68.79.881. Fax: +39 06 68 133 339
www.hotelbramante.com

Religious Guest Houses:

Casa d'Accoglienza S. Spirito
Borgo S. Spirito, 41.
Tel: +39 06 68 61 076. Fax: +39 06 68 130 574
www.santospirito.ssmitalia.org

Istituto Maria Santissima Bambina
Via Paolo VI, 21.
Book through www.monasterystays.com (search LAR208)

Domus Carmelitana
Via Alberico II, 44.
Tel: +39 06 684 0191. Fax: +39 06 68 401 9200
www.domuscarmelitana.com

Residenza Madri Pie
Via Alcide de Gasperi, 4.
Tel: +39 06 631 967 and 06 633 441
www.residenzamadripie.it/

Near the Station

4 Star Hotels:

Hotel Aphrodite
Via Marsala, 90.
Tel: +39 06 95 227 496. Fax: +39 06 95 226 730
www.hotelaphrodite.com

Hotel Diocleziano
Via Gaeta, 71.
Tel: +39 06 48 900 767. Fax: +39 06 47 45 891
www.hoteldiocleziano.it

3 Star Hotels:

Hotel Assisi
Via dei Mille, 29.
Tel/Fax: +39 06 44 53 813
www.hotelassisiroma.it

Hotel Flower Garden
Via del Viminale, 7.
Phone: +39 06 4782 4096
www.hotelflowergardenrome.com

Hotel Madison
Via Marsala, 60.
Tel: +39 06 44 54 344. Fax: +39 06 481 9090
www.hotelmadisonrome.com

Hotel Nord Nuova Roma
Via Giovanni Amendola, 3.
Phone: +39 06 488 5441. Fax: 39 06 481 7163
www.hotelnordnuovaroma.it

Religious Guest House:

Istituto Sacro Cuore
Via Marsala, 42.
Book through www.monasterystays.com (search LAR251)

INDEX

Saturnalia 33
Savello Park 109
Scavi (Excavations under St
Peter's) 3, 4, 50, 51–3, 68,
248
Senate House (Curia) 26, 92
Senate of Italy 147
Sergius, Archbishop 111
Servian Wall 34
Sessorian Palace 99, 100
Seven Pilgrimage Churches
see Pilgrimage Churches
Shelley, Percy Bysshe 161,
233
Sistine Chapel 2, 4, 29, 43, 57,
67, 146, 174, 191, 193–5
Sobieska, Maria Clementina
61, 133–5, 201
Somaschi Fathers 112
Spanish Steps 2, 138, 158,
160–2, 220
Spellman, Cardinal Francis
Joseph 203
Spencer, Fr Ignatius 204
St Paul's Cathedral, London
45, 55
Stefano, Giovanni di 92, 192
Stotzingen, Abbot Fidelis von
113
Street, George Edmund 162
Subleyras, Pierre-Hubert 181
Suetonius 211
Sutherland, Graham 192
Sibyl 146, 166, 194, 232
Synagogue 129

Tacitus 10, 11
Talking Statues 43, 151, 157,
162, 199
Tarquin kings 31
Taxis 185, 191, 247, 248
Temple weights 115, 122
Temples:
 Antoninus and Faustina 37
 Apollo 130
 Castor and Pollux 34
 Ceres 114–5
 Claudius 203
 Hadrian 228
 Hercules Victor 118
 Isis 121, 151
 Juno 27
 Jupiter 27, 29, 30, 31
 Minerva 152
 Mithras 15
 Peace 20, 22
 Portunus 118
 Romulus 37
 Saturn 33– 4
 Sun 215
 Venus and Rome 21
 Vespasian and Titus 36
 Vesta 33
Tenerani, Pietro 75
Termini see Railway Station
Testaccio Cemetery 161, 233
Theatines 198
Theatre of Marcellus 130–1
Theatre of Pompey 35, 184
Thomas Becket 103, 112
Thorvaldsen, Bertel 60
Tiber Island 127–9
Tintoretto 30
Tipping 248
Titian 30, 187
Titulus (general) 15

Lightning Source UK Ltd.
Milton Keynes UK
UKHW020056020919
348915UK00002B/103/P